21/'

✓

RESE~~RVE~~

RENFREW COUN~~TY~~

HEADQUARTERS: Marchfi~~eld~~

CARE OF BOOKS. Readers are asked to ~~take great~~
in their possession.

TIME ALLOWED FOR READING. Books may be retained for two weeks,
and are due for return not later than the latest date stamped below.
A fine of one penny will be charged for every three days the book
is kept beyond the time allowed.

RENEWALS. A loan may be extended if the book is not required by another
reader.

-6. ~~MAR~~ 1959

-2. NOV 1960

-7. MAY. 1962

16. JUN. 1962

-2. JUN. 1964

21. JAN. 1966

Ref. no 14~~92~~

Due for Return

6: Nov. '67.

~~4177~~

Due

23·5·69

17. MAY 1969

B91483

RESERVE

THE MEANING OF THE
MONASTIC LIFE

THE MEANING OF THE MONASTIC LIFE

by

LOUIS BOUYER
of the Oratory

LONDON
BURNS & OATES

This translation of Le Sens de la Vie Monastique
(Editions Brepols, Turnhout and Paris, 1950)
was made by
KATHLEEN POND

NIHIL OBSTAT : CAROLVS DAVIS, S.T.L.
CENSOR DEPVTATVS
IMPRIMATVR : E. MORROGH BERNARD
VICARIVS GENERALIS
WESTMONASTERII : DIE XVII JANVARII MCMLV

MADE AND PRINTED IN GREAT BRITAIN BY
SPOTTISWOODE, BALLANTYNE AND CO. LTD.
LONDON AND COLCHESTER,
FOR BURNS OATES AND WASHBOURNE LTD.
28 ASHLEY PLACE, LONDON, S.W.1
First published 1955

CONTENTS

PREFACE

THE purpose of this book is primarily to point out to monks that their vocation in the Church is not, and never has been, a special vocation. The vocation of the monk is, but is no more than, the vocation of the baptized man. But it is the vocation of the baptized man carried, I would say, to the farthest limits of its irresistible demands. All men who have put on Christ have heard the call to seek God. The monk is one for whom this call has become so urgent that there can be no question of postponing his response to it; he must accept forthwith. He does not wait for the figure of this world to pass away, to see him who ever stands behind its veils. He anticipates, abandoning everything in this world, in order to meet God here and now.

But this is tantamount to saying that this book is equally for every Christian. If it is true that the call: 'Be you perfect as your heavenly Father is perfect', is addressed in one way or another to everyone who wishes to be a child of God, the obverse of what we have just been saying is true. In every Christian vocation lies the germ of a monastic vocation. It may develop to a greater or a lesser degree; its very development can take on many different forms. But this germ cannot be smothered without at the same time killing the germ of the Christ-life in us. One cannot, in fact, be a child of God, without hearing in one's inmost heart the voice which cries: 'Come to the Father', and without being ready to respond by a total sacrifice.

Modern authors praise the spirituality which derives from St Francis de Sales for having at last given up wanting to model the Christian living in the world upon the monk. Such praise is somewhat ambiguous. If we admire the wisdom with which the saint succeeded in distinguishing between the essence of monastic life which, once more, is to be identified with integral Christian life, and its accidentals—if we congratulate ourselves that he has discouraged Christians living in the world from imitating the externals of monasticism, while helping them to adopt and adapt its vital principles, nothing can be better. But if it is implied that such spirituality would allow some people to hope for a Christianity without austerity, without striving after intimate communion with God, without penance and without interior life, no more serious accusation could be levelled against the so-called disciples of

St Francis de Sales. Prayer and penance are the bases of every Christian life, because without them charity is nothing more than a word devoid of meaning. To exclude them, or to push them into the background, is to refuse to allow the Gospel to become our whole life. But one cannot give Christ a limited place in one's life. If we refuse to give him all, he will give us nothing.

If we may use more ambitious terms let us say that the meaning of this book, if it has one, is to show that there is no integral humanism other than a radically eschatological humanism. True, the Christian must love the world, in the sense in which it is said in St John that God so loved the world that he gave his only-begotten Son . . . But that does not mean that the Christian must aim at settling down in the world and using the Gospel to that end. Such an interpretation would be the most ridiculous as well as the most scandalous of paradoxes. What is meant is that the Christian must aspire to saving the world from itself by first saving himself from it. 'The Lord is nigh: let this world pass and thy Kingdom come . . .', the sincerity with which we repeat these words of the early Christians will be the test of the genuineness of our Christianity.

It is not improbable that such prefatory remarks will shock many modern Christians. If so, it is all to the good; it is to wake them from a golden dream that this book has been written. Like many of our contemporaries, we were brought up in the illusion that side by side with the negative, crucifying asceticism of past centuries, there was room for a constructive, positive asceticism which would reject nothing in this world but would consecrate all in it to the glory of God. Experience of life, and in particular that of the priestly ministry, has been confirmed by the study of Scripture and tradition: such an illusion is merely a temptation, the first and most elementary of the temptations the devil tried our Lord with. Like all temptations, it is based on a false presupposition arising from a confusion. That the Christian effort must aim at an all-embracing consecration of self and of the world with all its glory and untarnished joy is beyond question. But the cross is precisely the Way which leads to this end, and there is no other. If this book succeeds in convincing some that there is no such thing as 'Christianity without tears', it will have fulfilled all the author's desires.

Louis Bouyer of the Oratory.

['D' after a Scripture reference = Douai version; otherwise the Knox version has been used.]

PART ONE

THEORY

I

THE SEARCH FOR GOD

Wᴴᴬᵀ is the meaning of monastic life? The question is of paramount importance. People adopt monasticism as a way to something. To embark upon it without knowing where it leads is like rushing into a blind alley. *Ad quid venisti?* If this question is not always present to the mind of the monk, or if he is not capable of making a response which comes from his whole soul, his labour is vain: to quote the Apostle, he fights as one beating the air.

Now it may be that one can give very different answers, all of which will be more or less true. But until we have found the right answer, we shall not get at the essence of the matter. As long as we stop short of the whole truth, monasticism will be like a plant without deep roots. It can bear leaves, some flowers perhaps, but certainly not fruit. Eventually it withers and falls to the ground. Or again, what is perhaps worse, it withers where it is, but it continues to occupy the ground to no purpose. Then it incurs the double reproach of failing to fulfil its purpose in the Church, and of concealing that purpose by seeming to be made for something else.

The most usual reply to our question is perhaps also the one nearest to the truth. It includes the truth but does not define it sufficiently clearly. 'Monastic life', it may be said, 'is the contemplative life.' Nothing is truer, in a certain sense, for it is essential to monastic life that it should be a form of life in which contemplation predominates. Indeed nowhere is contemplation pursued so effectively, practised so purely, as in the life of the monk. Nevertheless, this definition remains too vague. Contemplation as such is not a specifically Christian thing. The Therapeutists who won the admiration of Philo could have described their ideal in these terms. And in fact it was from them that Philo derived his inspiration in his treatise *Of the Contemplative Life*. The same would have to be said of all oriental sages. There is no compelling reason why we should consider a life so defined as necessarily religious. That Aristotle sees in the βίος θεωρητικὸς only the peak of what we should call the intellectual life, is proof of this.

At the opposite extreme to this too general reply will be found one which is too narrow. 'Monastic life is the life of penance.' The advantage of such a definition is that this time it starts from a concept which is specifically Christian. Penance was the first theme proclaimed by the Baptist to prepare the coming of the Messias, a theme with which the Messias' preaching would at once link up. Penance is equally, as we shall see, a mark, a fundamental mark, of Christian monasticism. Penance must never be lost sight of unless we wish to lose sight of the reality of the human environment into which monasticism is fitted, and to which it is adapted. But penance is only a point of departure. He who stops there and goes no further will see no more than the beginning of the way. What is more, he will be doomed to mistake, or quite simply to be ignorant of, its direction. The latter indeed can only be gauged from the end, not from the starting-point.

Such a view, indeed, approaches monasticism by way of modern institutions which, together with a fervour which is immensely valuable and important, show a dangerous tendency to take the part for the whole, what is immediately obvious for what is fundamental. Furthermore, there is reason to fear that we may adopt this notion merely under the influence of a romanticism which is carried away by easy contrasts. The monk who repeats to himself without intermission *memento mori* is repressing a disorderly appetite for life which is purely instinctive. There is a close connection between the two, as psychoanalysis has no difficulty in showing.

Shall we then accept a definition commonly received by our contemporaries, from the clergy downwards: 'the purpose of monastic life is the perfect celebration of the liturgy'? Although attributable to a monastic revival which obviously owes something to the *Génie du Christianisme*,[1] this third definition could claim more than one ancient authority in its favour. In how many charters of medieval foundations do we not read that the monks are '*propter chorum fundati*'? It may be said that in any case such a definition has the merit of expressing an undeniable fact: In the West as in the East, monasteries are *the* centres of liturgical worship. Moreover, as will be seen, the place which the liturgy occupies in the externals of monastic life has an equally important counterpart in the interior life. We cannot, however, be content with saying that the liturgy is the aim of the monastic life. In so far as the liturgy, in the original meaning of the expression, is a 'public service' in the Church, it is not to monks that it is entrusted but to the

---

[1] Chateaubriand, *Génie du Christianisme* (Paris, 1856).

clergy as a whole. If, in fact, at the present day, monks have become an important part of the clergy, such a circumstance, whatever proportions it may assume, remains accidental. All great monastic legislators, from St Benedict downwards, pass it over. To define the life of monks by their collective and unceasing performance of this 'service' in as perfect a manner as possible, would be to confuse them with the canons regular, who are something quite different. What really distinguishes monks *qua* monks is not an external function, however closely this may be bound up with the internal reality. Neither is it—one should not be afraid to say—a 'service', however exalted the notion of such a service may be. The meaning of monastic life will be found in a reality which is fundamentally interior, and whose end and purpose is within itself, and is far from having to be sought in anything utilitarian, however altruistic and disinterested the notion of such utilitarianism may be.

A fortiori these last reasons are sufficient to prevent us from supposing, as do men of the world for whom the name of 'Benedictine' immediately suggests 'scholar', that any form of learning could become the end of a monastic institute or of monastic life. Yet we should perhaps pause to examine this idea a little. It merits careful consideration. Firstly, it is undeniable that it corresponds to an historical fact. The medieval monasteries, both those of Byzantium and those of the West in Carolingian times, were the storehouses of an intellectual culture which must surely have almost entirely perished without them. If they had not existed, or if they had been something other than what in fact they were, it is beyond question that the Renaissance, considered in some of its essential features, would not have been possible. That is to say, they are responsible, even if indirectly, for deep-rooted and permanent elements in our culture, without which it cannot even be conceived. To this must be added the fact that in the foundation of certain great monastic institutions (as, for instance, the Vivarium of Cassiodorus), or, more frequently, perhaps, in their subsequent development (as in the Congregation of St Maur), the highest intellectual interests have undeniably played their part. Let us beware of seeing in this a de-formation, as the advocates of the second definition ('monk' is equivalent to 'penitent') would be inclined to do. Even from the point of view of monasticism, men like Mabillon are too much of a credit to their Order for it to have any scruple in accepting the relatively extrinsic credit which they have earned for it by their literary work.

There is indeed a type of intellectual culture which is the natural product of monastic life, even if it cannot become its objective.[1] For, as we shall see, it derives spontaneously from an essential monastic practice on which we shall have a good deal to say later—the *lectio divina*. And the bond between the two is of its very nature so effective that one could go so far as to say of monks who prove incapable of the culture in question, that they are probably equally incapable of the *lectio divina*! That much having been said, however, the arguments that are valid against the idea that liturgy is the purpose of monasticism are at least equally valid against putting any form of learning or culture in that place.

There is yet another meaning which men have sought to give to monastic life, and which cannot be put aside without investigation. But for the historians, people nowadays would not trouble about it. From the historians' point of view, however, much could be found to justify this last theory. We refer purely and simply to the apostolate. Although our present-day ideal of the monk and monastic life ignores such a consideration more or less completely, the past accords it very great weight. One may indeed wonder whether there have ever been missionaries who have exercised so vast and so determining an influence as the monks, particularly the Benedictines of the 'Dark Ages' and of the High Middle Ages. If on the most conservative estimate we take the banks of the Seine as the southern boundary of the 'North', the conversion to Christianity of the nordic countries, to speak of those alone, is their work. It must be added that if ever a work, apostolic in its own nature, went spontaneously hand in hand with the task of spreading civilization in the widest sense of the term, that is the case here. It is to the monks that France owes it that she is a land of wheat, as much as it is to them that she owes it that she has become a Christian country. However unusual the statement may appear there is perhaps no case of Christian humanism in history as complete as that—I mean no case which has made itself felt in the social and (to use Péguy's expression) 'carnal' realities, as much as, and more than, in the intellectual sphere. But the chief lesson which should be drawn from this is perhaps that Christian humanism is a success of the kind one never achieves so well as when one's real objective is elsewhere. What is certain in any case is that an apostolate which is the very reverse of what the moderns call proselytism is, as it were, for the whole of Christian

[1] I would add, in parenthesis, that it can only, moreover, remain the fruit of monastic life so long as it is not made its objective.

society, indeed even for society in general, the 'charisma', the 'special gift' of monastic society. We are obviously referring to an apostolate which is based upon and has its roots deep down in reality, which pays no attention to mere appearances, and is more the fruit of being than of action. The mediocre efficiency—up to the present—of modern methods of the apostolate, taking their pattern as they do from political propaganda, would lead one to suppose that in this sphere too monks still have some service to render to the Church and the world. But they will only do so precisely in so far as they remain themselves. The surest means of not succeeding in this objective would be to take for the end itself what should only be a result of it.

For, quite definitely, the meaning of monastic life is not, and cannot be conveyed by, any of the things we have just mentioned. However right it may be that they induce devotion, enkindle enthusiasm, neither the apostolate, learning nor high intellectual culture, nor even the liturgy or the life of penance, nor the contemplative life considered in itself, can orientate and define the life of the monk. If he is a true monk, what he is seeking cannot be some *thing*. It is some *One*.

When the postulant presents himself at the monastery, St Benedict puts him into the hands of one of those *seniores*, those older brethren, whose wisdom, which is at the same time completely supernatural and completely realist, plays such a large part in ancient monastic literature. But the older brother—'the abbot' in the original meaning of the word —far from attempting to secure the recruit at all costs, proceeds to strip his vocation of all false attractions. However anxious he may be to 'win souls', or rather, because he is supposed to know what that means, he will have—not without a certain humour which reminds us of the close connection between sanctity and sanity, both moral and intellectual—to pour cold water on the neophyte's fervour. St Benedict urges him to reveal to the postulant all the austerity, hardness and monotony that await him in the monk's life, and to do so without using the velvet glove. All this is aimed not so much at instructing the postulant about the monastery as at informing the monastery about the postulant.

And on that subject St Benedict is direct and formal. *Super eum omnino curiose intendat et sollicitus sit si vere Deum quærit . . .* After which the only things mentioned are the *opus Dei*, obedience and correction. There is therefore no question either of culture or apostolate. The most that can be said of contemplative life is that it is taken for granted. The life of penance is implied in the last two things mentioned.

The liturgy or, more precisely, the *opus Dei*, is explicitly named, but only in subordination to the fundamental question: 'does he really seek God?'

Let us state the fact without beating about the bush: a monastic institute which ceased to put this question to its postulants, or which inserted some different question in its place, would cease *ipso facto* to have any right to the name monastic.

The search, the true search, in which the whole of one's being is engaged, not for some thing but for some One: the search for God—that is the beginning and end of monasticism.

If it is to be *truly* God whom we seek, we have to seek him as a person. Martin Buber, in fact, the Jewish philosopher whose meat and drink has been the mysticism of the Hassidim, in which a last living thread of the tradition of the prophets lingers on to the present day, has expressed this very adequately: a person is only sought as a person, in dialogue. It is only in the 'I to Thou' relationship that the person remains personal for us. Someone of whom we get into the habit of speaking as 'he' is no longer a person for us. Whether we realize it or not, 'he' is no more than a thing.

The monastic vocation (is not this the meaning of the word 'vocation', which signifies 'call'?) thus presupposes that God is someone who has revealed himself to us by a word, someone who has called us. And to respond to the monastic vocation is to respond to this Person.

A word has broken the silence and has awakened us from the dreary solitude in which our soul, lost among things, had fallen asleep. This word calls for a response, which takes the form of a request to hear the call repeated, to hear it more clearly, never more to fail to hear it, in order to listen and respond to it continually. Think of the child Samuel asleep in the temple. A voice is heard, a voice which addresses him. A voice which says nothing more than his name: 'Samuel!' And the child exclaims: 'Speak, Lord, for thy servant heareth!' Think again of St Antony, 'the Father of monks'. He is in church. The Gospel is being read. He hears the word of Christ: 'If anyone will be my disciple, let him deny himself, take up his cross and follow me. . . .' He understands that this is no idle word, that it is to him that Someone has spoken; that it is God who has spoken and that it is to him, Antony, that he has spoken. . . . At once he responds to the call and puts into practice what he has just heard. The monastic vocation is that, or it is meaningless.

A divine word, the word which announces the Gospel, one day sank deep into our heart. Suddenly we realized that the call was to ourselves. And we set out in search of him who was calling, calling to him in our turn, calling him with an appeal into which we put our whole heart, our whole life.

The Canticle of Canticles is the poem and drama of this call and response. The voice of the beloved has pierced the night. And this voice can now never be forgotten. The spouse can no longer think of anything else. The memory of it is delightful and yet unbearable. Delightful because this fleeting word by its very tone promised a joy which will surpass all other joy. Unbearable because, with this memory in the heart, there is now no way of finding rest again. Impossible not to set out, not to leave all things forthwith, to find once more the Presence to which this word bore witness. For a moment the beloved was quite close. Nothing could make his presence doubtful to her who has been awakened at his voice. In memory she can hear this voice unceasingly. But she wants to hear it again, no longer merely in memory: to hear it again *now*, and always. She wants to find again the presence which has been offered to her and then withdrawn, precisely because the word was a call. She wants to find it never to lose it more, and so, in the night, to the night whence the voice has arisen, she makes answer. That is, she sets out in her turn, she sets out and she too calls . . .

The voice I love! See where he comes, how he speeds over the mountains, how he spurns the hills! Gazelle nor fawn was ever so fleet of foot as my heart's love. And now he is standing on the other side of this very wall; now he is looking in through each window in turn, peering through every chink. I can hear my true love calling to me: Rise up, rise up quickly, dear heart, so gentle, so beautiful, rise up and come with me. Winter is now over, the rain has passed by. At home, the flowers have begun to blossom; pruning-time has come; we can hear the turtle-dove cooing already, there at home. There is green fruit on the fig-trees; the vines in flower are all fragrance. Rouse thee, and come, so beautiful, so well beloved, still hiding thyself as a dove hides in cleft rock or crannied wall. Shew me but thy face, let me but hear thy voice, that voice sweet as thy face is fair.[1]

And then the response of the spouse:

In the night watches, as I lay abed, I searched for my heart's love, and searched in vain. Now to stir abroad, and traverse the city,

[1] Canticle 2. 8–14.

searching every alley-way and street for him I love so tenderly! But for all my search I could not find him. I met the watchmen who go the city rounds, and asked them whether they had seen my love; then, when I scarce had left them, I found him, so tenderly loved; and now that he is mine I will never leave him, never let him go. . . .[1]

Vox dilecti dilectæ! Therein Origen could visualize not only the whole content of the Canticle but the whole content of the ascetic and mystical life.

Note how the echoes of this voice which has arrested our attention, of the call which it addressed to us, and the inescapable nostalgia which drives us to find it again at whatever cost, fumbling, tripping up in the darkness, are indeed ineradicable in the human heart. Each man's conscience, the collective conscience of mankind whence each individual conscience emerges in its turn, recognizes this call in its inmost depth. A restlessness which develops increasingly as conscience itself becomes more sensitive, clearer and purer, welling up from its very source. And this restlessness remains an enigma for the human conscience so long as it fails to attain to this idea, this memory of the call arising in the night, of the call which, for want of having been listened to immediately, is heard no more. It remains with us, as a memory, but a fascinating memory, a memory which would absorb the whole of present life.

The Platonic myth of reminiscence has no other significance. It might almost be thought that we had formerly seen another light and in it contemplated another world: and that then we fell into a heavy nocturnal slumber. But the fact remains that all beauty, all thought with which the sight of the world in which we are is charged, is inevitably evocative of something else. Does it not create in us a desire, an attraction, out of all proportion to that which it can offer us? Thus everything we question on the matter tells us repeatedly, by its failure to respond, that he who is still waiting for us is beyond our horizon. . . .

All things say this to us repeatedly? Yes, indeed, but rooted and involved as we are in this world, how inclined we are to let ourselves be captivated by the sheer music of these voices, while at the same time we gradually grow deaf to their meaning! The further we are drawn into the world, both in the course of our life and in the unfolding of history, the more does its matter seem to grow coarse and thick. One

[1] Canticle 3. 1-4.

might almost say that it gradually becomes opaque to the light coming from afar off which at first moved our very hearts. But is it not rather we who are striving to lull to sleep the unbearable call which breaks in on us anew, by plunging into delights which become less capable of satisfying us, the more we strive to drown therein this inescapable memory?

Wordsworth in his 'Ode on the Intimations of Immortality' has expressed the drama of the man who makes himself deaf to a voice which is calling him beyond this world, only to find that he thus loses this world's very joy.

> Our birth is but a sleep and a forgetting:
> The soul that rises with us, our life's star,
>   Hath had elsewhere its setting
>   And cometh from afar;
>   Not in entire forgetfulness,
>   And not in utter nakedness,
> But trailing clouds of glory do we come
>   From God, who is our home . . .

Nevertheless, over the growing child, the world exercises its own attraction: that of the labours, troubles and happiness which do not extend beyond its confines. One day perhaps he will perceive, not without some anguish, that the childhood which he had fled from has departed from him of its own accord.

> There was a time when meadow, grove and stream,
>   The earth and every common sight
> To me did seem
>   Apparelled in celestial light,
> The glory and the freshness of a dream.
> It is not now as it hath been of yore:—
>   Turn wheresoe'er I may
>   By night or day
> The things which I have seen I now can see no more.

Yet they are the same things which are offered to our gaze. But the gaze, because it has willed to rest on these things, can no longer see beyond them. Man, however, cannot deceive his heart: he knows quite well

> That there hath passed away a glory from the earth!

A glory? Let us call it a reflection or better, an echo. It is this divine voice, stifled by the whole weight of human history, but not stifled before it has left in the heart of man a gaping void in which all other promises vanish. It is this voice, forgotten yet at the same time unforgettable, which is heard anew in the Gospel. Then for those who have truly understood, that is, who have understood that it is to them that it is addressed, there is no further possibility of doubt or delay. 'They think that they regret the past,' said Newman, 'when they are but longing after the future. It is not that they would be children again but that they would be Angels and would see God: they would be immortal beings, crowned with amaranth, robed in white, and with palms in their hands, before His throne . . .'[1]

But this time there is no room for doubt. What the word we have heard once more invites us to is a departure. We must part from everything, leave everything just where it is, abandon everything without going back on our abandonment. If not, who knows if the word will ever be heard again? And never to hear it again would be tantamount to ceasing to live. We must leave everything, for a quest that will have no ending.

For the mystery is this: here on earth the word will never be heard, except to call us to go after it across a new silence into a deeper solitude. Not only once but continually and unceasingly does the attraction by which the Presence draws us after itself make itself felt. To have found the Presence, here on earth, will always mean seeking it more deeply. He who allows himself to be captivated by this voice will never again be able to stay still and settle down. He will have no alternative but to advance ever further into the night and silence of self-stripping, of emptiness, of nothingness.

The word which calls us is the word which created us and which wills to create us anew. But it will not create us anew unless we have become once more, as it were, a new void, to be breathed on by the breath of life. We shall only embrace the Presence on the cross. . . .

Here we are touching on the fundamental theme in the oldest systematic form of monastic spirituality, such as it can be found in St Gregory of Nyssa or Evagrius of Pontus. The former tells us: 'To find God is to seek him unceasingly. Here, indeed, to seek is not one thing and to find another. The reward of the search is to go on searching.

---

[1] *Parochial and Plain Sermons*, IV. 17, p. 262. It should be noted that this text dispels, by explaining it, the illusion of a pre-existence in which Wordsworth, basing himself on Plato, was entangled.

The soul's desire is fulfilled by the very fact of its remaining unsatisfied, for really to see God is never to have had one's fill of desiring him.'[1]

This is not merely the theme of ecstasy, but of what Gregory of Nyssa would call ἐπέκτασις, that is, not only a going out of oneself but the continual going beyond self. As Gregory says further on:

> When the soul, as far as it can, has entered into the participation of his benefits, the Word draws it afresh to a sharing in his transcendent beauty by renunciation, as if it no longer had any part in these benefits. Thus, because of the transcendent character of the benefits which it is continually discovering in proportion as it makes progress, it always seems to the soul as though it is only at the beginning of the ascent. That is why the Word repeats: 'Arise' to one who is already risen, 'Come' to him who has already come. He who truly rises will always have to rise; there will always be a great distance to run for him who is running towards the Lord. Thus he who climbs can never cease from climbing, going from fresh beginning to fresh beginning—beginnings which never have an end.[2]

We can see that this Word who seeks us and finds us, that we may make response to him by seeking him in our turn, is the whole essence of the Gospel and the whole of Christianity. And in its turn monastic life is nothing else, no more and no less, than a Christian life whose Christianity has penetrated every part of it. It is a Christian life which is completely open, without refusal or delay, to the Word, which opens itself and abandons itself to it. This is the response that the Word expects—expects and elicits, for it is the creating and re-creating word.

St Augustine has left us an incomparable image of the movement which animates it—for, as we see, monastic life is essentially a movement and not a 'state'. We should say, if we dared, that it must be as it were the myth of monasticism, taking the word myth in the Platonic sense, not of legend but of poetry, not of the pathetic fallacy, but of truth too rich and too great to be exhausted or delimited by speech. It is the inner epic of the Hart, the hart we meet in Psalm 41.

Quemadmodum desiderat cervus ad fontes aquarum, ita desiderat anima mea ad te, Deus. Who is it who sings in this way? It is ourselves, if we will have it so.

---

[1] *Vie de Moïse*, P. G., t. 44, col. 405 CD.
[2] *In Cantica Cantic., Hom. V*, P. G., t. 44, col. 876 BC.

It is the whole of the Church.[1] The catechumens sing the *Quemadmodum* when they go to the baptismal font. But those who have already received the faith are still more thirsty for the vision. As the hart longs for the source of water, let us who are baptized long for the source of which Scripture speaks in another place: With thee is the source of life. For it is he himself who is both source and light: in thy light we shall see the light! What, in fact, is the Hart saying? My soul is athirst for the living God—What thirst is he speaking of then?—When shall I come and appear before the face of God! That is what I thirst after: to come and appear before his face. I thirst in my pilgrimage. I thirst in my course. I shall slake my thirst at his coming. But when shall I come? This coming which for God is so prompt, how it tarries when measured against the eagerness of my desire! When shall I come and appear before the face of God? The longing which speaks in this way is that which says elsewhere: I have asked one thing of the Lord, this will I require of him: that I may dwell in the house of the Lord all the days of my life. Why this request? To contemplate, he says, the beauty of his house. When shall I come and appear before the face of the Lord? Meanwhile I meditate, whilst I run, whilst I am on the way, before coming, before appearing: 'My tears have been my meat day and night while they say to me daily: where is thy God?'

Whatever in fact may be the joys of the world, the soul sees nothing in them but emptiness. But the very pain of this emptiness feeds longing.

Whilst the joy of the world breaks out around us, as long as we are in this world we are in exile, far from the Lord, and here they say to me each day: where is thy God? But to the pagan who says that to me, could not I, too, say: where is thy god? Yet he points out his god to me with his finger. . . . It is true that he has found his god, a god who can be visible to fleshly eyes.

Yet it is not that I, too, have not someone I can point to; but he who insults me has no eyes that can see him. He can show his god, the sun, to the eyes of my body, but to what eyes shall I show the creator of the sun? . . . And yet I too seek my God, not only in order to believe, but, if I could do so, to see! I see, indeed, all that my God has made, but I do not see my God who has made all that.

[1] The quotations on this and the pages immediately following are from St Augustine—see reference on p. 18.

The Hart, or the soul, then, runs through the whole world, demand-
ing the presence to which everything bears witness but which nothing
reveals.

But because, like the Hart, I long for the source of the waters and
because there is the source of life and knowledge . . . what shall
I do to find my God? I will consider the earth: the earth has been
made. Great is its beauty: but it has an author. How marvellous are
the seeds and all that grows: but all that has a creator. I point to the
majesty of the sea, extending everywhere: I am amazed, I admire,
I seek its author. I raise my eyes to the heavens and towards the
beauty of the stars; I admire the splendour of the sun, shedding light
on our labours, of the moon cheering the darkness of the night.
All these things are marvellous, worthy of praise and more than
amazing: they are already more than earthly: they are heavenly.
But by them my thirst is still not satisfied. I admire, I praise these
things: but it is for their author I am athirst.

Passing beyond the greatest splendours of the world, the soul enters
into itself again. It sees that it is nobler than the body and that it is
itself, and not the body, that seeks, and by whose searching the body
is moved. And to see itself it has no need of bodily eyes; but, on the
contrary, it withdraws from all bodily realities which hamper and disturb it, it withdraws into itself, to see itself in itself, to know itself in
itself.

The God of the soul, would he not be in some way like to it? In
fact, God cannot be perceived except by the soul; but the soul perceives itself when it does not yet see him. It is in fact seeking for
something which is truly God and which those who say: where is
thy God? cannot insult. It is seeking for truth that is immutable
substance that cannot suffer corruption. But the soul itself is not
thus: it falls back, it makes progress, it changes, it suffers ignorance,
it remembers, it forgets; at one time it wants this thing and at
another time it does not want it. God is not affected by such
mutability. . . .

Neither the one nor the other search, that within or that without,
has found its end, then: the source of light and life.

Seeking my God among visible and corporeal things, I have not
found him. Seeking his substance in myself, as if he were like to me,

I have not found him either. I understand that my God is greater than my soul itself. And so to reach him by my intelligence, *I have meditated on these things and I have poured forth my soul beyond itself.* For when will my soul really come to what is beyond the soul, if not when it is poured forth beyond itself? If it remained in itself, it would see nothing but itself. And when it saw itself, it was not God whom it saw. . . . I have then poured forth my soul beyond itself, and there remains nothing more for me to reach out to, save God alone.

Here, indeed, we are at the apex of the ἐπέκτασις.

There, in fact, beyond the soul, is the House of God where he dwells, whence he looks out on me, whence he created me, whence he governs me, whence he watches over me, whence he encourages me, whence he calls me, whence he directs me, whence he guides me, whence he leads me to the goal.

This House of God is the inaccessible light of his transcendence. But the great mystery of faith is this: this God who dwells so far above us, above all things created, and who yet makes himself so near to us by his love; 'this God who dwells in the secret of his most high dwelling-place, has also a tabernacle on earth. His tabernacle on earth is the Church which is still on pilgrimage. But it is there we must seek him, because it is in his tabernacle that we find the way which leads to his house. . . .'

The whole economy of our redemption, that is, of our return to the Father lies in the paradoxical duality of this mystery: that the God who dwells in light inaccessible offers to us his veiled presence, in the *chiaroscuro* of faith, that he may lead us to his clear and radiant presence. '*It is for this that I will enter into the place of his tabernacle.* For, outside the place of his tabernacle, I shall go astray in my search for God.' In the tabernacle, on the other hand, that is in the Church, the Hart finds the imprints, the immediate traces of the divine presence. He discovers them in the redeemed souls which form this tabernacle, in the sanctity which God infuses into them.

In the spiritual worship which they render to God, the Hart perceives the echo of the heavenly liturgy itself. '. . . In the tabernacle[1] he moves forward among these things. He even passes beyond them. And wonderful as the tabernacle may be, he is overwhelmed when he

---

[1] That is, the Church on earth.—Tr.

reaches the house of God himself.' For the house of God is this sanctuary in which everything obscure becomes clear.

That is what he finally recognizes and understands. Growing up in the tabernacle, he (then) reaches the House. While he is admiring the members of the tabernacle he is led on to the house of God. He is aware of a certain sweet attractiveness; he pursues an indefinable secret charm, as if, from the house of God, some melodious instrument had given forth its sound. Whilst he was moving forward in the tabernacle, he heard interior music, he allowed himself to be guided by its sweetness, which penetrated everywhere and re-echoed till it filled the place where he was, tearing him away from all noises of flesh and blood, and so he came to the House of God.

When an earthly dwelling-house reverberates with song and symphony, we know a feast is being celebrated there. It is the occasion of a birthday or wedding.

In the house of God, the feast is eternal. There it is no passing event that is celebrated. It is the eternal feast, the choir of the angels, the sight of God present, the joy that never fades. It is a continual feast day, without beginning and without end. Of this eternal, everlasting feast, an ineffably gentle and melodious echo rings in the ears; provided, that is, that the world does not cast its tumult upon them. But for one who moves forward in this wonderful tabernacle of God, the heart is melted on hearing the festal harmonies, and the Hart is borne away enraptured towards the source of the waters. . . .

Yet such rapture is only a flash. Soon the weight of the flesh and of the world makes itself felt. And the first drops of water that the Hart tastes enkindle in him desire for the sources, that is hope, his only present consolation, and also his continual pain.

Yet, brethren, because so long as we are on earth and our perishable body makes the soul feel its weight, we remain in exile far from the Lord and our earthly habitation drags down the soul which is absorbed by every kind of care, if it happen that the clouds disperse and that, impelled by our desire, we succeed for a moment in hearing the murmur of the springs, and manage to glimpse something of the divine dwelling-place, then, weighed down by our weakness, we none the less fall back to our habitual level and linger once more over our customary preoccupations. And as there we found matter for rejoicing, here we do not lack matter for lamenting. For indeed the Hart, nourished day and night with his tears, is borne away in rapture by desire towards the springs, that is towards God's inmost sweetness, his soul reaching out beyond itself, in order to touch what is beyond. He then moves forward within the wonderful tabernacle right to the House of God, led by the beauty of a music within him which he recognizes and understands, to despise all that is external, so that he may experience rapture within himself. He remains no less human for this, and here below laments no less, still clothed in weak flesh, still tossed to and fro among the stumbling-blocks of this world. He then turns back upon himself. Coming down from such a height, and seeing himself in such sadness, he compares it with what he had begun to see, and towards which, once seen, he had sprung forward, and says: *Why art thou sad, O my soul, and why dost thou trouble me?* We have already been rejoicing over an indefinable interior sweetness, we have been able to glimpse, with the fine point of the soul, were it only for the space of a momentary flash, something of the immutable. Why dost thou still trouble me and why art thou sad? Thou dost not doubt thy God! Thou art no longer without a reply for those who say to thee: where is thy God? Already I have experienced something of the immutable. Why dost thou still trouble me? *Hope in God.*[1]

It was this search indeed, as we can imagine, which led Pascal to put on the lips of God the words: 'Thou wouldst not seek me if thou hadst not already found me.'

*   *   *

Yet if I dared to suggest a corrective to such a phrase, I would say that it does not yet express the full depth and wonder of the discovery, which is in the search itself.

Let us go back once again, patiently, to what we said at the beginning: the person is sought as a person only in dialogue. It is because one says to him 'thou', that the person is *someone* for us. But one cannot say 'thou' to God unless it is he who has taken the initiative. That is why our search will never be anything but a response. And the more progress we make, the more it will really be that that we discover. It will be recognized that before we sought him, he was already

[1] St Augustine, *Enarratio in Psalmum XLI, passim.* Père Maréchal, S.J., has given a good commentary on this text in vol. 2 of his *Etudes sur la Psychologie des mystiques* (Paris, 1937), pp. 180 ff., although he forces certain terms a little.

seeking us. 'You would not be seeking for me,' God might say to the soul, 'if I had not already found you.'

Finally the further we advance into the night in which his call has come to us, a call which first took us out of ourselves and then seemed to leave us solitary once more, the more we shall realize that the night itself was filled full of God. We shall see—and this will be the most unexpected, the most revolutionary of our discoveries—that it was in reality simply we ourselves who created this darkness. When we think we are seeking God with our whole being, we continue, the old man in us continues, to flee from him secretly and despairingly. That alone creates the darkness; that alone creates the distance. But when we think we have overtaken him we shall recognize that it is he who has over-taken us and that throughout our quest he had never ceased to be not so much before us as behind us. . . . The discovery of grace, the discovery of love which loves us without looking for any return, which loves us although we are sinners, which loves us in our sin, but which alone will lead us, by obscure ways known to him alone, from sin to sanctity, that is, in the last analysis, the great discovery. Then it is that God reveals himself to us as one who speaks to us, as one whose word for the second time draws us out of nothingness to being, as one whom we have not so much to seek as to discover seeking us. It is he, the Shepherd who left the ninety-nine sheep in safety to seek and save that which was lost. It is he, the Father of the prodigal who goes out along the road to welcome his son when he has scarcely started out to meet his father, and takes him in his arms.

Thus behind the mystical theme of the Hart coursing after the waters, as St Augustine has just developed it for us, there remains the comple-mentary theme for us to recognize—what I should call the prophetic theme of the Hound pursuing the Hart. This is the whole subject of a poem of Francis Thompson, *The Hound of Heaven*, perhaps the most majestic picture ever given of the divine *Agape*:

> I fled Him, down the nights and down the days;
> I fled Him, down the arches of the years;
> I fled Him, down the labyrinthine ways
> Of my own mind; and in the midst of tears
> I hid from Him, and under running laughter.
> Up vistaed hopes I sped;
> And shot, precipitated,
> Adown Titanic glooms of chasmèd fears,
> From those strong Feet that followed, followed after.

> But with unhurrying chase,
> And unperturbèd pace,
> Deliberate speed, majestic instancy,
> They beat—and a Voice beat
> More instant than the Feet—
> 'All things betray thee, who betrayest Me.'

The Hart pursued by the Hound of heaven seeks a refuge in all creatures. But earthly friendships elude him who is the object of divine pursuit. And things themselves are powerless to protect him from it, were he to flee to the margent of the world, were he to trouble the gold gateways of the stars with his lamenting:

> Fear wist not to evade, as Love wist to pursue.
> . . . .
> But whether they swept, smoothly fleet,
> The long savannahs of the blue . . .
> Still with unhurrying chase,
> And unperturbèd pace,
> Deliberate speed, majestic instancy,
> Came on the following Feet,
> And a Voice above their beat—
> 'Naught shelters thee, who wilt not shelter Me.'

Are not at least children in their innocence unaware of the blessed curse that lies upon him who is pursued by God? But as he imagines that he will find in their eyes the response to his own look of longing eagerness for human and created sympathy, it seems to him that their Angel snatches them away from him. And no more than those of men do the children of nature offer him the sympathy which he thought he had discovered in them. What he finally recognizes in what he had taken for 'the laughing eyes of the morning or the red sobs of evening' is his own illusion: he knows now that they cannot understand man. Yet the chase slowly draws nearer:

> Nigh and nigh draws the chase,
> With unperturbèd pace,
> Deliberate speed, majestic instancy;
> And past those noisèd Feet
> A Voice comes yet more fleet—
> 'Lo! naught contents thee, who content'st not Me.'

The soul is now stripped of all her defences and all her arms. In anguish she waits for the final stroke. She sends up a cry of reproach and pain:

> Ah! is Thy love indeed
> A weed, albeit an amaranthine weed,
> Suffering no flowers except its own to mount?
>
> . . . .
>
> The pulp so bitter, how shall taste the rind?

Yet the mist, into which all things and all loved beings have been withdrawn one by one, sometimes partly clears, allowing as it were a glimpse of the pinnacles of eternity. It does not close in again until he who has been calling appears in his 'robes purpureal'. Can he then only gather in a harvest of death?

The question remains unanswered. But:

> Now of that long pursuit
> Comes on at hand the bruit;
> That Voice is round me like a bursting sea:
>
> . . . .
>
> 'Lo, all things fly thee, for thou fliest Me!
> Strange, piteous, futile thing,
> Wherefore should any set thee love apart?
> Seeing none but I makes much of naught' (He said),
> 'And human love needs human meriting:
> How hast thou merited—
> Of all man's clotted clay, the dingiest clot?
> Alack, thou knowest not
> How little worthy of any love thou art!
> Whom wilt thou find to love ignoble thee
> Save Me, save only Me?
> All which I took from thee I did but take,
> Not for thy harms,
> But just that thou might'st seek it in My arms,
> All which thy child's mistake
> Fancies as lost, I have stored for thee at home:
> Rise, clasp My hand, and come!'
>
> Halts by me that footfall:
> Is my gloom, after all,
> Shade of His hand, outstretched caressingly?

'Ah, fondest, blindest, weakest,
I am He Whom thou seekest!
Thou dravest love from thee, who dravest Me.'

'To seek God,' to seek him as a person, as the Person *par excellence*, and not only as the 'Thou' to whom all our love should be addressed, but as the 'I' who has first approached us, whose word of love, addressed to the primeval chaos, drew us forth from it in the first place, and, spoken to us in our sin, draws us forth from it again: to be a monk is nothing else than this. To be a monk, then, is simply to be an integral Christian. And regarded in this light, the Christian himself is simply the man restored by the Word of the Gospel to the vocation which the creative Word destined for him: to respond to the Word of *Agape* by the word of faith, in order eventually to meet God face to face. Commenting on the *Canticle of Canticles*, Origen tells us that the Church, under the old dispensation, only heard the Bridegroom's voice, whereas in the new, she is offered the sight of his countenance. And he adds that the development of the Christian life is made up solely of this transition. The monk is the one who does not limit himself to accepting it in some measure passively, by yielding to grace slothfully and reluctantly. He is the one who responds with all his heart to the call which he realizes comes from the very heart of God. He is of the number of the violent who will not allow the divine Kingdom to fall upon them as it were unawares, but who take it by storm in advance. For that he has staked his all, he has burned his boats. To the man who believes that his life consists in what he possesses, he seems to be consenting to, even to be deliberately seeking, a fatal renunciation. To the man who knows that being is of greater value than having, and that being which is of value is not that which passes but that which endures, he will seem the only true humanist. For man is born only as subject to the divine Word and he will only be fully himself the day when, freed from the nothingness which holds him prisoner, fully surrendered to the Word which calls to him, he will at last come to discover the Face which promised him being in promising him his own image.

II

ANGELIC LIFE

Let us recall the saying of Newman we quoted in passing: 'They think that they regret the past when they are but longing after the future. It is not that they would be children again but that they would be Angels and would see God . . .'

The whole of Christian antiquity understood man's vocation as a call to share the angelic life, in so far as that life can be understood as the vision of God. Just in so far, therefore, as the monastic vocation is simply a call to the most perfect and most direct realization possible of the vocation of man in general and Christians in particular, it is perfectly natural that the term 'angelic life' should have been applied to it pre-eminently. As the Constitutions of the English Benedictine Congregation continue to remind us, *primarium officium nostrum est in terra præstare quod angeli in cælo*, 'our primary function is to play on earth the part played by the angels in heaven'.

The meaning of the application will already be obvious, then. To say that monastic life is angelic life does not signify primarily or mainly that it is a life of the utmost purity. But it means that it is a heavenly life in so much as heaven, in the Scriptures, is the place where we see God. The monk is one who puts into practice, or at least strives to put into practice, every moment of his life the Apostle's saying: *conversatio nostra in cælis est*. Once more, nothing finer or better can be said of monastic life than that it is a Christian life breaking all ties with the world, all bonds, that may prevent it from being complete. In the Scriptures the Christian life seems to be as it were animated by a movement, an impulse, which can only be described as 'ascensional'. That was the meaning, symbolical if you like but not merely symbolical, that Christian antiquity saw in the mystical phenomenon of rapture which was accompanied in the case of the saints even by bodily levitation. We have the example of the ecstasy of St Teresa of Avila and St John of the Cross who, while conversing with one another of divine things at the gratings of Carmel, were raised from the ground together without their being aware of the fact. Or again, there is in

3

the Bible the example of the assumption of Elias, borne up to heaven in a fiery chariot. The earthly career of the Son of God reaches its culmination and is perfected in the Ascension, his Resurrection being only its penultimate stage. That the Ascension was not an incomprehensible abandonment of his followers but the crowning of his work of redemption, had already been made clear in the discourse after the Last Supper: 'it is expedient for you that I go away . . .' and the Epistle to the Hebrews—an epistle which throughout is in fact simply an exegesis of this mystery—enables us to understand this when it says that Christ has penetrated into the highest heavens, into the Holy of Holies of heaven, as our forerunner. Similarly, every Eucharist, celebrating this 'exodus', this passage from earth to heaven which Christ our Lord was the first to accomplish, doing so as representative of us all, culminates in the elevation of the *Per quem hæc omnia*; and then only, like new-arrivals in the divine presence, do we dare to address with the glorious liberty of the sons of God, him who dwells in light inaccessible, saying finally: 'Our Father who art in heaven . . .'

Such an anticipation of our destiny by faith and sacrament which is already fulfilled in the person of the second Adam, is St Paul's justification for telescoping things in a way which at first sight is disconcerting: 'you are risen, you are seated in heaven with Christ. . . .' The whole teaching is set out in detail in the Epistle to the Hebrews, in a very litany of astounding statements: 'You have come to the mountain of Sion, to the city of the living God, to the heavenly Jerusalem, to the myriads of angels, to the festal assembly—the panegyris, to the Church of the first-born who are inscribed in heaven, to God, universal judge of the spirits who have attained perfection, to Jesus, mediator of the new covenant, and to his purifying blood (*i.e.*, mystically offered at the heavenly mercy-seat) which pleads more eloquently (in the very presence of the heavenly Judge) than that of Abel.'[1]

If we wish fully to understand the meaning of Christian life, and therefore of monastic life, we cannot attribute too much importance to this theme, to this ascensional motif, which we find in ancient

---

[1] Heb. 12. 22–24. The above translation has been made directly from the French text. The Knox version runs as follows: 'The scene of your approach now is Mount Sion, is the heavenly Jerusalem, city of the living God; here are gathered thousands upon thousands of angels, here is the assembly of those first-born sons whose names are written in heaven, here is God sitting in judgement on all men, here are the spirits of just men, now made perfect: here is Jesus, the spokesman of the new covenant, and the sprinkling of his blood, which has better things to say than Abel's had.'

spirituality. Any view of man's vocation which, in the last analysis, tied him down to earth would of necessity mean a disastrous mutilation of Christianity. Man is what God wills him to be only when he accepts and more than accepts—when he desires with all his heart, to advance beyond himself. But such an overstepping of self presupposes and involves a swift and glorious flight beyond the confines of this world. The only life which is worthy of man, the life that God, if one may dare to say so, expects of him, is not merely a human, but an angelic life.

In early Christianity there are, of course, other fundamental themes besides that of the Ascension. In the first place we may mention the theme of the return to paradise, although this has become more or less confused with that of the millennium, *i.e.* an earthly reign of Christ, in a world regenerated by a first resurrection. Now this would surely allow us to fix our aim on less alarming perspectives. For could not our hopes now be directed to a regeneration of the physical universe only, to a glorification of the risen flesh? In this way a blessedness would be found which would satisfy the soul yet without exceeding its compass. Why cannot our hope rest simply on a regeneration of our universe, on a glorifying of the risen flesh, which would thus find beatitude which would satisfy the soul, and at the same time remain well within its compass?

It is, of course, superfluous to dwell on the passionate efforts of so many contemporary Christians, not merely to interpret the themes of the millennium or of 'paradise regained' along these lines, but even to treat such themes as supplying, within the *flammantia mœnia mundi*, the final and complete satisfaction of the totality of human aspirations— and that in spite of the light thrown on such aspirations by the Gospels. In so far as they continue to claim the title of 'children of the resurrection', such Christians seem to interpret this resurrection as if it were to make them for the second time 'children of earth' instead of children of heaven.

The evidence of Catholic tradition, it must be pointed out, is utterly opposed to such a view. It, too, believes in the resurrection of the body and in the transformation of the world which will be centred upon it. Its faith in these things is perhaps stronger than that of our 'modern' Christians, since for Catholics these expressions are in no sense more or less dubious metaphors. They are certainly *not* just exuberant rhetoric, intended merely to adorn man's effort: namely the achievements of what Scripture would call 'flesh and blood'. They are the

theological expression of faith in a new creation, which, just as fully
as in the case of the first creation, must be the work, wholly divine,
of God alone who will raise the dead not in any mere figure of speech,
but in actual fact.

To repeat, however, for tradition such a vision is not that of the end,
but of the beginnings. Not only is the millennium, in patristic thought
as in apocalyptic literature, always a period which is merely inter-
mediary (and, moreover, already wholly supernatural), but the idea of
the return to paradise—and, in precise terms, to the *earthly* paradise—
appears in the eyes of the Fathers as the explicit expression of a return
to a preparatory phase which the Fall interrupted. St Irenæus, Origen,
St Ambrose, Theophylactus, to quote only a few names, are explicit:
the Christian's return to paradise is only a first step, just as the introduc-
tion of man into paradise in no way signified his final installation there,
but, on the contrary, the preparation for the trial that was to give him
access to heaven, to the eternal dwelling-place of God among the angels.
This explains why in the early Church the life of paradise in the true
sense of the word was simply the life of the baptized. Eternal life, on
the other hand, is a heavenly life. The life of paradise is brightened by
angelic and even divine visitations. Eternal life is life in the divine
dwelling-place itself, and that is why it is unfolded in that uninterrupted presence of God which is the prerogative of the angels. Between
the two, as between Christ's resurrection and his session at the right
hand of the Father, there must necessarily be an ascension.

In this connection there is a third essential theme in the spirituality
of early times, which may be considered as providing a link between
that of the return to paradise and that of the ascension into the highest
heaven. It is the eastern theme of 'raptus', being taken up. The garden
of Eden was situated in the east: that is, at that point of the earth's
surface where 'the immortal Sun' was to rise, 'the immortal Sun who
by his rays restores life to us', and whence he was to raise us with him
to the 'Inaccessible' temple of the divinity. The Christ-Orient, drawing up with him to the sanctuary of heaven that humanity which he
snatched from the depths of Sheol, so that it can no longer be forced
to cling to the earth's surface—such is the supreme vision of traditional
Christianity. Such is the vision the monk must foster in himself, a
vision of which he, above all men, is forbidden to make the smallest
diminution.

Perhaps it will be said that we are here moving in a world of symbols.
That is doubtless true: these realities are so ineffable that we cannot

attain to them otherwise. But let us beware of using the word symbol in such a way that we empty such realities of their content. The line of cleavage between a spirituality which would fain be interested in God only in so far as he can be of use to this earth of ours, and a spirituality which is interested in the earth only in so far as it becomes a means leading man towards God, occurs precisely at this point. The first can borrow from Christianity all the elements it likes; it will never be fundamentally Christian. The second is Christianity pure and simple; without those additions or modifications which, whereas they claim to explain or to justify, only succeed in diminishing and adulterating. That is why the movement, the impulse which is involved in the second type gives us the very meaning of monasticism.

If we are to understand all this we need to discover anew the all-embracing vision of the world and of history that our forefathers had. Too often, alas, our Christianity, shrunken and shrivelled as it is, has retained only the merest vestiges of such a vision.

Reduced to such a form we no longer understand even such vestiges and they may easily appear to us as relics surviving from a bygone age which we would willingly jettison. Thus in the light of the considerations we have entertained up to this point, Pascal's remark, 'man is neither angel nor beast, and the unfortunate part about it is that he who would play the angel becomes a beast', will appear as a natural objection. We are, indeed, far from failing to recognize the profound truth of this thought and we intend to extract its full meaning a little later on. But, if we take it in a narrow sense (which is not at all what Pascal had in mind), it becomes completely false and no longer expresses anything—if we may be forgiven the expression—but a theology seated between two stools, that is, a Christian ideal which is fossilized and abortive.

On the other hand, for the whole of Christian antiquity, man, in virtue indeed of the original plan of his creation, was essentially an angel of substitution. To call him to angelic life is, then, in no sense to call him to a mutilation; on the contrary, it is to remind him of his integral vocation, the only one which can enable him wholly to achieve perfection. If he fails to follow it, he will be nothing but a misshapen monstrosity, neither angel nor beast, indeed, but no more of a man for being neither the one nor the other.

The whole of Scripture presupposes (in many places the idea comes to the surface, though it is never systematized) the existence of another creation, doubtless prior to that of the six days, or perhaps one should say 'superior' to it: namely, the creation of the angels. As soon as God manifests himself, he does so surrounded by *elohim*, by celestial beings. When he would put the finishing touches to the work of the hexaë-meron, he deliberates with them and says: 'Let us make man to our image.' After man's sin, God addresses the *elohim* once more: 'Now man has become like one of us, capable of knowing good and evil. Let us now prevent him from stretching forth his hand and plucking the tree of life, eating its fruit and living for ever.'

Continuing as it does the old rabbinical tradition and retaining the entire cosmic or supra-cosmic framework within which the vision formed by St Paul or St John of the drama of redemption is circum-scribed, the tradition of the Fathers has never admitted the existence of a material world apart from a larger creation, from a spiritual universe. To speak more precisely, for them the world, a whole and a unity, is inseparably matter and spirit. What we call the material world is only the reflection of a reflection. The world is primarily a living, free projection of the Ideas of God, all up till that point collected together in his divine Logos. These Ideas over which the Spirit of life has hovered and which are, as it were, each and every one animated with a life of its own, have become created spirits. The choir they form is, as it were, the created image of the uncreated Image of the Eternal Father, the Logos.

But they in their turn exercise thought and by that very fact are in the image of their Creator. Then his fiat, reaching out to the thoughts of his thoughts as if they were his own, projects them in their turn outside themselves and outside him. And this is the visible world, the common objectivization, so to say, of the multiple angelic thoughts, just as the invisible world is a distinct objectivization of the manifold aspects of the unique thought of the Father. Thus the Word is both monogenous in eternity and first-born in creation.

We should therefore think of the material universe as a mirror held up to the spiritual, as a garden in which these spirits are gathered and which is made over to them, since it is to their image that it has been made. It is, as it were, the fringe of their garment: the waves of its light are like the scintillating robe with which the Creator has been pleased to adorn his invisible creature. Whence the idea which goes so far back in Jewish tradition (it is particularly apparent in the accounts of the exodus and of the construction of the tabernacle) that all things here below are reproductions of heavenly models. And on this another idea, so frequently met with in St Paul in particular, is gradually grafted, that in the plan of creation there are mysterious contacts between the angels and the elements of our world, so much so that the Epistle to the Hebrews was to declare that everything in the present economy has been subjected to the angels. They are the rulers of the cosmos, the *archontes* (*i.e.* princes) of the present world.

Thus the pregnant Wisdom which gives to the crystal of creation its rainbow-like beauty disperses and gathers up again in the interplay of a many-sided unity and of a harmonious multiplicity, the resplendent light of that Word, dazzling, incandescent, all-holy, who in the Apocalypse is the *Imperator* of the Cosmos.

In that first dawn of creation evoked by the book of Job, 'When the morning stars sang in chorus and all the sons of God shouted for joy',[1] the established universe rested joyfully on this foundation. It was indeed under the image of an immense choir resounding with the divine glory in the unanimity of love orchestrated by the Word, that Christian antiquity represented the primordial world to itself. In this wholly spiritual universe, at the beginning all was song. To the hierarchy of the created powers within this unity corresponds the sympathy and symphony of the cosmic liturgy in which the countless myriads in that festal assembly of which the Epistle to the Hebrews speaks, glorified the Creator with a single voice.

Across this continuous chain of creation, in which the triune fellowship of the divine persons has, as it were, extended and propagated itself, moves the ebb and flow of the creating *Agape* and of the created *eucharistia*. Descending further and further towards the final limits of the abyss of nothingness, the creating love of God reveals its full power in the response it evokes, in the joy of gratitude in which, from the very dawn of their existence creatures freely return to him who has given them all. Thus this immense choir of which we have spoken, basing ourselves on the Fathers, finally seems like an infinitely generous heart, beating with an unceasing diastole and systole, first diffusing the divine glory in paternal love, then continually gathering it up again to its immutable source in filial love.

Yet a dissonance has been introduced into the universal harmony, for an obstacle has arisen which attempts to arrest the stream of being flowing out into creation from the divine *perichoresis* of the Godhead.

---

[1] Job 38. 7. 'When the morning stars praised me together, and all the sons of God made a joyful melody.'—Douai.
'To me, that day, all the morning stars sang together, all the powers of heaven uttered their joyful praise.'—Knox.

Among spiritual creatures a whole segment of the great mystic rose flowering around the Trinity has become detached and, as it were, torn open. At its tip is one of the highest, if not the highest, of the created powers: Lucifer, the morning star *par excellence*, the Prince of this tangible world on which the last wave of light broke, the last echo of the great Eucharist resounded. What has happened, then? What has intervened? Simply, pride. So marvellously raised up by the Creator's grace, so near the centre and source of all things, the created spirit yet willed to set itself up as the centre, as if it in itself were capable of being the source. With it, those who followed it, turning away their gaze from the divine model from which they had emanated, flung it into the mirror of things, no longer being willing to contemplate or love anything but their own image. At the same time they formed a screen against the spontaneous movement of response which was rising up to the Creator from the most remote strata of creation, so eager were they to attract this to themselves.

But, as soon as this unhappy deviation had occurred, that part of the universe now dominated by pride, cut off from the source of love and turned aside from the centre of glory, discovered that it was being crushed by pride and was crumbling beneath it. The first darkness came with the hovering wings of the destroying angel. Leaving the choir where eternal life palpitated, the world, our world, entered the cold kingdom of death.

Claiming to become leader of the cosmic choir in place of the Word, and ultimately to usurp even the place of the Father at the origin of all things, Lucifer indeed was the first to consummate the fundamental lie, becoming, in accordance with the words of Christ, the father of lies. Desirous of capturing and fixing the movement of life himself, he could not transmit but only paralyse it.

Yet in that very fact would be found the root of possible salvation for the world which had gone astray. Being essentially subordinated to the spiritual world, the material world has been given over to it in a positive manner by virtue of the very design of the Creator. The lot of the one is thus linked with the lot of the other. Yet it is not identical with it. For all creation, of the material as of the spiritual world, remains the work of God alone. The Godhead alone could give autonomous being to angelic thought as to his own thought, could provide the created spirit with its mirror in the sensitive creature, as the Godhead itself had been primarily reflected in the created spirit.

God, who willed to save the world which had fallen under the empire of the devil, would then simply give to the creation of the world an extension which was not foreseen by the angels, thus preparing for them a discovery which would increase their confusion.

God was to bring to life this countenance of the created spirit which was reflected in the pure and transparent waters of prime matter, the countenance over which Satan in his narcissism had, until the fall, lovingly hovered. In conferring autonomous existence on that part of spiritual reality that existed potentially in matter, God raised up, in the very heart of that physical creation which had been defiled by a pure spirit, a spirit, clothed in flesh indeed, but whose innocence could restore the universe.

It is no doubt true that the fall and the violence of the devil have cast a veil of darkness over the whole of this world of which he had been prince from the beginning. But as to the existence of this world committed to the devil in a trust which he abuses, it will always, for all his efforts, elude him. As in the case of all being, and whatever may be said, the origins of the tangible world are ultimately in God alone. Thus it is God alone who knows what he can yet bring into existence in this kingdom which has been usurped by another.

Not only is the world free from that 'other' in its essence, but the very thing he loves most in it: his own image, will elude him. In other words, all the potential spirit there was in matter will spring to life under the movement of God's own Spirit. Our earth, drawn from the chaos, blossoms once again as a new garden of God and in this Paradise man himself appears. Restoring directly to the world the divine image which its blinded prince had disfigured in himself, Man is created as the possible Saviour of the world.

This second moment of creation is the source of an entirely new order of things. Hitherto, from the uncreated Spirit had proceeded the created spirit, then matter, mirror of the finite spirit, had extended the finite spirit in its turn, as if in another infinite. Now the dim beginnings of a new order appear to compensate the failure of the first. From matter itself, in its return movement towards the Creator, a new spirit emerges. It will embrace matter in the ascensional movement of its own creation, and will establish it once more in the cycle of thanksgiving, of the cosmic eucharist which has been frustrated by Satan. Thus the World, fallen with its prince, will be liberated from darkness and death by one who was the very child of earth, who has joined himself to the company of the sons of God.

Yet Satan, confronted with this counter-thrust on the part of the Creator, was by no means disarmed. In virtue of God's original design which is without repentance, the world in which man has appeared, if it eludes Satan's grasp at its highest and lowest points, remains his in all that lies between.

In the sphere of all this physical reality of the flesh in which man's very spirit has emerged, the devil has all too much room in which to tempt him, however incapable he may be of touching the deep springs of man's intelligence and freedom. In the earthly paradise the devil is at home. There he can freely develop the initial suggestion of evil under a form applicable to this new kind of spirit that man is. Equality with God could not be claimed by these proud spirits of light for a being made of the slime of the earth, so the Tempter interweaves specious enticements to sensual delight.

Man will yield. The potential redeemer of the earth will be the supreme conquest of the rebel spirit. Satan, incapable of repressing, will prove himself, alas, only too capable of seducing that liberty which he had felt surge up beneath him, as a possible taking back by God of the empire which the demon had stolen from him. And that is the second drama, an extension of the first: the fall of man re-echoes the fall of Satan. Instead of the world, in man, being snatched away from the empire of the devil, it was now, through man, thrown into the bondage of sin and death. Through man's consent to the revolt of the angels, the underlying liberty of the world, which seemed, in the human creation, to have won the day over the calamity caused by the demons, becomes subservient to it.

Thus we see how man appeared in the universe as an angel of sub-stitution. A new Lucifer, he was to occupy the place left empty by the first Lucifer in the choir of the universal eucharist. Born of the very world that its first prince had involved in his ruin, Adam, the world's new master, was destined to reintegrate it into the *pleroma* of divine love, to bring it once more into the kingdom of light and life.

But—surrendering his liberty as he did under the sway of the devil, what he did was to give the latter, not only a victory he had not expected, but a closer domination over things. For the future, because of man, the earth comes under a positive curse.

God, however, is not at an end of his resources. The revelation of the creative possibilities of his Love has not reached its term. As on the first occasion God regained the world by re-creating in it the divine image which those who should have been its own transmitters had

defaced, so for the second time, God will regain man himself by
introducing into the world the eternal model of this image: the Word
in person. This re-ascension of the creation which man had inaugurated,
this rectifying of the line of creation which has descended primarily
from God to matter through the created spirit, is to continue. After the
created spirit has risen from matter itself despite both the first and the
second fall, the uncreated Spirit will raise up humanity to heaven itself.
As man, an incarnate spirit, was born in innocence from matter profaned by the pure spirit, so in turn the Son of God made flesh will be
born from defiled humanity, from sinful flesh, though escaping its
defilement. The divine Spirit works on guilty humanity as he had
worked on darkened matter. As Yahwe had planted the garden of
Eden in a world already haunted by malevolent presences, as he had
caused man, created in his own image, to flourish there, there now
appears in the self-same human race tainted by the sin of Adam, the
Virgin Mary, 'living paradise' as she is termed by the Fathers. When
the Spirit hovers over her, Mary becomes Mother of God, giving
birth in him to heavenly humanity, just as matter became man's
mother at the origins of earthly humanity. Thus the man born of the
first Adam will be saved and the world which fell with him will find
itself raised up in the second Adam.

The more bitter the frustration of God's first initiative of salvation
in Adam, the more striking will be the success of the second in Jesus.
Henceforward, not only will the sons of the earth and the earth itself
in them and with them be raised up to the choir of angels, there to fill
up the void made by Satan, but the Son of Man, gathering up the whole
of mankind in himself and retrieving the whole of creation in that
humanity, is henceforth to be identified with the eternal leader of the
heavenly choir: with the Word, with the eternal praise of the Father's
Love. Finally creation, separated from the Creator by Satan, finds itself
united to him again in Christ. At its term it returns to its source, not
to be reabsorbed there, but to come, finally, to an unfading flowering.

Thus the cosmic liturgy is not indeed merely restored but reunited
to its divine exemplar. Through the incarnation of the Word in humanity, which is itself an incarnation of the created spirit, all things are
recapitulated in their divine Model and the choir of spirits is gathered
up into the very heart of the Godhead. Christ leads humanity back to
the earthly paradise through the Resurrection: through the Ascension
he brings it back to the angelic sphere whence the prince of this world
had fallen to ruin. Finally, entering right into the heavenly sanctuary,

he makes us sit down with him at God's right hand, he makes us, and the whole universe with us, re-enter heaven, taking us with him right to the very heart of the Father from whom all fatherhood proceeds. In the whole Christ, in the heavenly humanity of which Jesus is the head, man, associated with the angels' choir, is initiated into the very canticle of the Word himself. The divinization which Satan's pride had dreamed of, that his lie had promised us, is here reflected, but in quite another sense, by the humiliation of the eternal Son. Instead of being the prey of egoism, which is the 'mirage' of pride, it will be the miracle of humility, supreme gift of love.

It is thus that this vocation of the angel of substitution, which gives its meaning even to the creation of the first man, is accomplished, despite the betrayal of trust of which he was guilty. In a state of unhoped-for perfection, through the new creation (that in which the final man appears) God-made-man, in order to make man divine, brings about this new creation himself.

In these perspectives (which, once more, are those of the Fathers, or to speak more accurately, the providential plan which tradition helps us to discern throughout the Scriptures), it will be understood that Christianity is summed up in the journey which leads straying man back to the angelic life, in accordance with the deepest truth of his being. The patristic interpretation of the parable of the lost sheep shows us how this way, this truth, this life are all found in Christ. The ninety-nine sheep in the fold are the cosmos of the spiritual creation, of which our own world, very far from being the whole, is only the lower fringe. The hundredth sheep, gone astray, is mankind, with its own particular world, the material universe, of which it is the head. The shepherd leaving the fold in the depths of night to plunge into the dark and lonely ravines of a mountain lying under a curse in search of the one lost sheep, is the Word stooping down, even to us. As if the immensity of the angelic world which had remained faithful was nothing to him and to the Father in comparison with the frail creature shut out by its own fault in the dead of night, we see him coming forth from his Father's house and going down to the deepest part of the chasm. Sharing all its sufferings, stripping himself of his divine glory, he finds the sheep in the abyss. Then he lifts it on his shoulders and, bent under the burden, retracing the painful road which it had trodden, he brings it back to the fold. As they both come in sight of the sheepfold, shepherd and sheep covered with the same wounds, their blood mingling, the unanimous joy of the faithful sheep, who are always present in the Father's sight, is transfigured. It is as if, discovering an aspect of divine love and Wisdom hitherto unknown, the cosmic eucharist was expanding to infinity.

Here, in other terms, we have the prodigal son found again by his Father, brought once more into the banqueting hall where the eternal feasts of those who are 'always with him' are celebrated. Our earthly eucharist, mystically reproducing that 'of the great Shepherd of the sheep', is then seen as our reintegration into the eternal liturgy by the Word himself, whom Philo had already termed the High Priest of creation. This is precisely the vision that the Apocalypse sets before our eyes.

In Chapter 4 we are shown the uninterrupted glorifying of him who sits upon the Throne in the heavenly places. The four Living creatures as elements of the material creation, the twenty-four Elders as representatives of the angelic worlds, ceaselessly glorify him before whom the seven lamps of the Spirit burn. With them, after the Elders who cast their crowns before the throne, plucking their zithers with the plectrum or raising their golden cups full of incense, the myriads upon myriads of incorporated spirits continually repeat the trisagion: 'Holy, Holy, Holy, is the Lord God, the Almighty, who ever was, and is and is still to come. . . .'

In Chapter 5 a new figure appears. Clothed in the weakness of a suffering flesh, marked with bleeding wounds which shine eternally, he is yet at the heart of light inaccessible, and takes his place at the very centre of the emerald rainbow, his wounds shining with the most unbearable splendour of immortal brightness.

The same voices that glorify the Invisible now chant: 'Power and Godhead, wisdom and strength, honour and glory and blessing are his by right, the Lamb that was slain . . .'

Then, after him, appears a new multitude, composed no longer now of angels, but of men. A multitude of every race, of every tribe, of every people and of every language presents itself before the throne and before the Lamb. They are arrayed in white garments, they have palms in their hands and they too sing their song. But it is a new canticle in which appears a new word, that of salvation, which tells of the specially wonderful manner in which God's love has been shown forth to them: 'Salvation is to our God who is seated upon the throne, and to the Lamb.' They are, indeed, the souls of the redeemed. The Lamb has brought them back from slavery and, henceforth, they follow him everywhere, even to the bosom of the Father, virgins like him, and like him free from even the shadow of a lie.

Such then is the primordial vision in which the meaning both of creation and of Christianity is fixed for ever. The whole of creation is simply one spiritual reality: a vast choir of spirits opening out like a vast luminous but fragile corolla around the Trinity, the eternal Heart and undying chalice of all things. And Christianity is the inexplicable descent of 'one of the Trinity' into outer darkness in order to find the one petal which has lost its setting in the marvellous crown. It is the descent of the Word and our ascent with him. With him we must return to this choir where the voice which our world was to bring into the orbit of divine praise is silent.

The silence which is imposed on this false voice, which we know all too well from its lying and death-dealing whispers in the night, must be imposed by the voice of the Word. Then, in the place left void by Lucifer, the petal of our humanity, white and crimson, washed in the redeeming Blood and marked with the glory of Christ's divinity, will close the restored circle of all creation with a jewel more splendid than that whose lustre was extinguished.

Here and here alone lies the whole meaning of human existence. Here below, indeed, as St Paul tells us, we have no abiding city. And that is why here on earth we must always be as strangers and pilgrims. The city we are waiting for is in heaven. Our fatherland is the heavenly Jerusalem. It was Abraham who sought it first, and after him all the other patriarchs and prophets, all the witnesses to God and the Lamb. It was for the heavenly city that Abraham left, forgot indeed, his earthly country and buried himself in the desert, heeding nothing but the heavenly Voice that was calling him. Otherwise, as the Epistle to the Hebrews says again, if their nostalgia had been merely for some earthly country, it was open to them to go back there. But the country they sought as they moved in the midst of their pillar of light, and which we in our turn are seeking, is a different city. It is the one whose gates are closed neither day nor night. It is the one on which all the treasures of creation are to converge. But it is one which has no need of the light of sun or moon or of any other luminary, for the Lamb and he who is seated upon the throne are the only lamp which lights it.

Towards this heavenly city a mountain leads us upwards, the mystic mount of Sion, described in the fourteenth chapter of the Apocalypse.

The redeemed, once they have crossed the river of baptism, move upward to the city in a white throng. This company, ecstatically echoing the timeless adoration of the hypercosmic powers in hymns to their newly-won salvation, mounts up towards Christ, the cornerstone, meeting place of heaven and earth, of the Church of the first-born whose names are written in heaven and the Church of the redeemed on earth. In these heights to which 'the virgins, those who have not defiled themselves with women' are advancing, we can see the monastic life. For, it cannot be said too often, monastic life is simply the perfect flowering of the Christian life. The monastery is simply the apex of the pilgrim Church. Or, if you prefer, it is the anticipated realization of its eternal destiny. And it is so because, like the heavenly city, it is essentially a choir of adoration, a liturgical society.

According to the grandiose imagination of Dionysius, the Pseudo-Areopagite, the ecclesiastical Hierarchy is in fact merely the image and extension of the heavenly Hierarchy, by which the latter in some sort draws humanity to itself. And the monastery is merely an earthly society completely identified, or tending towards identification, with that Hierarchy, *i.e.* that sacred Order, whose principle is the adoration of the invisible Father by all creatures in a harmony effected by Christ, the divine Orpheus. Its daily life is only an extension of the Eucharist in which we are brought back, in the Mystery of Jesus, to the unceasing worship of the Father by the incorporeal spirits.

As St Gregory of Nyssa says so magnificently:

> The whole of creation is but one single temple of the God who created it. But, sin having intervened, as the voice of those overcome by evil became silent, as joy no longer resounded in the heavens and the harmony of those who celebrated this liturgy was destroyed; and as the human creature no longer took part in the sacred festival of hypercosmic nature—the trumpets of the prophets and apostles gave forth their sound, like those trumpets of rams' horns of which the Law speaks, for they were preparing for the coming of the true Unicorn, the monogenous Word. In accordance with the power of the Spirit, they have thus provided a sustained echo for this word of truth, so that the ear of those whom sin had hardened might be opened and there might be once more a single festival celebrated in harmony, with tabernacles of the earthly creation placed next to the sublime and super-eminent Powers which stand around the heavenly altar. . . . Then, lift up your hearts, that they may enter the choir of spirits, taking David as master, conductor and leader of the choir, and sing with a single voice with him the sweet phrase which I repeat: blessed is he who cometh in the name of the Lord.[1]

[1] *Oratio in diem natalem Christi*, P. G., vol. 46, col. 1128–9.

The monastery is the tabernacle referred to, placed at the summit of the mount of contemplation, close to the everlasting dwellings. For, just as the division of the spirit between the divine realities and earthly realities, between the single word of Truth and multiple lies of the tempter caused us to succumb and slip down into the abyss, so the virginity of those who follow the Lamb whithersoever he goeth, that is, the perfect harmonizing of their thoughts and desires in their aspiration toward heaven, will reunite them to the choir, which has but one mind and heart.

Even to those whose lot is the life of flesh and blood, God, in his love for men, has given the grace of virginity, so much so that although human nature had fallen under the sway of the passions, virginity, stretching out a helping hand to it, enabled it to participate in purity, setting it upright and leading it to look on high. And that, I believe, is why the source of immortality, our Lord Jesus Christ himself, did not come into the world by the way of marriage, wishing, by the mode of his incarnation, to reveal this great mystery, namely, that purity alone is worthy to receive the *parousia* and the coming of God. . . . Such then is the power of virginity that it dwells in heaven near the Father of spirits, that it takes part in the choir of the hypercosmic powers and so works the salvation of men. Being the means by which God enters the life of men, it raises man to the desire of heavenly goods, it establishes a bond of familiarity between man and God and through it harmony is produced between natures hitherto estranged from each other.[1]

As was said at the beginning: it is not purity that is directly envisaged by the term 'angelic life' applied to monastic life, it is the heavenly character of a life in the presence of God, wholly consecrated to the glorifying of that presence. But we can see here the significance that virginal purity (obviously essential to the monastic state) takes on if we consider the superhuman aim which it finds by its new association with the cosmic liturgy. As Plotinus said long ago of the souls grouped around the One: 'When they sing, the choir always form a circle around their leader. But it may happen that it turns away towards the audience. Yet it is only when it turns towards the leader that the singing is true and the circle perfect.'[2]

[1] St Gregory of Nyssa, *De Virginitate*, Ch. III, P. G., Vol. 44, col. 324.
[2] *Enneads* 9, VIII, 38.

In monastic society as in the incorporeal society in heaven described in the Apocalypse, the divine presence remains the one and only centre. And the community of monks grouped around the altar, in all it does and primarily at the Office, but not only at the Office, is the community of praise, the church of the divine praise: *ut in omnibus glorificetur Deus*. This is to say that the monastery should be, as it were, the earthly incarnation of that divine *Agape* that the choir of angels reflects directly from the Holy Trinity. There one must be able to sing in very truth: *Ubi caritas et amor, ibi Deus est*. It is indeed in fraternal love consummated, and there alone, that God is willing to dwell. It is by that alone that he wills to be praised. Is he not himself the unchanging perfection of a mutual love? But it is also essential that cenobitical society should never forget the altogether heavenly character of its foundations. It must sing the *Ecce quam bonum et quam jucundum habitare fratres in unum!*, not in any sense as an indication of a state of rest in a pure but earthly happiness, but as a cry of exultation which transports it *in cœlestibus*, and higher still, *in sinu Patris*. As praise alone can be its basis, praise alone should be the end of this union of virgin souls. The bond of their fraternity has nothing natural in it: it is all entirely sacred, proceeding solely from the Father of lights. It is the common prayer, first in the Eucharist, and then throughout the psalmody of the Hours, which gives it its form and character. The Great Byzantine communities, the 'akopmetes', 'those who never lie down', sought to give a tangible manifestation of this in the *laus perennis*. Divided into several choirs which relieved each other at the oratory without intermission, they were unwilling that the common liturgical celebration there should cease even for an instant. This example is not for literal imitation, but its spirit should be that of every monastery. In the daily life of each monk it will show itself in a peaceful but constant effort towards continual prayer, again in accordance with the spirit of those other eastern monks who, by the prayer of Jesus of which we shall speak later, sought always to have the Name of Jesus on their lips that they might keep it always in their heart.

These are wonderful perspectives which enable us to see in the monastery the advance-guard of the pilgrim Church marching towards heaven. For the Church, it is indeed the living witness of the divine promises: of the new world in which God will be all in all and towards which the gaze of faith must never cease to be lifted. A promise and more than a promise: a realization even now anticipated or, at least, dimly outlined. . . .

4

But, it will be said, does not such an ideal in fact separate the monk from his brothers in humanity? Does it not, by force of things, lock up within a closed community this fraternal *Agape* which, being catholic, should permeate the whole of humanity?

To think this would be indeed to depend on sight and not on faith. It is because they are *in statu angelorum* that monks can love their brothers in humanity, as they should, with the most effective love. It is because they are like to the angels that they can be, like the angels, the 'guardians of their brethren' in all truth. The mountain of Sion is the citadel of Jerusalem at the same time as it is its sanctuary, *because it is its sanctuary*.

In so far as by the body they still belong in spite of everything to earth, monks can and should perform certain terrestrial obligations in regard to common human society. They have in fact magnificently acquitted themselves of such obligations in the past. But that is not the real service which they render nor is it the indispensable part of their work. God alone knows, the angels perhaps alone know with him, what is done for the world by this society which in the midst of the world is no longer of the world. God alone knows the manifold richness, the supernatural protection brought into the world through these openings into heaven . . . *Super muros tuos, Jerusalem, constitui custodes: non tacebunt die noctuque, neque cessabunt laudare Dominum.*[1]

[1] On the biblical and patristic conception of the relations between the angelic and the human worlds, as we have sketched them in this chapter, we venture to refer the reader to Appendix A of our book on the *Life of St Antony*, Ed. de Fontenelle, 1950. Cf. also in the *Dictionnaire de Théologie Catholique*, P. Arnou's article 'Platonisme des Pères', on the subject of the Augustinian view of the intelligible world.

III

DEATH, AND NEW LIFE

Monastic life, being the fullness of Christian life and the first-fruits of the life of heaven, introduces us into the angelic life by way of what we have called its eschatological humanism. But man cannot enter upon the angelic life without first dying and rising. 'No man can see God and live': the very sublimity of the considerations to which we have been devoting our attention up to the present demands that we should now boldly examine this saying without further delay, and ponder over its full meaning.

When Moses was on Sinai and God promised to be with him to lead his people, Moses asked God: 'Give me then the sight of thy glory', and God answered him: '. . . My face . . . thou canst not see; mortal man cannot see me and live to tell of it.'[1]

And when Manoah, who was to be the father of Samson, saw the angel of Yahwe rising up in the flame of the sacrifice, he exclaimed spontaneously: 'This is certain death; we have seen the Lord. . . .'[2] In the vision of Isaias, the seraphim who stood in Yahwe's abiding presence to serve him veiled their faces with their wings in order not to see him.[3]

As the Epistle to the Hebrews declares: 'It is a fearful thing to fall into the hands of the living God',[4] and again: 'Our God is a consuming fire.'[5]

All these texts have a single meaning: 'No man can see God and live': this means that the vision of God would bring death to a human being. The idea contained in this saying is a basic idea of the whole of Jewish revelation which we have lost all too completely, for with it we have lost the sense of the sacred, that is, ultimately, the sense of God. If anyone has not understood (let us think again of the seraphim in the vision of Isaias) that not only for men, but for all other creatures too, God is the Sovereign, the Utterly Other, the Pure, the Inaccessible, then he does not know what God really is. His religion will never be

---

[1] Exod. 33. 18, 20. [2] Judges 13. 22. [3] Isa. 6. 2. Cf. 5. 5.
[4] Heb. 10. 31. [5] *Ibid*. 12. 29 (résumé of Exod. 24. 17).

more than an idolatry. The divine reality is such that contact with it is crushing for our poor reality, for all reality other than itself. It recalls us, it recalls all other things, to their own nothingness.

Yet the New Testament deliberately invites us to this divine vision. 'Blessed are the clean of heart', said Christ himself, 'for they shall see God.'[1] 'We shall see (him) face to face', declares St Paul, and he adds: 'Then I shall recognize God as he has recognized me.'[2] And similarly we read in St John: 'Eternal life is knowing thee, who art the only true God, and Jesus Christ, whom thou hast sent',[3] for, says St John, 'No man has ever seen God; but now his only-begotten Son who abides in the bosom of the Father, has himself become our interpreter.'[4]

Does all this mean that the terrible statement of the Old Testament, 'No man can see God and live', was to be abrogated by the New? No, but it now acquires new meaning. It is in fact essential that man, in spite of everything, in spite even of the sin which draws down on him the wrath of divine holiness, should come to see God. That is his destiny. It is the fulfilment of the great prophetic promise: 'Those eyes shall look on the king in his royal beauty.'[5] And this vision is to give him life, true life, the very life of God. 'In thy light we shall see light, with thee is the source of life.'

But, as St Paul says: 'Flesh and blood cannot inherit the kingdom of heaven.' In other words, the natural creature, defiled by sin, cannot come to God and to the source of life which is in God, without undergoing a total refashioning. He still cannot, will never be able to see God and live, except now in this sense that it is essential that he die in order to see God, and, thus, live no longer with a life in itself mortal, but with the life of the immortals, with the life of the angels in heaven. The Epistle to the Hebrews which, it will be remembered, presents Christ to us as our precursor and guide to the heavenly tabernacle, even to the very presence of God, tells us that he himself has penetrated there, 'by way of the veil, I mean, his mortality',[6] *i.e.* by passing through death. And to us St Paul says: 'You have undergone death and your life is hidden away now with Christ in God.'[7]

We see, then, that it is not a matter of choosing in some way between a mysticism of the Cross and a mysticism of resurrection, as has sometimes been imagined. Christianity knows only one mystic way, that of ascension. But ascension to heaven presupposes an ascent by the cross. The one involves the other. The one brings about the other.

---

[1] Matt. 5. 8.   [2] 1 Cor. 13. 12.   [3] John 17. 3.   [4] John 1. 18.
[5] Isa. 33. 17   [6] Heb. 10. 20.   [7] Col. 3. 3.

They are so linked as to be insuperable. St John, particularly, shows so keen a sense of this truth that in his writings the two themes, death and exaltation, appear as if fused in one continuous vision. 'And this son of Man must be lifted up, as the serpent was lifted up by Moses in the wilderness; so that those who believe in him may not perish, but have eternal life', it was said to Nicodemus.[1] The context shows that the reference is to the ascension: 'No man has ever gone up into heaven, but there is one who has come down from heaven . . .'[2] But what immediately follows includes reference to the cross: 'For God so loved the world, that he gave his only-begotten Son . . .'[3] Later, Christ was to say to the Jews, linking together still more closely the act of the man who would deliver him up to death and the glory which the Father would draw out of it for him: 'When you have lifted up the Son of man, you will recognize that it is I myself you look for and that I do not do anything of my own authority . . .'[4] Finally, in his last public discourse Christ exclaims: 'Yes, if only I am lifted up from the earth, I will attract all men to myself.' We think immediately of his glorifying and rightly so. The evangelist immediately adds: 'In saying this, he prophesied the death he was to die.'[5]

Before stressing the counterpart of life, of divine life inseparable from Christian death, let us examine the paramount necessity of death, without which the Christian life, the angelic life of the monk, will never be more than an illusion without substance.

The paramount necessity of dying implied in entering into the heavenly life, carries to its logical conclusion the simple injunction formulated by Christ when he said: 'No man can serve two masters, God and Mammon . . .' One cannot live, like the monk, wholly for the world to come, unless one has abandoned everything in this present world. And dying means just that.

There is, indeed, an irreconcilable antagonism between the world to come, the world of the kingdom of God, and the present world, for the latter is the world where the devil reigns. 'Love not the world, nor that which is found therein', St John tells us, 'for the whole world is in the power of the Evil One', and he himself quotes the Master's inexorable statement: 'I pray not for the world . . .'

There is not, of course, in the Gospel any dualism between a world of matter, as such evil and condemned, and a world of spirit, intangible, immortal. All that has been made has been made by God. All, as it left

---

[1] John 3. 14, 15.   [2] John 3. 13.   [3] John 3. 16.
[4] John 8. 28.   [5] John 12. 32-33.

his hands, was good. All, re-created by the power of the resurrection, must become so again.

But what the word 'world' means in the texts we have just cited (particularly in the earlier ones) is, properly speaking, an 'economy', an organization, of all things. 'World' indeed for the ancients is not a simple convenient designation for an inorganic mass which merely gathers together beings and things. The ancient idea of cosmos always implies an order, a unified order, within which, as in a network (which is itself much more than an abstraction: it is basic being), everything, beings and things, find themselves enclosed. It is in that sense that the present world is condemned by the world that is to come. The coming of the future world must annihilate the present world because, once again, the world to come is the kingdom of God whereas the present world is the kingdom of Satan. Doubtless such an annihilation will be only a prelude to the resurrection. But the resurrection, the new creation, cannot be accomplished without passing through the intermediate stage of a new chaos. 'The corruptible must put on incorruptibility, the mortal, immortality.' But it remains that 'flesh and blood cannot inherit the kingdom of God'. If we suffer, if we die with Christ, we shall reign with him; but we shall not reign without having suffered, without having died. 'If anyone will come after me', he said, —'come after him', where to?—to the bosom of the Father—'let him follow me', along what road?—that of the cross, for there is no other which leads *in sinu patris*.

Thus then, in the very measure in which the monk outstrips the present life to attain eternal life, he must have broken so completely with this world as to be dead to it. St Paul tells us this once more: 'If by dying with Christ, you have parted company with worldly principles, you must be heavenly-minded, not earthly-minded, you have undergone death: and your life is hidden away now with Christ in God.'[1]

In these circumstances we can perhaps understand the disconcerting familiarity with death which was sought after and desired by the first monks, by all great monks. Let us beware of the double pitfall of seeing in this a morbid deviation—some sort of necrophilia—or (what would be equally wrong) of toning it down, of lessening its seriousness. St Antony, whose vocation was entirely bound up with the hearing of the words of Christ which we have just quoted: 'You cannot serve God and Mammon. . . . If anyone will be my disciple, let him

[1] Col. 2. 20; 3. 1–3.

take up his cross and follow me', St Antony, the father of monks, took up his abode not in just any cave, but precisely in a tomb. The early monks of Egypt or of Palestine were to imitate him. Ancient Russian spirituality, in which a monastic life full of a spirit of joy and paschal lights flourished, derives from the extraordinary personality of St Antony of Petchersk, who was actually walled-up during his lifetime. Even to-day Mount Athos, that storehouse where the spirituality of the Desert Fathers is preserved intact, considers its recluses, its hermits who are immured while yet alive in some grotto in the mountain, as the models of its asceticism.

These facts, apparently so odd, must by no means be interpreted in the light of more or less romantic ideas. Here we are not in the presence of a simple *Memento mori*, or a piece of grotesque mimicry. It is not, indeed, a matter of reminding ourselves that one day we shall certainly have to die. It is a matter of being really and truly dead. 'You are dead and your life is hidden away with Christ in God.'

This follows directly from the monastic profession if it is true that we should see in such profession, according to the earliest tradition, a sort of new baptism. Now there is no other Christian baptism than baptism into the death of Christ. 'You know well enough that we who were taken up into Christ by baptism have been taken up, all of us, into his death.'[1] 'If one man died on behalf of all, then all thereby became dead men', says St Paul again. 'Christ died for us all: so that being alive should no longer mean living with our own life, but with his life who died for us and has risen again.'[2] In effect, he finally explains to us, 'For me life means Christ: death is a prize to be won'.[3]

But we want to know more precisely what is the only acceptable sense in which we are to take this formula which makes a new baptism of monastic profession, in spite of the fact that there is obviously only *one* baptism, the baptism which begins every Christian life. The answer is that the mystical death implicit in every baptism, which for those Christians who are not monks is, directly, only an interior reality, without an immediate extension into objective reality, becomes actualized purely and simply through the monastic profession. Monastic profession achieves that effective detachment from the world which is identical with death.

Otherwise, if it is not that, it is nothing more than a scandalous comedy. Why, indeed, is the monk dispensed from the common social obligations of humanity? Why has the monk no longer to labour

[1] Rom. 6. 3.   [2] 2 Cor. 5. 14-15.   [3] Phil. 1. 21.

for the earthly city? Why has he not to toil to bring up a family? Why, in principle, as the Code of Justinian recognized, is he even freed from any obligation of defending his country when it is threatened or invaded? The reason for all these things is the same for the inhabitant of the monastery as for him who is buried in the cemetery. It is that neither the one nor the other any longer belongs to earthly humanity. The statement in the Epistle to the Hebrews: 'We have an everlasting city, but not here; our goal is the city that is one day to be',[1] applies to him literally.

If these are only empty words, if they are not really true, if the monk does not literally lead a 'dead life', he is only a sham monk, he is not a monk at all.

Yet the chief objection is immediately obvious. Unless, like the monks of Hindu Jainism, we are to make of the monastic profession a veritable suicide—whatever we do, the monk in point of fact remains very much upon the earth, and the life he will lead after his monastic profession, just as before, will remain an earthly life in its substance as in its details.

What, then, is the real point of all we have been saying? When we have got as far as the putting of this question, we are on the point of discovering the meaning of mortification. It is here indeed that those other words of St Paul, 'Death is daily at my side',[2] and 'You must deaden then these passions in you which belong to earth',[3] should be considered, for now they can be understood.

It is not a matter of a purely 'spiritual' death: that would mean nothing at all. It can only be a question of a real, in other words, a physical death, just as our presence in this world is physical. The physical reality of this death will be one with the reality of the essential renouncements included in the monastic profession: the renunciation of the things of this world by poverty, renunciation of the body by chastity, renunciation of the will (that is, of its free use in concrete actions) by obedience.

To detail the application of these demands will be the object of our discussions on monastic practice. Here, where we are primarily investigating the theory of the life, what is important is to stress the reality of all these exigencies. If it is only *in principle* that one renounces, if it is only renunciation of an abstract ownership and not of the concrete use, one is not a monk at all. What distinguishes the monk from the Christian who is not such, is that he binds himself not only to

---

[1] Heb. 13. 14.   [2] 1 Cor. 15. 31.   [3] Col. 3. 5.

the principle of renunciation (everybody is bound to this by baptism), but to its effective reality, a reality as immediate as possible.

Let us hasten, moreover, to add, that renunciation in principle, if it is not just a farce, must mean for all renunciations in fact. But for the rest of us, its binding force is more or less mediate. For the monk it is immediate. Once again, the monk is one of the violent who are not content with being prepared to welcome the kingdom of God when it comes, but who claim to take possession of it immediately. But this claim is a farce in so far as it is not accompanied by a renunciation which becomes immediately effective. We shall only live *here and now*, as the monk undertakes to do, the life of the kingdom, in so far as we die *here and now* to the life of this world. 'And yet I am alive', says St Paul, 'or rather, not I, it is Christ that lives in me.'[1] The second part of the phrase can only be real and effective in the exact measure in which the first has become so.

This brings us at one and the same time to what gives its significance to the mortification of the monk—what makes of him, as we have said, something other than a morbid necrophile—and to what makes that mortification possible. 'I live, yet now not I, but Christ liveth in me'— this statement is to be taken in conjunction with the one we have already mentioned more than once, but whose content we are far from having exhausted: 'Henceforth you are dead and your life is hid with Christ in God'—and the apostle immediately adds: 'Christ is your life and when he is made manifest you too will be made manifest in glory with him.'[2]

What does this mean if not that this death finds its significance and its possibility in life—but a life at present hidden, although in no wise destined to be so always. In other words, what gives its meaning to the 'dead' life of the monk, that which alone renders it possible, is that it is the life of faith, life in faith.

Without faith monasticism would be the most senseless undertaking conceivable. Without faith, it would be doomed to end in failure, in nonsense, a sheer impossibility. But, conversely, given faith, the death which is so deeply inscribed in monasticism becomes transfigured, just as for St John, let us remind ourselves once more, every mention of the Cross becomes transformed into a mention of the glorious ascension. And just as faith alone gives its virtue to monasticism, so monasticism alone gives to faith, to the life of faith, to life in faith, the fullest development of which it is capable here below. Nothing is more

[1] Gal. 2. 20.   [2] Col. 3. 3–4.

characteristic of the *Life of Antony* by St Athanasius than the way it reduces everything to faith, but an integral, totalitarian faith.

Faith alone, indeed, can give a meaning, the only acceptable meaning, to this paradoxical love of death with which the monk seems to be obsessed. It is very necessary here to see the whole problem, or rather the whole mystery.

How is it that the monk can achieve the perfection of Christianity precisely by anticipating death, when in Holy Scripture death appears as the supreme and final enemy of God? As the author of Wisdom says clearly: 'Death was never of God's fashioning',[1] in which St Paul agrees with him when he tells us: 'Death came owing to guilt',[2] seeing Death and Sin simply as characters who lend their masks to the same actor in the cosmic drama: the Devil. Is not seeking death, then, to seek the devil? To this question there is an obvious and immediate answer which contains the whole solution. If the monk goes forward to meet death, it is simply because Christ has done so in obedience to the Father: '. . . accepted an obedience which brought him to death, death on a cross.'[3] The monk in this respect is simply taking seriously St Peter's statement: '. . . he suffered for our sakes, and left you his own example; you were to follow in his footsteps.'[4] In desiring death, in tending towards it, he has no other desire than to be, in accordance with the inspiration of St Paul himself, 'moulded into the pattern of his death.'[5] It is in the measure in which the monk wills to be assimilated to Christ according to the full grace of baptism, that he wills to deliver himself up to death, that he says like Christ, in Christ: 'This my Father loves in me, that I am laying down my life, to take it up again afterwards. Nobody can rob me of it; I lay it down of my own accord . . . that is the charge which my Father has given me.'[6]

This reply, it should be said, contains the whole solution. It is only in Christ that this reaching out for death, apparently so shocking, acquires a meaning, its proper meaning. But to say this is at once to change the focus of the problem. If it is in Christ alone, in conformity with him, that the mystical significance of a deliberately crucifying asceticism is to be found, what then is its meaning? How can God, the God of whom we have been told that he did not fashion death, who says himself, 'It is an enemy who hath done that', how can he ask his Son, and all his children by adoption, to die?

We have reached the heart of the mystery. No rational solution

[1] Wisd. 1. 13. [2] Rom. 5. 12. [3] Phil. 2. 8.
[4]. 1 Pet. 2. 21. [5] Phil. 3. 10. [6] John 10. 17–18.

can satisfy us. It is a mystery we just have to accept. But, in order to accept it, we have to sound its depths.

It is precisely because death is the final, the supreme enemy of God, that Christ goes forward to meet it, and the monk after him. Christ only came into the world to lead man back to paradise, whence he would be able to rise to the vision of God. The monk follows Christ in order to return there too. Now what is it that holds mankind back from paradise? What is it that cuts man off from intercourse with the angels, but the chains which his sin has forged and which bind him to Satan? But the supreme test of this power which the evil one has acquired over humanity is precisely death. Death, which God has not made, is as it were the creature of the devil, the monstrous master-piece by which he keeps mankind far from God. It is thus impossible to conquer the devil, to liberate man and lead him back to paradise, without facing up to death. Until a man has reached that point, the essential thing has still to be tackled. So long as the devil has not been encountered in this place, in this stronghold that is peculiarly his own, we cannot say that he is vanquished, mankind liberated, and angelic life restored.

Thus the deliberate confronting of death by the monk brings us back to the fundamental aspect of monastic asceticism in the tradition of the Fathers. I mean its aspect of struggle, of strife, and, more precisely, of struggle against the demons.

In the *Life of St Antony*, the monk's vocation is clearly one of conflict. The monk becomes truly a monk, is really initiated into monasticism as such, in so far as he discovers this aspect of it by experience. To speak more precisely, he does not leave the novitiate, he does not enter real monastic life until the moment when he recognizes from his own experience that, according to St Paul's expression: 'It is not against flesh and blood that we enter the lists; we have to do with princedoms and powers, with those who have mastery of the world in those dark days, with malign influences in an order higher than ours.' [1]

Why does the monk retire to the desert? Is it that he may there enjoy the solitude, tranquillity and detachment which favour the pursuit of the interior life? If we are to take any account of the relevant ancient literature, such a view is completely inadequate. As Karl Heussi has shown so perfectly, to go no further than that is to neglect what seemed to all the early monks the most important thing of all.

[1] Eph. 6. 12.

If the monk buries himself in the desert, driven there by the Spirit of God, it is precisely for the same reason that, according to the Gospels, Christ himself went there; to be tempted by the devil, or more accurately, there to be put to the test by him and victoriously to pit his strength against him—the strength of divine grace.

The underlying idea, which may seem strange to us, but one which the Fathers have taken from Scripture and from the tradition of Israel (and for them it is as important as it was for their sources), is that the desert is the habitation of the devil. That they should think this, that Scripture should teach it, should not seem to us so difficult to understand after what we have said of the great vision of the spiritual world which was that of the whole of Christian antiquity. Let us recall that man is a first redeemer of the world. He is an angel of substitution, appearing in the very heart of the world which has been estranged from God by the fallen angels, in order to lead it back to God by his obedience. Consequently, in every place in the world where mankind is present and subsists, not yet swallowed up in death, the might of Satan is threatened, his kingdom is frustrated, his very presence is less powerful. Conversely, wherever man has not yet appeared, the devil remains sole master of the terrain. Consequently, in the desert, and there alone, he is at home. For the man clothed with the spirit of God in Christ, therefore, to bury himself in the desert will be to provoke the devil in his own lair.

But, more important still, such considerations now enable us to understand fully the deliberate choice made by the first monks in the midst of their solitude, of taking up their dwelling in deserted tombs. If the desert is the place where the devil, not yet driven back by the presence of mankind, remains immediately present, the tomb is the place where he has recovered that position, where he has snatched an initial victory, for by there crushing his rival, Man, he has wrested back from him the disputed territory.

Thus the astonishingly realist mind of the ancients saw Satan as particularly close, and very sure of himself, in the vicinity of tombs. In going to seek him there, they flung at him their boldest challenge. For it is in the form of death that the devil most clearly shows his influence in this world. If he is vanquished there, his defeat will be a total one. The supreme manifestation of God must be life, the divine life, communicated in the incarnation and final resurrection of Christ and of his mystical body.

In the same way death is the supreme manifestation of Satan. And that is why, without accepting death, we cannot finally triumph over him. Thus it is in death that the monk, like Christ, must overcome Satan if he is to overcome him at all.

People have sometimes been shocked to see ancient authors of monastic lives take over more or less wholesale, in order to sing the 'agon'—the struggle of their hero, the fantastic lives which were the delight of pagan antiquity, the best known of which was Antisthenes' *Heracles*. But the deep significance of such an adaptation should be understood. It is similar to that which likens Christ to Hercules, a comparison also very familiar to the Fathers, which Ronsard was to take up again in a poem not devoid of beauty which he entitled *L'Hercule Chrétien*. In order to understand this, let us think of Euripides' Alcestes. Thanatos, the god of death, runs up to the tomb into which the queen, Alcestes, has just been lowered. But at this moment Heracles arises, overthrows Thanatos and restores the dead girl to life. In this legend, the Fathers have caught the image they needed to make their contemporaries understand the intervention of God, in Jesus Christ, in the course of world history. Christ is himself the real Hercules of whom the legend only dreamed; alone, he has been able to confront him whom the second Epistle to the Corinthians calls 'the god this world worships',[1] him who, says the Epistle to the Hebrews, 'by his death would depose the prince of death, that is, the devil; he would deliver those multitudes who lived all the while as slaves, made over to the fear of death'.[2]

And the monk who is the supreme imitator of Christ is so precisely in the measure in which he is found to be entirely conformed to him in what is the essential act of his mission: death freely accepted, death conceived of as a struggle, as a struggle not only with ourselves or with the world, but as *the* struggle with the enemy of God.

Perhaps the chief interest of these considerations is to throw light on an essential point. In giving himself up to death, it is not death itself which the monk is seeking. There is no place in his thought or affections for any sort of necrophilia, simply because it is in no sense death that he loves and wills. What he wills is not death in itself but what Christ wrought by dying. For death as such the monk experiences all the horror natural to man and, moreover, sees therein the subject of a really supernatural horror: the specific mark of the demoniacal kingdom which he wishes to crush. Yet if with all the force of divine grace, that grace of conformity to Christ to which he wills

---

[1] 2 Cor. 4. 4.   [2] Heb. 2. 14–15.

to surrender without resistance, he reaches out towards death, as Christ in this world reached out towards the Cross, it is in the spirit of the Easter troparion which the Byzantine liturgy never tires of repeating: 'By *his* death he has vanquished death, giving life to those who are in the tomb.' What he loves, what he desires, is the Cross of Jesus, and in the cross it is not death which attracts him, the death which is all that those who stop short at appearances see, but the triumphant life which faith alone reverences there.

There is nothing more important than to become deeply imbued with these truths. If this view of the faith should come to be obscured, the whole of Christian asceticism, that school of life, of superabundant life, of eternal life, would immediately become discoloured like a decomposing corpse. If it is no longer the death of *Christ*, with all that is unique about it, that we desire, if it is just death, the Spirit immediately deserts our asceticism which is no longer redolent of anything but corruption. St Paul says of the apostle, the perfect Christian, 'we carry about continually in our bodies the dying state of Jesus', but he immediately adds, 'so that the living power of Jesus may be manifested in our bodies too'.[1] This final phrase immediately loses all its significance if, in the main, emphasis is allowed to rest on death itself and not on its complement: the death of *Christ*.

We have said already, and it cannot be too often repeated, that it is in so far as it is a life of faith that the monk's life must be a death-life. But this means that it is not just any such life, but a life the death of which is wholly enlightened by faith or, more accurately, by what faith has revealed to us of absolute uniqueness in the death of Jesus Christ. Since early Christian times, too often and too constantly, the attitude of the Christian ascetic in the face of death has been approximated to that of the Platonist philosopher. Platonism, it must be recognized, has lent to Christian asceticism, and more particularly to monastic asceticism, certain formulas, certain images that are particularly apt. But such formulas and images are only acceptable if they are wholly transfigured by their new context. If, on the other hand, as happens in Christian milieux where the sap of Christian life is no longer active, such formulas and images revert wholly to their original meaning and thus come to give their own light and atmosphere to our meditation of the Gospel, then the divine light becomes darkness.

The whole of Platonist philosophy, like the whole of Christian asceticism, can be considered as a preparation for death, as a disposition

[1] 2 Cor. 4. 10.

to accept death, as a seeking for death. And again as in Christian asceticism, this is not at all through a morbid taste for destruction, but through a deep desire of life, of true life, of immortal life. Like the monk, Plato desires death only as a way, not for itself, but for the beyond to which it leads, and this beyond he too conceives of as life, the life which is nothing *but* life.

But there the similarity ceases. The Platonist expects this life from death itself. It is a life in the possession of death which death will give to him. To receive it, all that is necessary is to die completely, not through constraint, but voluntarily, deliberately. For the obstacle to true life is precisely what death destroys: the life of the body.

The body is only a tomb for the soul. Once the soul has understood this and, far from resisting death, surrenders to it completely, as a happy reparation of the wild folly which made her come down into the body, she will be able to live again in the real sense.

For the Christian there is nothing of all this. If he seeks life in death, it is certainly not from death that he looks for life. If death is to-day effectively the master of life, it should rather be said that it is its tyrant, a tyrant which dominates it only to crush it. Death will never give life: life will be regained only by a mighty struggle. It is not purely and simply by dying that we shall live, but by dying such a death that it kills death itself—and it is only the death of Christ that can do that. For it is not the life of the mortal body which has injured the life of the soul. It is, on the contrary, the death of the soul which has injured the body and made it mortal. Life will be won back by the resurrection, not of the soul alone, but of the human being in its unity, inseparably body and soul. And if the passage through death can lead to the resurrection, it is only in as much as the soul, which has become alive again in Christ, has been made capable of burning away the death of the body as with a red-hot iron and of causing it to evaporate in its own flame.

The monk goes forward to meet death because he believes that this miracle, the greatest of all, has been accomplished in the death of Christ: because he believes that Christ was Life, the very Life of God, and that in making physical death his own, he has robbed the evil one of all his power and all his empire which are annihilated by this very act. Again he goes forward to meet death because he believes that Christ now and for the future lives in him: and finally because he believes that what has taken place in Christ will be reproduced in himself, in the same manner.

The death of the monk, so desired and sought after day after day, is then only the supreme evidence of his faith, his faith in Christ vanquishing death in himself, his faith in Christ present in his followers to vanquish it in them. The monk's mortification is ultimately nothing more than his witness given to Christ, the witness of his faith, which makes it clear that it is not only an intellectual thing but an engagement of the whole being.

And here we come to the final, and also the fundamental idea of monasticism, the sole justification for its appearance in the history of the Church. This idea is that monasticism and martyrdom—martyrdom, let us recall, in Greek, merely signifies witness and nothing more—are but one and the same thing. Monasticism arose in the Church at the very moment, at the end of the third and beginning of the fourth century, when martyrdom was disappearing. Monasticism in the Church is nothing else than martyrdom reappearing under a new form required by altered circumstances.

In the beginning the Church stood forth in open conflict with the world. Then the world seemed to make its peace with her. But could the Church, will she ever be able, to make her peace with it? Certainly not, if with Holy Scripture we understand the world in the sense we were speaking of just now. If the world no longer outwardly forces the Church into the contest, it is the Church who, interiorly, must take the contest upon herself. Here on earth, indeed, she could not cease to be militant, that is combatant. For the Church to compromise with the world, to accept deliverance from the conflict with relief, would be to renounce for ever the chance of eventual triumph. Only he who has striven will be crowned. He alone who has striven unto death will receive the unfading crown promised to the victor. The crown of glory is only for those who have worn the crown of thorns. . . .

That, ultimately, is the meaning that death had for the martyrs, and that will determine the meaning it must have for monks.

The authentic Christian martyr is in no sense the Stoic who has arrived at a joyful indifference to all creation such as Corneille presents to us in the guise of Polyeucte. If we want to look for a faithful portrait of such a martyr in literature, it should rather be sought in Eliot's St Thomas Becket in *Murder in the Cathedral*. He delivers himself up to death without trembling, but not without suffering—without rhetorically rejecting the whole of the rest of creation, but, on the contrary, in an outburst of love which bears him towards his brethren and towards the Father at one and the same time. The Christian martyr does not give himself up to death through hatred of life, not even of corporeal life, but on the contrary because he knows, like him whose sufferings he imitates and continues in his own flesh, that 'there is no greater love than to lay down his life for his friends'.

But the martyrs of history must speak for themselves. No one can do so better than the first of them whose authentic writings have pre-served his *novissima verba* for us. Let us examine them again with all their richness, vigour and life, a life immolated that it may bear fruit and be born again, free now of the restrictions of egotism and infinitely varied in the wholeness of Christ's (mystical) body. I refer to St Ignatius of Antioch, the bishop of the second century, brought from Syria to Rome to suffer martyrdom there. His entire journey was starred with epistles, which are like the itinerary of a Christian soul marching on to God along the royal road of the cross.

The epistle which prepares the Romans for his coming is filled with a glorification of the cross which is not a glorification of death as such, but of death with Christ.

I write to all the Churches and I would have them all know that I die most willingly for God, if at least you do not prevent me. [The Romans in fact were in the process of procuring his reprieve through more or less powerful influences.] I implore you: do not show me an untimely kindness. Let me become the food of beasts for by their means I shall be able to find God. I am the wheat of God and I am ground by the teeth of beasts that I may be found pure bread of Christ. Caress the beasts rather, that they may be my tomb and leave nothing of my body, so that in my falling asleep I am a charge to no man. It is then that I shall be a true disciple of Jesus Christ: when the world shall no longer see my body. Entreat Christ for me: so that, through their means, I may be found a sacrifice to God . . . Oh that I might enjoy the beasts that have been prepared for me! I hope they will be swift with me, and I shall cajole them that they may devour me promptly, not as they have done with some of whom they have been afraid and whom they have not touched. If indeed they should be unwilling through stubbornness, I shall know how to force them. Forgive me: I know what is good for me. Now I begin to be a disciple. Let nothing, of things visible and invisible, through jealousy, hinder me from finding Christ. Fire and cross, herds of beasts, tearings and rendings, dislocation of bones, mutila-tion of limbs, the crushing of my whole body under the millstone,

5

let the worst scourges of the devil fall upon me provided only I find
Jesus Christ.

Pleasures of the world and its kingdoms—all are nothing to me.
It is good for me to die and so to cleave to Christ Jesus, rather than to
reign over the ends of the earth. He it is I seek: he who died for us,
he it is I want, he who rose again for us. The birth pangs are upon me.
Forgive me, brethren: do not prevent me from living, do not desire
my death. Do not deliver me up to the world, do not seduce me
with material things, for I want to be God's. Let me receive the pure
light. When I am there I shall be a man. If anyone has God in
him, let him understand what I want, and have compassion on me,
understanding what constrains me. . . . My earthly love has been
crucified; there is no longer any fire of material longing in me, but
a living water which is murmuring in me and which says within
me: Come to the Father; I no longer take delight in the food of
corruption nor in the pleasures of this life: what I desire is the bread
of God which is the flesh of Jesus Christ of the race of David, and
for drink I desire his blood, which is 'incorruptible love'.[1]

The first point that strikes us in this text is, if one may say so, the
motive that inspires the martyr's desire. He advances towards death
with the sole purpose of finding Christ there, or, what amounts to
the same thing, there to find himself in Christ. For him death is but
the place where he must meet Jesus, where he must in some way be
identified with him.

And this becomes clear if we notice a second point: namely, the
abundance of the eucharistic images, and at the same time their constant transference from Christ to the Christian. Ignatius desires that he
himself should become the wheat of God. His personal aspiration to
martyrdom becomes one with his desire both for the flesh of Jesus
crucified, and for his blood which, as he says with magnificent economy
of words, 'is love incorruptible'.

The parallel is all the more remarkable in that the eucharist is, with
martyrdom, the other great theme of the epistles of Ignatius of Antioch.
And the eucharist is for him at once the realization of the unity of the
Church in God, through communion in love incorruptible, and the
real consuming of Christ crucified and risen, who assimilates each and
every one of us to himself. One can thus sum up and synthesize the
whole of his teaching by saying that in his eyes martyrdom is, as it

---

[1] Chaps. IV–VII.

were, the counterpart of eucharistic communion. Or rather: it appears as the justification, and, in some sort, the experimental proof of the reality of the eucharist. Through the eucharist Christians enter into the catholic cycle of divine love which is communicated to the world in receiving and assimilating Christ crucified. Through martyrdom the reality of the *Agape* of God, which is diffused through their hearts, breaks out triumphantly and the reality of their assimilation to Christ becomes at the same time a fact of experience.

It is necessary to go thus far if we would give these burning words their full meaning. And this belief in the mystical realism of the presence of the risen Christ revealing itself in martyrdom, in the death of the martyr, is in fact the constant teaching of the authentic acts of the martyrs. Martyrdom, if we are to see it as the early Christians saw it, culminates in a genuine mystical experience in which the Christian seems almost to feel the reality of the assimilation which the eucharist has wrought between himself and the dead and risen Christ.

When young Felicity, awaiting martyrdom in her prison, cried out with pain as she brought her child into the world, one of her gaolers said to her: 'If you cry out like that now, what will it be in the amphitheatre?'—'No,' she replied without hesitation, 'Another will then suffer in me.' All the wealth of meaning contained in this simple phrase will be found in the acts of the martyrdom of Polycarp, where it is fully developed. These are the last words of the friend of Ignatius, the one who collected his letters:

Having raised his eyes to heaven, he said: 'Lord God almighty, Father of thy well-beloved and blessed child Jesus Christ, by whom we have received knowledge of thee, God of the angels and powers and of all creation, as also of the race of the just who live in thy presence: I bless thee because thou hast deemed me worthy of this day and hour, so that I may be counted among thy witnesses, and that I may partake of the chalice of thy Christ for the resurrection of eternal life, soul and body, in the incorruptibility of the Holy Spirit. May I be received among them before thee to-day as a sacrifice rich and acceptable, as thou didst prepare and reveal it beforehand and hast accomplished it, O thou who art the faithful and true God. For this and for all things, I praise thee, I bless thee, I glorify thee through the eternal and heavenly High Priest, Jesus Christ, thy well-beloved child, through whom is to thee, with him and the Holy Spirit, glory both now and in the ages to come. Amen.' When he had pronounced the Amen and finished his prayer, the executioners lighted the fire. A great flame spurted out and we to whom it was given to be witnesses of it saw a wondrous thing, which we have kept in memory to declare to others. The fire formed as it were a canopy and, like the sail of a ship swelled out by the wind, it surrounded the martyr's body: and he himself, in the midst of it, did not appear like flesh consumed, but like bread in the baking, like gold and silver burnished in the oven, and we inhaled the perfume thereof as if it were smoke of incense or of some other precious spice.[1]

The sacrifice of the martyr bishop here seems like a final eucharist in which it is he himself who is the altar-bread transubstantiated into Jesus Christ.

If with such writings we compare the accounts of monks as handed down to us by Christian antiquity, we shall be struck by finding in them the same transfiguration of death by the presence of Christ, of the Christ who 'by his death overcame death'. If, for instance, we read in the writings of St Gregory of Nyssa his account of the death of his own sister, the Abbess Macrina, which he had just witnessed, we find gathered together all the themes that we have been considering. This death—I will not call it an apotheosis, the associations of the word are too pagan—is truly the passing of the Christian into Jesus Christ, by a perfect cleaving to him in his final triumph, in his supreme struggle:

The sun was about to set but the power of her mind was in no way diminished, and seeing the beauty of her bridegroom all the more clearly as she drew nearer to her end, she made still more haste to go and meet him. So, fixing her eyes firmly upon him, it was no longer to us but to him that she spoke (her little bed was turned towards the East). With hands joined, she spoke in a voice so low that we could scarcely hear; but her prayer was such that we could not doubt that she was talking to God and that he heard her.

'Lord,' she said, 'you deliver us from the fear of death. It is to you we owe it that the end of this life is the beginning of a true life. You leave us to sleep for a time and you will awaken us by the sound of the trumpet which will sound at the end of the ages. You entrust to the earth as a sacred treasure the earth of our body which you formed with your hands, and you will call it forth again from the earth, clothing with immortality and glory that in us which is

---

[1] *Martyrdom of Polycarp*, XIV and XV

mortal and deformed. You have delivered us from the curse and from sin, having willed for the love of us to be burdened with both the one and the other. You have crushed the head of the serpent whose doing it was that man in disobeying you became his slave. You have broken the gates of hell and in overthrowing him who was master of death, you have opened to us the way of resurrection. You have given to those who fear you the sign of your holy cross to confound that irreconcilable enemy and put our life in security. Eternal God, to whom I have belonged from my mother's womb, whom I have always loved with all the generosity of my heart, and to whom from my childhood to this hour I have consecrated my body and soul, give me, Lord, an angel of light to lead me into a place of refreshment and repose, with the holy Fathers. You, my God, who have shattered in pieces the flaming sword the flash of which made us tremble, and who pardoned one of those who were crucified with you as soon as he appealed to your mercy, please remember me in your Kingdom. I too have crucified my flesh with you, for I have been pierced as it were with nails by fear and apprehension of your judgements. Let not this dread gulf separate me from your elect. Let not the spirit who is envious of the happiness of man appear in my path to hinder me from going to you. Let my faults disappear in your presence. And since you have a sovereign power of forgiving the sins of men, forgive me those which the infirmity of nature has made me commit in my deeds, words and thoughts, so that in leaving this body I may find myself purified from my stains and that thus you may receive my soul into your hands as a precious perfume poured out in your presence.'

In uttering these words she made the sign of the cross on her eyes, lips and heart. Gradually her tongue had become completely dried up by the extreme fierceness of the fever, and she could no longer speak distinctly nor be heard; we only knew that she was praying because of the movement of her hands and lips.

Night had now fallen and they brought a light. Having opened her eyes, she looked at it, and gave a sign of her desire to say Vespers. But, her voice failing, she expressed what was in her heart as best she could by the movement of her hands and lips. After having said Vespers in this way, she lifted her hand to her face to make the sign of the cross: this told us that Vespers were finished. And uttering a great and deep sigh her life closed as she ended her prayer.[1]

[1] St Gregory of Nyssa, *Life of Macrina*, XI.

Plato said that the whole of life should be but a preparation for death. We have seen in what sense that can be said of the life of the monk. Deaths like the one the account of which we have just read, or like that of Christ himself, are indeed transfigured by the life they crown and consummate. They are no longer the fate to which we were inexorably destined by sin. They are sacrifices freely consented to, by faith in Jesus Christ, by the faith which literally transports us into him: the sacrifice that a whole life of abnegation produces as its perfect fruit, at the hour when the master of the vineyard comes to claim it. Then, faith having taken possession of the whole being, when the hour of the power of darkness comes, there is no longer anything in the monk, or in the perfect Christian, which belongs to it. The hour of the greatest— of total, abandonment becomes the hour of victory: in the farthest depths of the darkness of the world, faith grasps the divine light and can say, of this very hour: 'Father, the hour is come, glorify thy Son in order that he may glorify thee. . . .'

Death is necessary, as we said at the beginning, because the life which we are seeking, angelic life, is that of the world to come, and because we cannot reach the world to come without dying to the present world. But to die to the present world by faith in Christ, in Christ dead and risen again, is no longer simply to die. It is to overcome the very power of death which dominated the whole life of the present world and made it a perpetual slavery. It is to find again, through the great act of reparation through faith and love, the divine sonship which we had lost. By dying to a human life which had become disfigured into the image of the devil by the very fact of becoming mortal, we are born again to angelic life, to the life which brings to life in us again the imprint of the Son of God, the unfolding Image of the Logos of light and life.

IV

LIGHT INACCESSIBLE

IT is the search for God that gives monastic life its whole meaning. It is thus an angelic life and therefore a life which has, as it were, forestalled death and attained to the first-fruits of the Resurrection. But all this is equivalent to saying that monastic life is a contemplative life: or if we wish to be more accurate, that its ideal must be the vision of God. Eternity, to which a Christian death will bring us, will indeed be filled with that vision of God face to face which forms the whole life of the angels and saints. And it is certain that only in eternity are we capable of this vision understood in the fullness of its meaning. Once more, 'no man can see God and live'. But already here and now, in the darkness of faith, a certain vision is possible, a vision that is in some sort of the twilight, and it is after that vision that the monk must strive continually.

As we have said, fundamentally the monk is one who is not content that God should remain for him a 'he', a being of whom one speaks in the third person. He is someone to whom God spoke at the beginning when he called him, and who then listened so intently to the call or who became so obsessed by it, that he burned to respond, so that communication between God and him is established, henceforth never to cease. The monk is a man like Jacob, saying to the angel who has visited him by night: 'I will not let thee go till thou hast blessed me.' And he will wrestle with him in the darkness until the first faint light of dawn enables him to discern the outline of the divine countenance. The monk is the man for whom God is a person: a person whom he can meet, whom he longs to meet, a person to meet whom he abandons everything else. 'Thine eyes shall see the King in his beauty'; this promise is the motive power behind the monk's whole effort, once it has led him to loosen his hold on all those earthly things which so delight others.

The monastic vocation would be, as it were, deprived of its central pivot, if we were to neglect this mystical element. Monastic life without such an incentive, would be nothing more than a soulless code of behaviour. And, even though he possessed all the perfection of the cenobitical virtues, the monk would not even begin to be a monk, if he did not experience within himself an invincible drawing to be 'alone with the One', *solus cum solo*.

This search for God of which we have already spoken at such length has no meaning at all if it is not that. And it will not do to say 'mystical graces are not given to all, there can therefore be no question of confusing the quest for such graces with the search for monastic perfection'. Such a statement is only true if by an abuse of terms we confuse the mystical life with certain particular psychological experiences which are no more necessary to perfection than they are desirable for all. On the other hand, there is a knowledge of God, a knowledge sufficiently direct to deserve at least the name of chiaroscuro vision we have given to it, without which there is no such thing as Christian perfection. A monk for whom such knowledge held no interest and who yet claimed to be seeking God as he should, would be like the man whom Kierkegaard speaks of, who knows perfectly well that none has yet reached the North Pole but who, for all that, takes it into his head to say to his friends and neighbours: 'I am going to the North Pole', when all the time he is merely thinking of going for a stroll in the direction of the harbour and has no intention even of embarking.

The genuine monk, who is such not only in external observances but interiorly from the heart, is a man who knows that he has undertaken the ascent of Mount Thabor. What is the significance of this ascent if it is not to lead to the summit where the divine glory radiating in the transfigured Christ will appear? To see the light of Thabor must be the monk's highest aspiration.

But no sooner has this been said than we must examine what there is in such a desire that may be preposterous. It is essential that the man who desires this thing, who is urged to desire it by the call of God and the promise of God, should also realize that he can desire it only in fear and trembling. We must realize that the light of divine glory, the light in which God dwells, the luminous cloud into which God himself invites us to enter is what Scripture calls a light inaccessible, like Mount Horeb after God's descent there, which a man could not approach without being struck as if by lightning. On the other hand, as we have just heard St Augustine remind us, the old pagan gods were easily visible. In a passage of singular magnificence, the poet Lucretius shows us the joy, so easily satisfied, of the devotees of Cybele in contemplating the face of their goddess; but what was this face whose sight filled them to satiety? A mere idol. Similarly, Lucius in the Metamorphoses of Apuleius, describing his initiation into the mysteries of Isis, exclaims with assurance: 'I have been raised up to the stars, then I came down again to my own place; I have crossed the threshold of Proserpine [the goddess of hell] and I have drawn nigh to all the gods. . . .' But this is only a pompous way of bringing in symbolic ceremonies in which the powers of nature were supposed to reveal themselves to the initiate. And what an initiate! As an English scholar, who is an historian of these mystery religions which were yet the most religious cults of antiquity, writes: 'These divinities were certainly not over fastidious in the matter of worshippers.'

The God of Israel, on the other hand, he whom we call our God, is a hidden God. Let us recall these texts once more: 'It is a terrible thing to fall into the hands of the living God. . . .' 'No man can see God and live.' When Isaias received the vision of Yahwe amid the seraphim, he exclaimed: 'Woe to me because I am a sinful man . . .' And was not the first reaction of Jacob on awaking from the dream in which he had seen the heavenly ladder, to exclaim: 'How terrible is this place; it is the house of God, the gate of heaven, and I knew it not.'

Beyond all other men the monk must be permeated with this holiness of God. He it is who, like Moses, has been called to climb the mountain which strikes death to others the moment they touch it. He will not come down again himself until he has been clothed with uncreated light. Let us remember Moses, coming down again from Sinai, unaware that his own countenance had become radiant. Woe to the monk if we forget that 'the place where he stands is a holy place'.

The monk who is aware that this divine invitation is addressed to him would be slow of heart to respond indeed if such awareness did not invest him with sentiments that should properly be called religious, restoring to that word a meaning which seems, alas, almost to have disappeared from our thought. 'Religion' is, in fact, or should be, an abiding sense of what God is and of what is due to him. In other words, it is the sense of the holy. But it cannot be denied that such a sense is strangely absent these days even among those called upon before all others by vocation or state of life to exhibit it. We are in point of fact misinterpreting the holy filial liberty to which the grace of the Gospel calls us in our relationship with God, when we look upon him either as a comrade, or as an inexhaustible source of benefits continuously open for us to draw upon. Yet it is quite certain that these are the only two images with which for the most part our relationship with God corresponds. And what this amounts to is, that it is no longer God whom we put under the name of God, but an idol made up of our entirely human, indeed all too human, thoughts and imaginations. Let us not then deceive ourselves: far from magnifying the Father's love, we are degrading it. For that which forms its unspeakable grandeur is that the One who thus loves us remains ever the same: that is, the Holy One, eternally without loss or diminution of his dignity or holiness.

About twenty years ago now, a German historian and religious philosopher endeavoured to define the notion of divine sanctity by a phenomenological analysis of what is specific, absolutely speaking, in the religious manifestations of mankind, precisely in so far as they are religious. We refer to Rudolf Otto's book: *The Idea of the Holy*. Without being able to approve everything in it, we can yet hardly underestimate the fact that it revived a concept which, so far as we are concerned, was completely dead. But the scandal this book gave to a number of pious authors or thinkers says much, in truth, for the need there was for such analyses. We may be permitted to wonder whether with such phrases as the 'good God', the 'little Jesus' and certain other childish idols of a Christian imagination which has become degenerate, God is not, as it were, dead for Christians themselves at least as much as for those rebellious souls whom Nietzsche has provided with the formula of their 'denial'. Are there any more terrible and more irremediable blasphemies than those we utter on our knees, imagining that we are thus glorifying him whom we insult? The derisory image we form of God, and which is what we use when we claim to be adoring him, offends him much more directly than hatred, which is, after all, a misunderstanding.[1]

If the monk's seeking for God is genuine, and if his search is seriously intended to end in meeting God and enjoying his presence, obviously it must begin by a total rejection of such caricatures. The monk would not be searching for God if he were to go about in pursuit of such wretched idols. The monk can have no sympathy, no weakness for such manifestations of a poverty of expression which is unconsciously blasphemous. He is first and foremost someone who knows that God

[1] The question is perhaps not quite as simple as this passage would seem to suggest. What of the simple folk who, if deprived of their, admittedly inadequate, concept of *le petit Jésus*, will be left incapable of replacing it with anything at all?—Tr.

is not that, that God is nothing like that at all. And if he does not know it, he cannot be a monk, for he cannot seek God—for what he will be seeking for in that case, whatever it may be, has nothing in common with the God who has revealed himself to the prophets and in Jesus Christ.

On the other hand, the monk is one who knows from the beginning that God is great, that he is the Lord, the Pure, the Inaccessible, the Wholly Other. Such are in fact the harsh but salutary truths of which the word 'Holy' should remind us.

God's holiness does not mean only, or even primarily, absolute moral rectitude. Such rectitude, of a perfection that cannot be diminished, is simply the manifestation of an intrinsic quality of the divinity which is indefinable and which makes it God. And it is this quality which the word 'holy' suggests rather than embraces, and which its different synonyms can only indicate indirectly, after the manner of the seraphim of Isaias, who cover their faces as they sing the *Sanctus*.

God's sovereignty (or rather the fact that all other beings but himself are in comparison with him, as it were, pure nothingness) is again only a relatively secondary element of his Divinity, like a reflection of his greatness on that which it infinitely exceeds. To say that his holiness makes him the Pure One, the Inaccessible, is thereby to say much more. It is to place him in a category completely apart. The original meaning of the word 'Holy' or 'Sacred' is precisely that: that which is apart. It is tantamount to saying that his greatness is such that the very word greatness becomes inadequate for it. In talking of him all our human words fail, the most sublime as much as the lowliest. They are like birds whose breath fails because they have ventured into air so rarified that it becomes impossible to breathe in it. Ultimately, every resource is taken away from us except this purely negative designation: the Wholly Other.

In that lies the meaning of an essential paradox to which it is necessary to draw attention forthwith. Despite the clear terms of which we have made use up to now in speaking of contemplation, it is a distinctive mark of both Jewish and Christian mysticism to insist on the obscure character of the contemplation of the true God. The brilliant anonymous writer who has hidden his identity under the figure of Dionysius the Areopagite has laid an emphasis on this other kind of image which has become famous. But it would be a mistake to suppose him to be its creator or that he introduced it into Christianity. If, for

him, mystical theology is defined as an entering into the divine darkness, this is in accordance with a tradition which, through St Gregory
of Nyssa and Origen, goes back to what is an essential theme in the
Bible; that of the luminous darkness of the radiant cloud into which
Moses entered as he ascended Mount Sinai, at the call of God himself,
to meet him and speak with him face to face. This theme was at the
centre of Jewish, before it took its place at the heart of Christian
mysticism. It is, in fact, wholly orientated to the blessed Shekinah of
light and life which hovered over the Tabernacle and afterwards filled
Solomon's temple. There it appeared as an impenetrable cloud, wrest-
ing from the king the cry: 'The Lord is pleased to dwell in mystery.'

It is here that the clear-cut cleavage between a mysticism which is
fundamentally Christian, such as that of Dionysius, and neoplatonist
mysticism becomes evident; although Dionysius has not hesitated to
borrow certain details of vocabulary and concept from the latter that
all too frequently have obscured his originality. Whereas the God of
Plotinus is the One, that is to say a human concept purified only by its
sheer simplicity, the God of Dionysius, as he tells us explicitly, is beyond
the One, because he is beyond any concept taken from creatures. Only
complete Darkness, so far as all earthly or heavenly lights are concerned, can be the dwelling-place of his inaccessible light. Thus
Dionysius opposes the theology of affirmation, which speaks to us of
God in terms which are positive but necessarily borrowed from created
analogies, to the theology of negation which can only suggest the
infinite to us by methodically denying every such affirmation about
him who is beyond every idea that any created or creatable intelligence
can form of him.

One has to reach this total obscurity in order even to begin to have a
mere inkling of what God is. To speak of him, to speak of seeking him,
is literally not to know what one is saying so long as one has not
grasped something of this *Mysterium tremendum*.

But the unsurpassable beauty of Christianity, the unrivalled grandeur
of the monastic vocation, are revealed when, having attained to this
holy fear of which we can truly say that it is the sole beginning of true
wisdom, we can see welling up there that which is to become the river
of overflowing joy. For the divine Mystery, which is the *Mysterium
tremendum*, the mystery which communicates a fear which is like to
no other fear and which has been revealed to us in the Gospel in its
fullness, reveals to us at the same time that it is also the *Mysterium
fascinosum*, the mystery which is supremely desirable.

In other words, it is only in revealing all its magnificence to us that this mystery also makes known its supreme force of attraction. God only begins to be known as the God of love where he is finally known as the Saviour who dwells in light inaccessible. Grace, the revelation of which is, purely and simply, the revelation of God in the Gospel, towards which all the fragmentary revelations made to the prophets pointed—grace is indeed 'the gift of God', of which Christ spoke to the Samaritan woman. And the magnificence of the gift of God is not only that it is a gift which God makes, but the gift by which God gives himself. In it the Inaccessible comes to us himself. Therein the all-Pure chooses as his dwelling-place us mere vessels of clay.

Long ago, when Jacob mysteriously wrestled with the angel, Yahwe himself, the God of holiness, provoked him into saying: 'I will not let thee go till thou hast blessed me.' He has not revealed his magnificence without revealing at the same time his unbelievable desire: that we should ourselves desire communion with him. And indeed the revelation of his magnificence cannot but saturate us, since we are such as he has made us, with an irresistible desire to contemplate him, to see him face to face. At the same time that it pierces us through with the reverential fear of his holiness, a single dark ray of which blinds the creature, and crushes the sinner, it cannot but inspire in us an insatiable longing to return to him who is our source and origin. In the presence of the Holy One, the human soul, like every consciousness created in his image, is seized with the presentiment that he is its infinite Good; a Good which surpasses all satiety, but which we can never again cease to desire, even when we have merely glimpsed it, a Good which henceforward cannot allow any other desire to live in us along with the desire of seeing our God.

Newman, in his poem 'The Dream of Gerontius', has given wonderful expression to this double and inseparable movement of man, the fallen creature, at the first revelation of divine holiness. Although he knows that this holiness will shatter him, will burn him through to the very marrow, he who has caught a glimpse of the nearness of the holy God cannot refrain from casting himself into his presence, thus eluding the angel who would hold him back. What matter if he is to be consumed in this unconsumable fire? Once he believes that he has caught even a reflection of that light he can no longer live unless immersed in it.

The psalms most deeply impregnated with the impression of holiness that the divine Presence in the Holy Place has produced in man are also those in which the longing for that presence is expressed with the greatest forcefulness:

> O God, my whole soul longs for thee, as a deer for running water; my whole soul thirsts for God, the strong, living God; shall I never again make my pilgrimage into God's presence? For the courts of the Lord's house, my soul faints with longing. The living God! at his name my heart, my whole being thrills with joy.[1]

To this desire, which has been elicited by the divine Word itself, striking man with fear in the presence of Yahwe's dread majesty, the New Testament has promised a realization beyond all expectation. 'No man has ever seen God', St John tells us, 'but now his only-begotten Son who abides, in the bosom of the Father, has himself become our interpreter.'[2] He will not hesitate to place on the lips of Christ himself this prayer: 'This, Father, is my desire, that all those whom thou hast entrusted to me may be with me where I am: so as to see my glory, thy gift to me.'[3] Finally he sums up his whole vision of Christianity in these words: 'But we know that when he comes we shall be like him; we shall see him then as he is.'[4]

St Paul, in his turn, expresses himself in terms which imply no less: 'It is given to us, all alike, to catch the glory of the Lord as in a mirror, with faces unveiled; and so we become transfigured into the same likeness, borrowing glory from that glory, as the spirit of the Lord enables us.'[5]

The monk is precisely the Christian who has recognized in Christ 'the way, the truth, the life', and who intends to act logically over this discovery, a discovery of such a nature that it should not leave any of those who have made it tepid or indifferent. That in Christ the hidden God is revealed, that the Inaccessible has himself come to us to lead us back to him—the offering by God himself of such a possibility should take possession of all our desire and should henceforth be the motive power of all our efforts. Once again, this is the case with the monk, if he is more than a monk in habit only. The monk, like the seer of the Apocalypse, has seen a door opened in heaven. And this door is he who can say: 'No man cometh to the Father but by me.' From now on, for the monk, everything resolves itself into passing through that door, into plunging into the vision which it opens on to the Invisible.

---

[1] Pss. 42 (Vg 41). 2, 3; 84 (Vg 83). 3.   [2] John 1. 18.
[3] John 17. 24.   [4] 1 John 3. 2.   [5] 2 Cor. 3. 18.

The Hebrews, let us repeat, had discovered in the Shekinah both holiness and the *hesed*,[1] both the immeasurable grandeur of Yahwe and his infinite merciful love. The column of fire and mist, the thunder-charged cloud of Sinai, had brought them prostrate before the Sovereign Lord, the Inaccessible. But in this cloud which bathed Moses in a light never gazed upon by mortals, they were initiated into an unprecedented alliance. The God of heaven, the God who does not dwell in any house made by man's hand had come down even to their level. More than this: he had given them his law. He had spoken to the man who represented them as friend speaks with friend. And this not only for a brief encounter without a morrow. The alliance had been sealed by the descent of the burning cloud upon the tabernacle of assignation, the tent where God and man had met. In future the God of heaven, the God to whom no man can draw near, has made himself the companion of his people in their travels in search of the city that is to come. And when this people seemed finally to have established itself upon Mount Sion, the God who dwelleth not in houses made by man's hand, yet condescended to invest the sanctuary of Solomon with the sacred cloud which at once revealed and hid his divine presence.

When the people's pride had constrained him to disown them for their illusory assurance of holding their God now always at their mercy, like a mere Baal of the Canaanite alliance, God destroyed the sanctuary in which they claimed to imprison him. But this punishment had been but the prelude and the means to a higher grace. As early as this the Shekinah could have said to the people: 'It is expedient for you that I go away.' In Ezechiel's vision of faith, the Shekinah fleeing from the profaned temple had shown itself as the invisible companion of the exiles in their exile, of the afflicted in their affliction, of the captives in their captivity. And the prophet's other vision, a vision of hope, had promised that the Shekinah should return to a supernaturally constructed sanctuary there to reign visibly, and to dwell eternally with the new people of a new and eternal covenant, who would be filled with life-giving contemplation.

That is what is fulfilled for us to-day. 'We were not crediting fables of man's invention, when we preached to you about the power of our Lord Jesus Christ, and about his coming; we had been eye-witnesses of his exaltation. Such honour, such glory was bestowed on him by God the Father, that a voice came to him out of the splendour which dazzles human eyes; This, it said, is my beloved Son, in whom I am well

[1] *I.e.* merciful love.

pleased; to him, then, listen—we, his companions on the holy mountain, heard that voice coming from heaven, and now the word of the prophets gives us more confidence than ever. It is with good reason that you are paying so much attention to that word; it will go on shining, like a lamp in some darkened room, until the dawn breaks and the day-star rises in your hearts.'[1]

At the Transfiguration, the luminous cloud in which God had hitherto veiled himself came down on Thabor. This time the disciples were invited to enter it. There they gazed on Jesus, whom they had hitherto known only 'according to the flesh', as the radiant centre of this divine splendour.

In other words, as St John hints in his Prologue, the Shekinah is established for the future in the human nature of the Saviour. There, in his risen body, the new temple, which is no longer the work of men's hands, it will remain for ever visible to all those who cling to it. And it is in the final transfiguration of this resurrection that we must in our turn contemplate him in faith, so that, in accordance with the phrase of St Paul which we have quoted, 'seeing the glory of God as in a mirror, we may be transformed into his image'.

Thus, this divine glory, this shining of a light without compare, of which God said in the Old Testament: 'I will give my glory to none other', we now contemplate in Christ 'as with unveiled face', according to St Paul's phrase. Again, as St John says: '*We have seen* his glory, the glory, as it were, of the only-begotten of the Father', the inalienable glory of God is communicated to us, for its light inaccessible has come to us in Christ. In him, through the power of the Spirit, it has pierced through the veil of the flesh which hid it from us. For the future, although no one has ever seen God, he who has seen Christ has seen the Father.

All this is tantamount to saying that the ascent of the Thabor of contemplation, and the entering into the luminous cloud where God dwells, and the vision of Christ transfigured, are all one. If the monk is someone who is overwhelmed by the realization of the divine Holiness, but who for that reason only desires the more to contemplate the divine glory, it is because he is primarily a disciple of Christ, or rather a friend of Christ, like Peter, James and John.

In what sense should this be understood? It is not merely a question of the monk's occupying himself with an effective and imaginative meditation of the life of Christ 'according to the flesh'. We are here

[1] 2 Pet. I. 16–19.

concerned with an ontological reality and with the faith which should take hold of that reality.

The monk is one who lives not only *with Christ*, but according to the extraordinary Pauline expression, *in* Christ. The sacramental meaning of the habit which he has put on, revivifying the significance of the baptismal robe, is to put on Christ himself. As his aspirations are identical with those of the martyrs, they can be summed up completely in the words of Ignatius of Antioch: 'to attain Christ' (one could equally well translate: 'to obtain him').[1] Or, better, with Antony, the Father of monks, he will have no other purpose but to accomplish literally the Apostle's saying: 'I live, yet now not I, but Christ liveth in me.'

We are thus brought back once more to the question: Does this mean undergoing what modern people understand by a 'mystical experience'? Yes and no. Yes in one sense, for if no special psychological condition can be assigned to the monk as his objective, it is certain that what we mean by such an expression, should appear normal in monastic life. Yet it would be better to say, using a richer and simpler term, that contemplation understood as St Gregory the Great, St Benedict's greatest disciple, understood it, is the natural climate of the monk.

> There is in contemplation [he says] a great effort of the mind, when it rises to heavenly things, when it fixes its attention on spiritual things, when it strives to pass beyond all that is visible, when it withdraws into itself in order that it may be expanded. And sometimes indeed, it is carried away and takes its flight above the darkness of its stubborn blindness, so that it reaches out in some measure to the infinite light, furtively and in an imperfect manner. But, in spite of all, immediately baffled, it returns to itself, and, sighing, re-enters the darkness of its blindness, as it goes out from this light into which it passed trembling.[2]

At the same time, we cannot repeat too often, this monastic contemplation is not primarily defined by the particular state of mind that it presupposes in him who is the subject of it, but rather by its supernatural object. To invert the order of things, in accordance with a tendency which is wholly modern, would be to take the shadow for the substance. This experience of Christian contemplation is not an

[1] Letter of St Ignatius to the Romans, 5. 3.
[2] Homilies on Ezechiel II, 11. 12 and ff.

individualistic experience which each man remakes for himself, as if he were in fact the first or even the only one to make it. It is not a question of discovering God. He has revealed himself once and for all. It has been done. 'All is accomplished.' There is no longer even any new revelation to be looked for. 'We have learned to recognize the love God has in our regard', said St John, as of a thing irrevocably done.[1] What could we possibly want to add to that?

For it is in no sense through an individual, private revelation that this knowledge was communicated. Jesus Christ, in whom God reveals himself in giving himself, is the sole Bridegroom of an unique Bride, the Church. The Church does not seek for the truth and knowledge of God. She has them. She no longer seeks anything but the city of peace where eventually she will be able to live alone with the Beloved. The individual Christian life *par excellence,* that is, monastic life, is then only an insertion by faith, the prayer of faith, and the reception of the mysteries of faith, into this life of the Church. It is by that and by that alone that such a life will enter into the heritage of the treasures of wisdom and knowledge which are hidden (and revealed) in Christ Jesus.

As a contemplative, the monk has thus in no sense to be a discoverer of new continents, nor, consequently, the subject of unheard-of or exceptional experiences. He has only to allow himself to be wholly absorbed by the realities of faith which were all set before him at the very beginning of his believing, but which a whole life of detachment and prayer will not be too much to enable him to penetrate and in some measure be penetrated by them.

It is in this sense that it must be said of the monk that he is the 'true gnostic' of whom not only Clement of Alexandria but also St Irenæus speaks, whose entire aim is to contemplate, in Scripture, in the holy Liturgy, in his soul now enlightened by biblical and eucharistic revelation, 'the mystery of God, that is, Christ'.

Scripture indeed, the Word of God, is and will always remain the fundamental sphere of monastic contemplation. Here again it is essential to understand Scripture, to approach and use it constantly in the spirit of the early Church so well expressed by Origen. For the monk, for the contemplative, for the 'gnostic', it is not just a book, even one having the distinction of divine authorship. It is something quite other than a book. It is a whole spiritual world, a whole new universe, a whole cosmos of living thoughts, which are the thoughts

---

[1] 1 John, 4. 16.

of God himself. To express this more adequately: it is the syntheses of
the thought of God upon our world, taking possession of the world
itself from within, in order to remake it after the pattern of the divine
ideal—like a new creative word, only infinitely more effective. It is
God's plan revealing itself to the soul and imposing itself on it in flashes
of fire. For this plan is in no sense an abstract idea, it is a mystery of life.
It is the mystery of the Cross, that is, the mystery of a person: the
Mystery of Jesus, God made man, and re-creating man and the world,
by dying the death of Adam, and by consummating in himself the
death of the world, so that the latter might be reborn in his own
resurrection.

But this personal mystery cannot remain a mere object of thought.
In the liturgical celebration (and let us remember that for the early
Church, every reading of Holy Scripture is at least an embryo of such
a celebration), the mystery becomes a present reality, *the* reality for us
henceforward, into which we enter effectively, or which rather takes
possession in us: 'the Christ in you, hope of glory', says St Paul. Celebrating the holy mysteries, we become partakers of the Cross, partakers of Jesus. Through the Mass, we share in the mystery of redemption, through Communion we communicate in the Redeemer himself.
And in the sacred psalmody Christ, the eternal Word of God, himself
speaks in us to God; the Spirit who intercedes in us with unutterable
groanings, finds again on our lips the very words he has for ever
inspired.

And so eventually we fulfil the saying of the Apostle which was
taken up in turn by the Father of Monks: 'I live, now not I, but Christ
liveth in me.' In other words, the life of faith, the life of the Mystery-
in-us, becomes our life pure and simple. And contemplation, in the
Christian and monastic meaning of the word, is simply that and
nothing else.

'To see God' thus—which is the exact meaning that St John gave
this word in his prologue—is not in any sense the same thing as neoplatonist ecstasy. It is indeed the gradual recognition, through personal
knowledge, of the great personal acts in which God has revealed himself to us as *Agape*—as creating and re-creating love—but it is through
personal knowledge, not in the sense of knowledge that we have
acquired by our own efforts but rather of knowledge to which we
have come to consecrate ourselves without reserve. Or, and this
amounts to the same thing, it is to recognize it because one has oneself
come to share in this holy humanity, because one has become open to

it by faith, and because the Spirit who overspreads it has filled us with his fullness.

It is by following this way that the monk, in so far as he no longer lives except by faith in Christ who has loved him, will discover, with the Church and in the Church, the dawn of the vision of Thabor. Thus he will recognize in Jesus Christ that 'God is light and there is no darkness in him', because 'God is Love'. And to recognize this by living faith, which should come to be as it were the breath of the monk's whole life, will be to love him here and now with his own love spread abroad in our hearts by the Holy Spirit.[1]

[1] On the whole light-darkness theme in Christian mysticism and in particular for a justification of the interpretation of the Dionysian darkness which is to be found here, cf. Vl. Lossky, *Essai sur la Théologie mystique de l'Eglise d'Orient*, Paris, 1944, pp. 29 and ff.

V

IN SPIRITU

IT is contemplation, the twilight vision of the light of Thabor, possible even in this life, that is, so to speak, the heart of monastic life. But it is the divine Spirit alone who can make this heart beat.

In fact, the monk is and must be the 'Spiritual' in the Church, the man of the spirit *par excellence*. All Christians have received the Spirit through the mystery of the Holy Chrism, but he does not manifest himself equally in all. We may even wonder if the gravest ill from which our Christianity is suffering is not that of having more or less 'quenched the Spirit', to use an expression of St Paul. What place does the consideration of the Holy Spirit and of his gift at the beginning of Christian life occupy in contemporary devotion? It is to be feared that to this question we could not make an answer which would be frank and at the same time encouraging. Fairly recently a religious has not thought it out of place to entitle a book on the Holy Spirit: *The Unknown God*. How is it that things have come to such a pass that this scathing term is possible?

It is probable that the deterioration which our thought has suffered in the matter of the theology of Confirmation has had no small part in this. The vague and impoverished notion which the close of the Latin Middle Ages transmitted to us has involved in the same neglect both the sacrament and him who is given to us in it. Thus who among us would to-day think of basing solid spirituality on the three mysteries of Baptism, the Chrism and the Eucharist, as Nicholas Cabasilas did as late as the fourteenth century? From the moment one sees nothing more in it than a grace to fortify and make us soldiers of Christ, and not the great gift of the Spirit, it is inevitable that the sacrament of Chrism should no longer figure as anything more than a sort of sacramental without any precise purpose. More imposing than others because it is reserved to the Bishop, it seems on the other hand to correspond to nothing very clear: people do not see that the metaphor applied to this sacrament implies that it contains anything more than there was already in the simple anointing with oil of the candidate for baptism. But this narrow teaching, as has recently been shown, rests entirely on the pseudo-theology of the False Decretals, and purely and simply ignores the ensemble of the chrismal theology of the Fathers. The first consequence of this, unfortunately, has been to tend to make us ignore the Spirit, by making us fail to recognize the fact that he is solemnly conferred on the baptized.[1]

Confirmation, in fact, is precisely the accomplishment, the perfection, of Christian initiation, being the communication of the gift to which this initiation is orientated as to its goal: the gift of the Spirit.

By his resurrection Christ has been made second Adam because he has been made life-giving Spirit. And he becomes in fact the head of a new race in so far as he animates it with this Spirit, who is the very Spirit of God. A Christian life which does not expand into life in the Holy Spirit thus remains radically incomplete. If, on the other hand, monastic life is defined as integral Christian life, it must essentially be the accomplishment of life in the Holy Spirit.

From all time the Holy Spirit has had, as it were, his privileged witnesses in the Church. The first were naturally the apostles and disciples after Pentecost. We see the Church of Jerusalem radiant with the flames of fire. In the apostolic age it was the martyrs who took over from the apostles the rôle of witnessing to the Spirit. We have already sufficiently stressed the charismatic character of martyrdom as the early Church understood it. Christ 'become life-giving Spirit' took tangible possession, it was thought, of the man who offered himself for the reproducing in his own flesh of the very sufferings of Jesus. We have only to recall the account of the martyrdom of Polycarp. And above all we remember the words of Felicity: 'Another will suffer in me.'

It is this that explains the extraordinary devotion to the confessors which the Christian people showed.[2]

The attitude of the faithful in their regard obviously presupposed that they were filled with the Holy Spirit, so much so that there were no charismata that were not to be expected of them. The very exaggerations of this belief are revealing. It seems that there were cases where people went so far as to consider that the fact of having been a confessor for the faith could take the place of priestly ordination. In any case, as the correspondence of St Cyprian about the thorny

[1] Cf. our article, 'On the Meaning and Importance of Confirmation', in *The Eastern Churches Quarterly*, Vol. VII, No. 2, 1948.

[2] The term 'confessors' in primitive times denotes, of course, Christians imprisoned in imminent expectation of martyrdom.

question set by the reintegration of the *lapsi* into the Church shows, there is no question but that confessors abrogated to themselves, with general approval, the capacity to absolve penitents. Martyrs and confessors were in turn to be followed by monks. Early monastic lives are unanimous on the way the faithful flocked to their places of retreat. What was asked of them? Two things: miracles and inspired utterance. The crowds which pressed around them were eager for the same things which the crowds who pressed around Christ eagerly sought. Innumerable sufferers from disease hoped for a cure at their prayer or from their mere touch. And troubled hearts were anxious to hear from their lips the inspired word which would bring them enlightenment.

It is this which enables us to understand a statement, so often to be met with in our early texts: monks, we are told, hold in the Church the place which the prophets held in the Old Testament. They are the successors of the wonder-workers who spoke in the name of God, such as Moses or Elias. With these prophets of the new covenant, however, there is something those of the old dispensation lacked. Not only do they manifest the presence of the Spirit, they transmit it. The perfect monk for the early Christians is always the spiritual Father. The term must be understood in its most literal and strongest sense. That is, that they were, at least it was thought so, really capable of a spiritual engendering, of a begetting into that life of the Spirit which is the true Christian life, whole and entire. Hence the word 'abbot' by which they are designated, derived from 'abbas', that is, 'father'. Primitive monastic custom did not restrict this title to the superiors of communities. It was the prerogative of any monk who had attained to the summit of monastic life, thereby becoming capable of communicating the Spirit.

On this point, as on many others, oriental monasticism has proved amazingly conservative. In Russia as late as the nineteenth century, we find on the lips of St Seraphin of Sarov these words to a disciple, who recorded them after a vision in which the holy Staretz had appeared to him in the light of Thabor: 'Give thanks to the Lord God for his infinite goodness towards us. As you have seen, I have not even made the sign of the Cross; it has been sufficient merely to have prayed to God in thought, in my heart, saying interiorly: Lord, make him worthy to see clearly with his bodily eyes the descent of the Spirit with which thou favourest thy servants when thou deignest to appear to them in the magnificent light of thy glory. And, as you see, friend, the Lord heard this prayer of the humble Seraphin immediately.'[1] A 'spiritual father' of the fifth century would not have expressed himself differently.

Let us then ask ourselves the question which Montovilov, Seraphin's disciple, had begun by putting to him: 'What then is life in the Holy Spirit?' It seems that we might answer with St Paul that life in the Spirit is the breathing of a new atmosphere which alone maintains in being the life which is the true life.[2]

The Spirit indeed, in the original biblical sense of the term, is the breath of life, but of divine life. It is the breath which, as it passes over the dry bones of Ezechiel's vision, will restore life to them. It is the breath which in the beginning had been breathed into the nostrils of Adam, and had brought forth its fragile image, the soul. Nevertheless, compared with the man in whom the Spirit himself lives and breathes, the first man, the living soul, was still only flesh. The last Man, on the other hand, that is the ultimate, final man, the risen Christ, is made 'life-giving Spirit'. This means that he has no longer merely the simple life of a Creature made in God's image, because endowed with intelligence and will. His life, in his human nature itself, is henceforward *the* life of God; his intelligence is henceforward filled with the very knowledge of God and his heart loves what God loves, with the very love with which he loves it.

The first result of this is that he enters into a new world. It is not only that the tangible universe is no longer the true home of him who has received the Spirit, but that the new universe which is revealed to him, although it includes the created spiritual world, definitely penetrates beyond the sphere of created things. The world that he in whom the Spirit lives knows, is a world that is no longer the world as a separate object, in some sort existing outside God. It is the world such as it was when God sent it forth in the act of creation: a world in which all beings and all things are in communion with each other through their communion with God. It is the world, immense yet one, of the divine Wisdom, in which the measureless fecundity of divine life is revealed in the hierarchized multiplicity of creation, but without being broken up or separated. For all things are there found gathered up in the unbreakable unity of the life and thought of God. All things there become transparent to God. There God himself becomes all in all things.

[1] Quoted by Vl. Lossky, *Essai sur la théologie mystique de l'Eglise d'Orient*, p. 226.
[2] Cf. I Tim. 6. 14.

The world of the Spirit is indeed the created world, but it is creation perfected, overcoming the rent made by sin, plunging itself once more into its source, animated by the unique Soul which is creation's life at the same time as it is that of God. It is the world which nothing any longer differentiates from the thought of God upon himself, which is no other than the thought which God has of himself. Thus it is the perfect fulfilment of that divine Wisdom in which all that has been made is found again in the final union with the Bride, who discovers her true personality in consummating her union with the Bridegroom, that is, the eternal Word. Mankind gathered together in the Church, the society of the world of spirits, the world itself in its uni-totality at length accomplished, the creature in its fullness, thus becomes the daughter of God in espousing the only-begotten Son. It is made 'one flesh with him', having with him henceforth but one Spirit; the Spirit of God.

This eschatological reality, that is, this reality of an ultimate eternity, towards which the world tends, in which the energies of the Kingdom of God have been liberated by the ascension of the Son made man, this reality of the world seen in the light of faith becomes for the new man, the man of the Spirit, *the* reality. In other words, instead of sensing it as something existing behind the physical world as it presents itself to the senses or the rational reason, it is in the depths of his immediate contemplation of it that man henceforth sees this world of the flesh. Thus, it is not only another world that the Spirit reveals to the man who is indwelt by him, but this very world itself, inasmuch as the Spirit reveals the meaning of it to him: the world towards which he is tending, that of which he is at present only a spoiled sketch which the divine workman is in the act of refashioning that at the end he may infuse into it his own life.

If indeed the Spirit reveals a new, or renewed, world to us, it is because he puts into us and makes us discover in others, a new life, a new life which is none other than the life of the Ancient of Days. We only discover this world, in which beings are no longer in opposition, either among themselves or with their Creator who has become their Father, when we ourselves live by the life that must animate it, that life that is the very life of God. And this life is *Agape*, that is, the love of which St John has said that 'God is Love'. The Spirit alone, indeed, can give experience of *Agape*. For the world knows nothing of it. It is the soul of the Wisdom which was hidden in God from all eternity, and of which the Church constitutes the manifold revelation.

For the Spirit consumed in his flame the sacrifice of reconciliation, humanly impossible of achievement, which Elias had prepared, just as he consumed that sacrificial love which effects unity between God and us, because it is in the strictest sense divine, namely, creative and redeeming love. Obviously it is not the sort of love that seizes on some good ready to hand, in order to enjoy it for itself. On the contrary it is the kind of love that strips itself of the good it possesses, that strips its very self. It is the kind of love that gives, a love that gives *itself*. God alone is capable, properly speaking, of giving—he to whom all things belong. And he alone, the infinite, can give himself continually with no loss or diminution. In God, the Spirit is precisely the Gift, in which the depths of the divine life, of the divine being, are revealed as something utterly different from the being of a creature who by making himself the centre of all things becomes paralysed. Thus, it is the Spirit communicated from God to man who will shed abroad in our hearts the love which creates, which *is* the life of God. The Spirit will enable us to live this life, all of us together, transporting us all into God himself, or, if you prefer, by bringing God into us, at the root of all our thoughts and all our affections.

When this has been said, it is possible to understand in what sense the Spirit procures the gift of prophecy, enlightens the monk and makes of him the guide of mankind in its search for the true homeland. It is not that the Spirit has revelations, what may be called new revelations, to communicate to us. As we have said before, everything which can be and is to be revealed has been revealed to us in the Gospel, since all has been given to us. But the Spirit unfolds to us the meaning of the Scriptures. The things of which the Scriptures speak, at the very dictation of the Spirit, could indeed have no meaning for one who has not this same Spirit in himself. So long as we understand them only in a material, piece-meal way, we do *not* understand them, and the fact that one may be an expert in exegesis makes no difference. We can penetrate their meaning only in the measure in which we see certain themes in the Scriptures standing out and then forming part of a general pattern. Throughout the providential history of Israel, throughout the progressive summing up of the whole history of the world in the history of this people of God, whose beginnings were apparently so insignificant, but of which the apocalyptic consummation will pervade the entire globe, the unity of this pattern is gradually made clear to those who have established in themselves a sympathetic understanding of it. Contrasted with the necessarily piece-meal, shortsighted wisdom of men, the divine Wisdom which goes from end to end of the world and contains all history, disposes all things in it, *suaviter fortiterque*. Making all things work together as he does to the good of those who love him, God reveals its all-embracing unity and simplicity in what St Paul would call the mystery. This mystery of Wisdom is Christ, is the Cross. It is Christ recapitulating all things in himself, making peace by his blood, reconciling the world with God, gathering together into one body the children of God scattered throughout the world. It is his Cross, revealing to us all the treasures of Wisdom and knowledge hidden in this divine abyss, which is *Agape*, and which the Spirit alone can fathom. It is the Cross filling the world, consummating its history and projecting it from a temporal order, corrupted by sin, into the eternal present of redemption. The whole of Scripture is filled with that and nothing else. But for him who has not the Spirit of God in himself, all this has no meaning. On the other hand, he who possesses the Spirit sees all this solely as the unfolding of the 'great mystery', of the 'Christ, the hope of glory in us', and from then on never tires of exploring its riches in detail.

Yet, the mystery of divine Wisdom cannot thus be grasped by a soul without Wisdom taking possession of that soul and making of it the instrument of its own realization. Similarly, the gift of prophecy is bound up by the closest links with the gift of miracles.

We are here referring to these two fundamental gifts of the Spirit considered in their radical and deepest meaning. Prophecy, in this sense, is the discovery of God's plan, revealed in Scripture and fulfilling itself in the world. It is an entering into the secret thoughts of the heart of God who enables us also to enter into the heart of man, since the latter was made by God for God and is only revealed to him who knows its divine Model, who is also his end. And the supreme miracle which orientates and sums up in itself all the others, is the work of the new creation, by which this divine plan, until then hidden in God, is realized in the world by the very power of God who has revealed it. The miracle is the divine *Agape*, deploying its energies through the world of nature, which sin has set in the rigour of death.

Just as the monk in his capacity as man of the Spirit will be a prophet, because filled with the vision of the divine Wisdom, so he will be a wonder-worker because the mystery of love which is the key to this Wisdom will operate in him and through him. Just as the Spirit creates in him spiritual senses which mean that even in the midst of this world he sees what God sees and as he sees it, so he creates in him a spiritual heart, through which creative and redeeming love permeates the world to create it anew. By his very contemplative prayer, in which his faith sees God's great design infallibly realized, his love—which, to repeat, is the very love of God himself shed abroad in our hearts by the Holy Spirit—brings it about in the order of fact. Thus in a manner which is purely interior and independent of any ordinary or indeed extraordinary manifestation which God may grant him, the monk, reintroduces the first-fruits of immortality into this world which is mortally wounded by sin. The presence of the monk in the world—unconcerned as he is with it precisely in order that he may be wholly God's—maintains the world in true life, by ensuring in its midst the effective presence of the only source of that life.

Yet, however lofty these considerations on life in the Holy Spirit may have been, they have not yet reached the heart of the matter. We only arrive at the culmination—which is also the central point of St Paul's teaching on the Holy Spirit, with the phrase in which we are told that 'the Spirit soundeth the very depths of God'. All effective influence of the Spirit, indeed, and of his presence in a soul acting in relation to the salvation of the world, finds its basis and its objective nowhere so well as in what the Spirit brings about in us in our relationship with God. For the Spirit to make us capable of such a supernatural activity in this world, it is necessary, indeed, that he should first of all establish in us a really supernatural contact with God. But this activity itself, far from giving its meaning to the meeting and union with God, will have no eternal value except in so far as it is, eventually, wholly at the service of union with God and of that alone.

Here we come up against a truth which ought to be regarded as fundamental in our whole view of Christianity, but which, it must be confessed, is too much forgotten in our times. Moreover if there is a truth to which the monastic life should bear witness, it is first and foremost this. The truth of which we are speaking is a simple one. It should follow as immediately evident from the great affirmations on divine holiness which we recalled in the previous chapter. It is simply that God, and not ourselves, must be the end and aim of our religion.

The aim of any religion which is not idolatry or disguised magic, must be, not the exploitation of God to the profit of man, but the bringing of man to glorify God. In any case there is no opposition between the bringing about of the true good of man and the glory of God. In the magnificent words of St Irenæus, *Gloria Dei, vivens homo,* that is, God places his glory in giving life to men. But, conversely, men will only live through God in the measure in which they turn to him for his sake, and recognize him as the sole end they must serve. Thus, the essential gift of the Spirit is no new resource of mind and heart which he places at the service of our temporal activities: the capacity of knowing and loving God which he infuses into us, alone deserves this title.

Monastic life is fundamentally, as we say, 'theocentric'. That is, it turns us away from ourselves and the world to direct us immediately upon God. It presupposes in us recognition of the value of God only as transcendent, but infinitely above all comparison with that of any created object or even the entire world in its highest perfection. The great gift of the Spirit is to reveal that to us and make us appreciate it, 'by faith operating through charity'.

To repeat, 'the Spirit alone sounds the depths of God'. The Spirit alone can give us a knowledge of God which exceeds knowledge which is either radically inadequate or purely negative. The Spirit, because he makes new men of us, men participating in the divine nature, as the second epistle of St Peter does not hesitate to declare, the Spirit gives us the only knowledge of God which is on his level, because it is a knowledge through connaturality.

We must, then, rise to the level of such affirmations. Strictly speaking no one knows God save God alone. By the Spirit it is given to us to know him in some measure, because he assimilates us to himself.

The real work of the Spirit, which causes him to reveal himself in us as the *Holy* Spirit, is that we should no longer live in ourselves but in another. The gift of the Spirit is the gift supreme which sets us free from the prison of individuality. He opens all that was closed. He breaks down all barriers. He annihilates all opposition. He is in himself the *coincidentia oppositorum*, the reconciliation of opposites, which the philosophy as well as the mysticism of Nicholas of Cusa—the Christian thinker who has perhaps most deeply felt the gulf between finite creature and infinite creator, and at the same time the necessity of crossing it—took for its unattainable ideal.

The great work of the Spirit is to carry us over into Christ, the Wisdom of God. To have the Spirit in oneself is, while remaining personally distinct from Christ, no longer to exist outside him. It is no longer to live locked up in the deadly autonomy which through sin has sharpened the distinction between God and ourselves. On the contrary it is this distinction that faith should take as its support, for in that way it may return to the free and fruitful unity of *Agape*. Through the gift of the Spirit we ultimately come to be conformed to the idea God had of us, as that idea exists in its perfect state. The Spirit, engrafting us into Christ, makes us live and be as God thinks us eternally in his Word. That is, he restores us to our place in the totality of the divine thought upon humanity and upon the world. He re-establishes the infinitely varied and harmonious richness of the relationships which God had willed for us and the rest of men. But, above all, he plunges us anew into the infinite unity of the Word, where our limitations vanish, where our own personal and inner life will be none other than the very life of God communicated to us. Thus we shall escape from our loneliness, from the solitude of every creature, of all creation separated from its Creator by sin. Henceforward, literally, 'It is no longer I who live, it is Christ who liveth in me.'

At the same time, precisely because we are restored after the pattern of our eternal Model, because we have come to take our place once again in the ideal which God conceived of us in creating us, our created nature, our very existence, far from being reabsorbed, comes finally to its fulfilment which had been retarded by the fall. For we are not really ourselves, or, what amounts to the same thing, we are not what God planned for us in creating us, until we become children of God. But we can only become children of God by being assimilated to his only Son. And this assimilation is effected only in the measure in which we have the Holy Spirit in us, the Spirit of the Father, the Spirit of the Son, by whom the Father and the Son are one in their very distinction. Our adoption by the Father, effected in the Son by the gift of the Spirit, is thus the culmination of creation. It can be said that until this adoption is an accomplished fact, creation has not achieved its end. The perfect monk, that is the monk who has become in the full force of the term 'the man of the Spirit', is thus clearly the eschatological man, the man of the last days, in whom the eternity promised to mankind is foreshadowed and inaugurated even here below.

In speaking, as we have done, of the most personal gift which the Spirit makes to us, we are brought immediately to the subject of the Trinity. For the persons of the Trinity cannot be thought of as persons unless considered conjointly. It is thus not surprising that the gift of the Spirit, the gift which in point of fact is nothing else but the Spirit himself and no one else, should be called in the Gospel purely and simply 'the gift of God', a gift in which God both gives and is given.

The Spirit in us is precisely the living bond of our belonging to the Holy Trinity. It is through this gift that the Trinity, which is a world to itself, the only really perfect world, becomes our world too.

The life of the Holy Trinity has its soul, as it were, in the person of the Spirit, because the Spirit, in a sense even deeper than that in which we have taken the word up to the present, is the Gift *par excellence,* whereas the life of the Trinity is a constant reciprocity in the mutual giving. But for us ourselves, the Holy Spirit is primarily the gift in which God is given to us and enables us to give ourselves. Indeed, this is the great gift of God, the gift that most properly should be called divine, if it is true that God is love and this love that God is, is a love which gives, a love that gives itself.

That indeed is why the gift of the Spirit to a creature represents such a flowering for that creature. All the frustration involved in the state of finite being, which sin has driven in on itself and shut up within itself, as soon as the Spirit touches it, breaks out into an unexpected spring which no winter will ever be able to wither.

There are perhaps no Christian documents which have expressed the idea of this divine springtime which is permeated by the action of the Spirit of God throughout creation more forcefully than the *Odes of Solomon*, those Johannine-like canticles of the early Church. The third of the *Odes* declares:

> He loves me.
> I could not have loved the Lord if he
>   had not loved me first.
> Who indeed can understand love if it is not
>   he who loves?
> I love the beloved and my soul loves him.
> Where his body is, there I am too and I will
>   no longer be a stranger to him.
> For there is no hatred with the most high and
>   most merciful Lord.
> I am dissolved in him for he who loves has found
>   him whom he loves:
> Because I love him who is the Son, I shall become Son.
> Yes, he who adheres to the immortal, will himself be
>   immortal.
> He who takes pleasure in life will live himself.
> Such is the Spirit of the Lord who lieth not,
>   who teacheth men to know his ways.
> Be wise, understand and watch. Alleluia.[1]

---

[1] III *Odes*, 2–13.

But it is particularly the eighth ode which describes the flowering in man of the love of God himself in spring-like language which immediately calls to mind the youthful joy of the Canticle of Canticles:

> Open, open your hearts to the joy of the Lord,
>   and let your love well up from the heart
>   to your lips,
>   to produce fruits for the Lord.[1]

It is indeed a flowering, but a flowering which presupposes a breaking open, a sacrificial rending, freely accepted by the creature who, in the egoism brought about by his sin, knows now that only the death of sacrifice can give him back the life of love.

> My heart hath been cleft,
> Its flower hath appeared
> And grace hath fructified therein,
> And hath borne fruits for the Lord.
> For the Most High hath opened me by his Holy Spirit,
> . . . He hath filled me with his love,
> And his wounding hath become salvation for me.
> . . . A water which speaketh has touched my lips,
> Generously sprinkled by the fountain of the Lord,
> I have drunk, I am inebriated with the living and
>   immortal water.
> And my inebriation was wise:
> I abandoned my vanity (*i.e.* my nothingness)
> And I turned to the Most High, my God.[2]

This theme of spiritual drunkenness, of sober inebriation was already known to Philo. We shall come across it again in the original text of a hymn of the Latin office:

> Læti bibamus sobriam
> Ebrietatem Spiritus. . . .[3]

It is closely related to the theme of mystical death which was to be so dear to Origen and was to nourish all the meditation of the Greek

---

[1] VIII *Odes*, 1–2.
[2] XI *Odes*, 1–8.
[3] Lauds hymn for Monday in the monastic breviary, 'Let us all joyfully drink of the sober inebriety of the Spirit.'

Fathers upon the theme of the Cross, as the means decreed by Providence for the divinization of sinful creatures. Both the one and the other embrace the idea, so essential to Christian mysticism, to the mysticism of the Spirit, of a rapture, that is, to repeat, of a going forth of man from himself, beyond the limits of created things, beyond the *flammantia mœnia mundi* of which Lucretius spoke, into the burning abyss of light inaccessible.

But side by side with these striking images which indicate the awful holiness of the sacred ground where the Spirit enables us to stand we find images of greater serenity in which reign incomparable joy and peace which the divine *Agape* alone can pour into the heart of man. Particular instances of these may once again be found in the *Odes of Solomon*; I mean the musical images which marvellously describe the sudden coming to life at the merest touch of the life-giving Spirit, of a world until then inert:

> As the hand moves over the zither
> and the strings speak
> So doth the Spirit of the Lord speak
> in my members,
> And I speak in his Love.[1]

The canticle of praise, praise that is exultant because loving, loving because loved, is, in fact, the spontaneous expression of the soul which, in God, is flowering and fructifying at the breath of the Spirit.

For the peculiar characteristic of the divine life as it is lived in the Trinity, by the Trinity itself, is to be at once open to receive from another and to give oneself. And in the Trinity, the special characteristic of the Spirit is to the bond of this union. He is the bond of this unparalleled unity of the divine being in which each person is only fully himself by being Loving Relationship. What the Spirit is in the Trinity he is also in us and it is thus that he brings it about that our persons, created as they are, come to the height of our perfection as creatures by being now nothing but loving reference to the Father, through the Son, in the Holy Spirit.

Through the Spirit, by experiencing life in the Holy Spirit, the innermost mystery of the life of God in the Holy Trinity is in some sort opened to us. We understand it through him in the measure in which, through him, we become sharers in it.

[1] VI *Odes*, I.

God, as Father, is at the origin of all things, of eternal as well as temporal realities. That is, he possesses his life, his being, only to give it to another. That other is the Son. Thus the Son is himself only by being given,[1] as the Father is himself only by giving himself.

But if the origin of the Son is a primordial giving of the Father, who brings it about that he is himself only by being Father, the mutual life of the Father and the Son is again only Gift. In the Son whom his essential love has, as it were, projected into existence, the love of the Father rests and takes pleasure. And the Son in return loves the Father and loves him with the same love with which he is loved by him, since everything, in the Son, likewise proceeds from the Father, and reproduces the Father with perfect fidelity. This gift, by which the Father communicates himself to the Son, and by which equally the Son is related, as it were, to the Father, so that their distinction is consummated in the union of a mutual love, is the Spirit, Love, the substantial Gift. Consequently, in the Trinity itself, the Spirit is that which enables the being that proceeds to be fully itself, by enabling it to return directly to him whence it proceeds, even within the very movement of love which bears the latter towards him.

This, too, is precisely what the Spirit is in us; he is the gift of the Father's love by which we love him himself in the Son, by which we become fully ourselves in becoming sons, that is by returning freely to our source, to *the* source, the Father.

In the cosmogony of Genesis, the Spirit is represented to us as an immense winged-creature hovering like fire over the watery and as yet unformed expanse of primordial chaos. Brooding, so to speak, over the world as a bird over its egg, what new being, moulded of matter and spirit, did this divine bird will to raise up from it? He willed to raise up man, child of God, a man living with the very life of God, true phœnix of immortality destined to arise from a dust that was, by essence, mortal.

The monk is the man whom the Spirit has raised up, not this time from the primordial chaos, which was still responsive to the creative Word and to the Breath of life which expressed itself by that Word. He is the man who has arisen from the sacrificial ashes in which death, freely accepted, has consumed sin with the old man inherited from Adam. But this man reborn of Christ, reborn no longer simply of chaos, but of death, is the man of the Spirit. He is not merely living soul, but man living by the Spirit. His heart of flesh has become the

---

[1] *I.e.* He *receives* the Divine Being from the Father.—Tr.

temple of the true God. In him God begins to be all in all things. Henceforward he is free of the earth. He rises from its dark depths towards the radiant heights whence the bird of flame swept down even to us. He no longer gazes on the burning bush merely from outside. He himself is burning without being consumed amidst the lamps of the Spirit, around the Lamb who was slain, standing near the throne.

VI

PER FILIUM

WHEN Jesus promised the gift of the Spirit to his disciples, he said to them: '. . . it is from me that he (*i.e.* the Spirit) will derive what he makes plain to you.'[1] The whole mission of the Spirit, in fact, points to Christ. As we have already said, he in whom the Spirit dwells finds himself as it were taken out of himself, to subsist henceforward in Christ. If, in accordance with the expressions just used, the whole mission of the Spirit points to Christ, it can also be legitimately said that its purpose is to direct us to him. To say, as we have suggested, that the perfect monk is a man of the Spirit, is tantamount to saying that he is the man in whom Christ is perfectly formed.

Actually, one of the fundamental themes of monastic piety has always been the imitation of Christ. Antony's vocation came from his hearing the words of the Gospel: 'If anyone will be my disciple, let him deny himself, take up his cross and follow me', in church. The monk is a man who hears this saying as if it were addressed to him in particular, and who strives to put it into practice. There and there alone the whole life of renunciation finds its significance. He is simply someone who has taken seriously the ideal held out to Christians by St Peter: 'He suffered for our sakes and left you his own example; you were to follow in his footsteps.'[2] The focal point of progress in the monastic life, along the painful road of penance which is its rightful path, is simply an ever closer conformity to Christ.

Yet the term 'imitation' is inadequate. To speak more precisely, it certainly expresses an essential truth, but for lack of more exact definition it may lend itself to equivocal interpretations. The imitation in question must go deeper than external copying. It must be a true assimilation. There are in fact two possible ways of imitating someone. One way is to regard the model from the outside and to seize upon a whole series of external mannerisms and habits and then to force oneself to reproduce them as well as one can. Such a way of imitation will always be lacking in internal cohesion, for it is but part of a piece-meal

---

[1] John 16. 14. [2] 1 Pet. 2. 21.

process which is the result of a more or less judicious *selection*. The 'copying' of the model thus obtained will always be lifeless. It will always be difficult to prevent it from becoming a caricature.

The other way of imitation is illustrated by the man who proceeds from the model, as effect from cause, instead of being adjusted to it artificially. And usually such imitation will be all the more genuine, in that the anxiety to copy, in the sense we have just explained, is absent. For it will result from an intuition arising directly from this being and its deep unity, instead of being the self-conscious action of the reasoning mind which is painfully occupied in putting together again what it ought to have begun by keeping separate. In this way there will be real relationship between the image and its model, just as there is between beings related by causality.

In the other case, on the contrary, the likeness will never be more than an artificial conjunction and not a natural continuity.

As soon as we are concerned with the imitation of Christ, imitation which is a mere (external) copying, is not only inadequate—it is absurd and offensive. To want to rush into it implies deliberate mis-understanding of him and ourselves. The danger of caricature then becomes inevitable and the caricature will become blasphemous. Christ is not to be imitated, because he is unique, the sole Well-Beloved of the Father. Nothing can be compared with him without being annihilated by the comparison. We only imitate him by being assimilated to him, in the deeper meaning of the expression, to such an extent that we are, as it were, gathered up in him and have become inseparable from him. St Paul's phrase is to be taken in the full force of its mystic literalness: 'I live, yet now not I, but Christ liveth in me.'

It is only in dependence on this primary truth that the other Pauline phrase can have a meaning: 'The Spirit bears witness to our spirit that we are the sons of God.'

There is, in fact, no other effective imitation of the Son of God than really to become children of God, not only, as St John reminds us, to be called by that name, but really to be what it signifies. There can, of course, be only *one* Son of God, and that is Christ. Consequently there is no other means of becoming children of God than in a certain manner to become Christ.

The teaching of the New Testament on the main principle of Christian life is in complete agreement with this conclusion. St Paul tells us that in being baptized we die with Christ in our natural life as children of Adam so that we may rise again in Jesus Christ. Now, as we have seen, what distinguishes monastic life from any other form of Christian life is that it strives to make this death as effective as possible here and now, in order that the risen life, lived in Christ Jesus, may be so too. The ideal monk, it may be said, will be the monk whom Christ has completely emptied of his selfhood, that he may take its place himself.

If all this is to be possible, we must admit that the relationship which is to unite us to Christ is quite different from that which unites or can unite two men in the ordinary way, or any other two personages in history. In fact it is worth remarking that St Paul describes this relationship in terms which are absolutely unfamiliar.

It is worth while to dwell on these expressions. There is no other means of understanding to the full the altogether special character which our relations with Christ must have. Without this, we naturalize Christianity and we no longer know our Lord, except 'according to the flesh', to quote St Paul once more.

A preliminary detail, of itself very revealing, is supplied by the verbs which St Paul invents to speak of Christ and of ourselves. They all have a common trait, the prefix *syn*, 'with'—here implying the idea of an action of which we become the subjects, but which is primarily that of another. Thus he speaks to us of suffering-with Christ, in order to be glorified-with him,[1] of rising-with him and of sitting-with him in the heavenly places,[2] of being vivified-with him,[3] of reigning-with him,[4] of dying-with him and living-with him,[5] in short—and this sums it all up—of being conformed to Christ.[6]

The adjectives, too, correspond to the verbs: as, for instance, conformable (σύμμορφος) (with the idea of being made conformable to the image of the Son, in Romans 8. 29, or that our bodies are conformed to the body of his glory, in Philippians 3. 21), or the untranslatable σύμφυτος of Romans 6. 5, which presupposes that we are to become as it were a single plant with Christ, grafted on him, engrafted into him by baptism.

Such expressions are either meaningless, or else they presuppose that the Christian life excludes autonomy and isolation. It implies that we enter into a sharing in the very life of Christ.

In this context, indeed, there is a typically Pauline expression which is both clear in itself and also compels us to give to the terms we have

---

[1] Rom. 8. 17.   [2] Eph. 2. 6.   [3] Eph. 2. 5; Col. 2. 13.
[4] 2 Tim. 2. 13.   [5] 2 Tim. 2. 11, cf. Rom. 6. 3.
[6] Phil. 3. 10.   The point of these references is, of course, to the Greek text.

just looked at the sense of a more than moral union. They indicate a truly mystical union. It is the expression 'in Christ'. Its extraordinary recurrence in the Pauline writings is the first point that strikes us. It can in fact be found there more than a hundred times.[1]

Doubtless the expression has not the same force everywhere that it has in certain texts at least. The poverty of the semitic languages in prefixes may, as we have said, have urged St Paul mechanically to fall back on the preposition ἐν, without always putting a formal intention into it. But, to repeat, it cannot be doubted that for him this formula has a most important significance, particularly when one compares his usual use of the expression *in Christo* and the strange verbs we have seen him invent. It means that we are not only associated with the *acts* of Christ, but rather that we are united with his being in a permanent manner. And even more: this life that is ours, from the moment that we are his, literally cannot be lived outside him. He is for us what the water is for the fish, the air for the bird: he is the atmosphere we breathe, the life-giving environment outside which we could not exist.

Strong as they are, these expressions still do not exhaust the riches of the mystical teaching contained in the expression *in Christo*: To arrive at such knowledge it is necessary to link this expression with two great Pauline notions which, to repeat, throw light on each other by their mutual relationship. The one is the idea that Christ is, as it were, a Second Adam, who is also the Last Man; and the other is the expression describing the Church as the Body of Christ.

The two concur to show us that our interior relationship to Christ is not only that of a living being in relation to his life-giving environment, it is the relationship of an organ in relation to the living being to whom it belongs. Christ is the Second Adam, and at the same time the Last Man, not indeed because, like Adam, he will be the source of a new race, but rather because he renews the ancient race by gathering it up again into himself. The Christian life is not a life which is led merely in dependence on Christ; it is the very life of Christ, coursing through us because we have been engrafted, incorporated into him by baptism. This relationship between us and him could only be compared to the relationship between the as yet unborn child and the mother who carries him in her womb, if it were not that it is in no sense an embryonic phase of our life, but the most mature expression of our personality.

[1] ἐν χριστῷ, or else, ἐν χριστῷ Ἰησοῦ, or ἐν κυρίῳ, ἐν αὐτῷ, in the phrases in which Christ is obviously the antecedent.

When this great reality has begun to take possession of our mind we can in some measure understand other expressions of St Paul even more disconcerting than all those we have met up to the present. Thus, to speak of Jesus and of what he is for us, he will use all sorts of nouns, as if Christ not only obtained the most precious realities for us, but himself *was* them for us. He will call him our wisdom, our justice, our peace and our reconciliation, etc. . . . For St Paul these expressions are to be taken quite literally. Entry into the life in Christ is like the entry into a new universe, where henceforward Christ and Christ alone is to stand for the whole of reality for us.

Does he not go even further, to the extent of using an unprecedented boldness of expression, describing Christ now not by nouns but by a verb in the infinitive, and by a verb which expresses the essential action, that of living? He was indeed to write in the Epistle to the Philippians, ἐμοὶ γὰρ τὸ ζῆν Χριστός, a phrase which literally is untranslatable and which loses much of its vigour when it is rendered 'Christ is my life'.

It should rather be expressed: 'For me life means Christ.'[1] Could our assimilation to Christ and at the same time his all-sufficiency for us, once we are his and he is in us by his Spirit, be pushed to greater lengths?

It is only when all this has been taken into consideration that we can begin to sense what St Antony was striving after when he sought to carry out to the letter the Apostle's saying: 'It is no longer I who live, it is Christ who lives in me.'

At the same time light is thus thrown on two of the fundamental doctrines of St Paul, that of the 'body of Christ' and that of the 'mystery'. It is here that the two poles of what we may call the mysticism of the monastic life are eventually to be found.

When St Paul speaks to us of the 'body of Christ', it is obvious that there are texts where this body is the Church, others where it is simply the risen body. In the first category are the expressions of the Epistle to the Ephesians: 'the Church, which is the body',[2] just as similarly in the Epistle to the Colossians we find this: 'He too is that head whose body is the Church.'[3] In the second category we have the great eucharistic text of the first Epistle to the Corinthians, in which the body of Christ received in the sacrament is compared with his blood.[4] But, in a third category, there are texts in which the term of 'body' applied

---

[1] Phil. i. 21.   [2] Eph. i. 23.
[3] Col. i. 18.   [4] i Cor. ii. 24.

to the Church is placed in direct relation with the eucharistic communion at the very moment when the latter is defined as communion in the 'body' of the risen Christ. Thus: '. . . Is not the bread we break, a participation in Christ's *body*? The one bread makes us one body, though we are many in number; the same bread is shared by all.'[1] These texts invariably prompt the question: Are there then, strictly speaking, two bodies of Christ, one 'physical', present in the eucharist, the other 'mystical', namely the Church? That was certainly not the way the Apostle saw things. For him there is only one body of Christ, his risen humanity. But the Church, existing only by participation in this humanity of Jesus, made 'life-giving Spirit', which is offered to her in the eucharist, is herself only 'the completion of him who everywhere and in all things is complete.'[2]

Thus, as St Augustine said, ultimately we are compelled to take the view that in Christianity, supernaturally, there is nothing other than Christ: the total Christ, *totus Christus*, Head and body, *Unus Christus amans seipsum*.

The second Pauline notion which we have just recalled, that of mystery, brings us to the same conclusion by another way. In the language of St Paul mystery is the great secret of the divine Wisdom. It is as it were the focus or central point of the divine plan conceived from all eternity and put into execution in these latter days in order finally to bring about the kingdom of God despite the revolt of his creatures. At the same time it is the deepest revelation of the resources of divine power and love, hidden from even the highest created intelligences. Folly to the Greeks, to the Jews a stumbling-block, the mystery is the cross of Christ, with all its power extended in time and space, with all its consequences. It is also indeed Christ himself, but 'Christ crucified', for it was precisely the crucifixion that was in truth 'a stumbling-block to the Jews, folly to the Gentiles'. The mystery is Christ and his cross, inasmuch as 'it was God's good pleasure to let all completeness dwell in him, and through him to win back all things, whether on earth or in heaven, into union with himself, making peace with them through his blood shed on the cross'.[3]   Or again, it is 'the presuming everything in Christ',[4] that is, the summing up in him of the whole history, so tragic in its beginnings, of man and the world, by bringing back all things, through the cross, to union with God and union among themselves in *Agape*.

---

[1] 1 Cor. 10. 16–17.   [2] Eph. 1. 23.
[3] Col. 1. 19–20.   [4] Eph. 1. 10.

The 'mystery', then, covers the same reality as the 'body of Christ', the same vision of final unity between ourselves and Christ, but adding to it the act by which this unity is effected, namely, the act of saving and re-creative love whereby Christ, in delivering himself up obediently to his death gave back life to us by the power of his resurrection. In other words it is by the 'mystery' that he is made the Second Adam, and so the end as well as the beginning of a new and eternal humanity, reborn from heaven after being born from earth.

If we examine the ideal of monastic life against such a background, we see that its purpose is to bring about, by the effective death of the old man, full participation in the mystery of the new man, so that we become *the* body of Christ, in the fullest possible sense of the term. In this way our meditation on the great Pauline themes leads us beyond them to others that are really Johannine.

It is from this perfect unity with Christ, towards which the thought of St Paul leads us progressively, that the thought of St John may be said to begin. The great allegory of the vine, or rather of the vine-shoot, of which Christ said: 'I am the vine, you are the branches', immediately takes us a step further on from the position where St Paul's thought of the 'mystery' or the 'body of Christ' ends. For St John, not only do Christ and ourselves form a single organism, of which he is the head, and of which we are the body; not only has what takes place in him a mysterious power of renewing itself in us; but Christ is at once the fullness of which we have only to receive, 'and grace upon grace'. The Johannine thought does not even stop at what St Augustine would call the total Christ, and what St Paul, in a less compact form called 'the Christ fulfilling himself perfectly in all'. For him, quite simply, Christ *is* all, immediately. It is not he who is to be extended in us. It is we who must, so to say, re-enter into him. He does not say: 'I am the root and you are the branches', but 'I am the vine-shoot, . . .' thereby implying that Christ and ourselves are neither more nor less than Christ alone.

At the same time St John throws light on the reason for this perfect fullness of Christ in himself, which has not so much to extend itself to us, as to gather us up into him. 'In him', he tells us, 'was life, and the life was the light of men.' 'Life', 'Light'—in St John these two terms may be said to exhaust the sphere of creative radiance. 'To live' is to be as God is. 'To see the Light', is to know him as he is. Now as St John says, in Christ 'we shall be like him; we shall see him then as he is'.[1] Christ, in fact, for him, is at one and the same time God himself and the fullness of all the divine radiance which the creature can reflect. For he is the eternal Word in which God, revealing himself to himself, at the same time reveals all he can and will give of him to the creature. Thus no individual being can add anything to Christ. On the contrary and emphatically, it is only by finding itself again in him that any being can at length fully be what it should be. 'Beloved, we are sons of God even now, and what we shall be hereafter has not been made known to us as yet. But we know that when he comes we shall be like him; we shall see him then as he is.'[2]

Even if the patristic reading of verses 3 and 4 of the prologue is doubtfully authentic, there is no doubt at all that it expresses a very specifically Johannine thought: 'All that has been made, was life in him.' In other words, it is, to repeat, only in Jesus who is the eternal Word, and not in their individual and separate existence, that beings will live with the 'true life', for themselves as well as for God.

We can now understand that St John knows only one Son of God, his only-begotten Son, Jesus. St Paul did not hesitate to call us sons, too, reserving for Christ the title of First-born. But for St John, however true it may be to call us children of God, since in fact we are so, there is no other Son than the only-begotten one. That is, we are children only in so far as we become one in him.

To grasp the ultimate meaning of monastic asceticism it is essential to have reached the summit of Christian contemplation of the Son. Death to self, the renouncing of one's own will, the crushing of the ego—all is explained by the single wish to anticipate the last day. Thus, in effect, we shall ultimately truly live, because we shall no longer live in ourselves, but in him, who is Life, who wills to be our life. Or, rather, he alone will live, in whom everything was created, in whom all that which was lost, and which he came to seek and to save, will be found again.

These thoughts bring us once more to the very fringe of the unfathomable mystery; that of the Trinity, of the eternal life of the Godhead. As we have said, to borrow the expression of Dionysius of Rome, this life is reduced to unity through the procession of the Spirit.[3] But in the first place, starting from unity of the Father as origin, the source and root of the whole Godhead, declared the theology of early times,

---

[1] 1 John 3. 2.   [2] *Ibid.*
[3] S. Dionysii, *De Trin. et Incarn.*, Denziger 8. 48 (17th edition).

is diffused and multiplied in the Son. And the Son realizes, in himself, the infinite life-giving richness of *Agape*, which gives the impetus and, as it were, the impulse to the divine life. The Son is thus necessarily the Only-beloved of the Father.[1] It is not sufficient to say that the Father loves him: what we must say is that he is all his love, that the Father who is love itself could love only him, for he could find nothing to love after him. He is the fullness of the lovable and the loved, perfectly responding to the fullness of the Father's love.

The creation of the world, even the creation of an infinity of worlds, could add nothing of lovableness to the Only-begotten. For he embraces in himself, for the Father, a world, an infinite and eternal world. In him, indeed, the Father contemplates all the possibilities of his creative Wisdom realized from all eternity. On him, he makes his Shekinah rest for ever, that Presence of himself in his work which gives the power of existing in the very source of being, and makes it resplendent in the heart of the light which knows no darkness. From him, finally, the whole of divine glory radiates, that is God revealing to himself all he is, in the diffusion of the inaccessible light.

Compared with that, our world will never be anything but a refraction through the void of some few rays of this infinite splendour. It will add nothing to it. It will not even acquire anything of it, except by returning to this source whence it has come, just as a spark would take nothing from a bush that burns but is not consumed.

But for the Father, the Son is much more even than all that. For he is not only this total infinity which the idea of a divine, eternal world presupposes. That world is included in himself, for, in so far as he is the fullness of Wisdom the world is not distinct from him. But he, as a person, as Son, transcends the very Wisdom of God in God's very heart. For love seeks not only the All, an all-satisfying fulfilment; it reaches out even more towards the Unique, the irreplaceable. In its aim as in its origin love is personal. In love, the whole being, the entire essence, gives itself and finds itself again. But in love, there is infinitely more, something of another order. What we mean by love is some *one* desiring to communicate with another, that is, with another self. If the first impulse of divine love is a word, is *the* Word, it is precisely there that the reason of it is revealed. The Word is communication not of something, but of someone to someone, whom he stirs into life and calls to. And it is to this divine Word, eternally giving utterance

[1] In Hebrew and Greek 'well-beloved Son' is synonymous with 'only son'.

without having to go out from the Father's heart to discover a filial heart there, that Newman's lines apply perfectly:

> I wish only to speak with thee for speaking sake,
> I wish to hold with thee conscious communion.

Christ, then, is from all eternity the Father's well-beloved, because he is in himself the world in which all creative richness of the life of the Father is unfolded in unsurpassable fullness. Again he is the Well-beloved by a higher title, because he is the Sole-begotten. For him who loves him and engenders him in loving him, he is the only one whose person is worth infinitely more than any world.

We too, then, can only be loved by the Father, and thereby even simply *be*, in the true and divine sense of the term, by being fused in some sense with this Unique being, by becoming members of his body, and thereby, elements of that whole which he bears within himself eternally.

Does this mean that Christian mysticism, the mysticism of Christ, of which monastic asceticism is but the condition, has as its objective, if not 'pantheism' at least some form of 'pan-Christism'? Does the dying to self, essential as it is to the life of the monk, that is, to the life of the perfect Christian, signify an annihilation of our personalities and, more generally, of creation as distinct existence?

To believe this would be to fall into a fundamental error which would entirely vitiate all we have been saying up to the present. If it is true that monastic life presupposes the mortification of all individualism, the very death of the self, yet it leads to the liberation and final maturing of the personality, that is, of *our* personalities and of the whole of creation, which will be, as it were, the ultimate person, whose final flowering, on the other hand, is to give history its meaning.

Here, poor human words, imperfect human analogies, obviously break down at all points. But, even if it were at the price of apparent contradictions, one must not allow any of the focal points of this wonderful reality to be sacrificed.

We cannot be as God wills us to be and as God sees us from all eternity, except in Christ. Our life will only be worthy of the name of life when it is no longer we who live, but Christ living in us. We must then return to him, our eternal model. We must die to ourselves to live again in the Only-begotten, in the Second Adam where God himself will be all in all. But that in no sense signifies any disappearance, nor even any reabsorption of ourselves into him. The gifts of God are without repentance, and if the division and separation of the fall is an evil which must be overcome, the distinct existence of creation, of each personal creature, is a positive good, eternally willed by God, which there can be no question of suppressing but only of perfecting.

How can this be reconciled with all that has been said previously? There is a simile, a fundamental theme of the whole of Christian mysticism, of the whole of 'Christic' mysticism since St Paul and St John, which alone can help us to glimpse it. It is the theme of Bridegroom and Bride, who are 'two in one flesh', the theme of the marriage feast of the Lamb.

For St Paul, the Church is at once the body of Christ, and the Bride of Christ, 'the fullness of him who is perfectly fulfilled in all'—terms which express her unity with Christ. She is the one whom Christ has loved, to the point of giving himself for her—terms which indicate that she is other than him, and not only other, but destined through him to a perfection of her own for which he has not hesitated to sacrifice himself.

In St John's view, the end of creation does not consist in a pure and simple return of all things to their divine model where their own 'figure' will fade away. It consists, on the contrary, in the appearance on the great day of a mysterious figure who until then will be hidden in God, namely, the Bride of the Lamb. '"Come with me," he said, "and I will show thee that bride, whose bridegroom is the Lamb." And he carried me off in a trance to a great mountain, high up, and there showed me the holy city Jerusalem, as it came down, sent by God, from heaven, clothed in God's glory.'[1] An expression which coincides with that of St Paul: '. . . Your life is hidden away now with Christ in God; Christ is your life, and when he is made manifest, you too will be made manifest in glory with him.'[2]

The Christian use of this nuptial imagery comes to us in direct line from the teaching of Osee, which was taken up again by Ezechiel, who represented Israel as the Bride of Yahwe, not indeed lovable in herself, but made so by the immense, the foolish generosity of the love with which God loved her.

Earlier the Canticle of Canticles, as also the Wedding-song, Psalm 45 (Vulgate 44)—*Eructavit cor meum verbum bonum*—had taken up and developed this theme (at least if we interpret them as Israel did) to the extent of drawing from it a whole mystical teaching on the marriage feast. What strikes us immediately as remarkable, even before we turn

[1] Apoc. 21. 10–11.   [2] Col. 3. 3–4.

to the New Testament, is the unprecedented use made of these images of the Bridegroom and the Bride. For the banal sexual symbolism of all nature religions, which have not developed beyond the magic stage, and which take over only the animal and sub-human elements from the relationship between man and woman, is substituted in fact a nuptial symbolism, that is, the symbolism of a union of persons. In the flesh assumed by the spirit, there is henceforward much more than flesh which is envisaged. What is envisaged is the mutual giving of two lives, of two centres of consciousness, of two beings who far from being fused into one by their union, each find self-fulfilment through the other.

But in order really to understand what this inspired symbolism means it is necessary to go back to the notion of man and woman given to us by the divine Word. In the account of Genesis, Woman appears as issuing from Man. She is simply a part of him who is detached from him, yet on the other hand, it is only by returning to him in marriage that she truly possesses the life, which remains the man's life, that she has received from him. Then alone does she become 'mother of the living', at the same time finding a name that is proper to her, that is, a true personality. Until then she had been only the shadow of man. Now, without ceasing to be 'flesh of his flesh and bone of his bone', but, rather becoming this again in the full implications of the original expression, she becomes his equal. Like him, like God whose image he himself was, she becomes truly the mistress of his life in becoming its donor.

With Christ and the Church, light is thrown on the obscure depths of this archaic narrative. For it is in relation to them that the mystery of Man and Woman is the 'great mystery' of which the Apostle speaks.

We thereby understand the true meaning of the nuptial mysticism of which St Paul has been, as it were, the initiator in Christianity, and to which Origen, on the eve of the first flowering of monasticism, gave the framework of its thought and the mould of its final expression.

The return of humanity to Christ in the Church, signifies, in the light of this, not an end and a cessation of created being, of distinct being, but a crowning, a perfecting which eternalizes it.

In the place of a limited being, shut in on itself, we have one that is made truly in the image of God, for our life there is substituted a life which is a mutual giving, like that of God, and, in some sort, a subsisting relationship, as that of the persons of the Trinity subsists.

In the created being who has renounced the deadly autonomy of sin, the true personality, far from being suppressed, only comes to light at the moment when the union with Christ is consummated. Each soul becomes a child of God, each one truly bears his image, and the whole of Mankind becomes the Daughter of God, in the Son. That is, far from being lost in the one to whom she cleaves and to whom she abandons herself, it is only there that she finally finds herself. In this experience, hitherto utterly unknown to the creature, an experience in which creation finds fulfilment, it discovers that there is a greater happiness to be found in giving than in receiving, and thus it discovers also the truth of the statement that he who would save his life, loses it, and he who resigns himself to losing it, finds it.

Mankind is aroused to live truly when it ceases to seek itself for its own sake and only seeks now itself *for* Christ and *in* him. Simultaneously, it discovers, let us note, that individual existence only comes to maturity in the union of corporate life. It is the Church indeed, and the Church alone, the sum total of regenerated humanity, who is destined to be the unique Bride of the sole-begotten Son, and who is here and now the betrothed of the Lamb. But this by no means implies that men should live in Christ at the cost of a fusion which would suppress the infinite variety of their individual characteristics. On the contrary, it means that the Church, in a much deeper sense than that in which the term applied to Eve, is the mother of the living. She is Mother, not in the manner in which Eve was, that is of a people whose very birth involved a division and separation and was the source of innumerable antagonisms. She is, on the contrary, the Mother of the people who are born from the gathering into a single body of the children of God, scattered by sin. She is our Mother, she is the heavenly Jerusalem, inasmuch as she brings us forth to the life that is lived in the love of Christ. And this means that through her it is given to us truly to live in the love which gathers us together into her, as she herself receives the true life in the love which joins her to the eternal Son.

Thus, the mysticism of the *Solus cum Solo*, that exists at the heart of the Church's life and is therefore to be found in monastic life, inevitably appears as the unfolding of the many petals in the unique mystical rose. There is no opposition here but the deepest, most intimate harmony. Each individual soul is destined for union with the Word within the union of the Church with Christ. The two control and condition each other. Or rather indeed, at the heart of things, the two are only one. It is on this note we must conclude.

On the one hand, there is no authentic mysticism in Christianity except in an ever deeper penetration into the life of the Church. To participate in the Catholic celebration of the mystery of Jesus is the only means we have of really living 'in Christ Jesus'. As St Augustine said, 'How should he who is not in the body of Christ, have the Spirit of Christ in him?'

But, on the other hand, the celebration of the mystery in the Liturgy of the Church would remain an empty formality if everyone did not make it a matter of the deepest concern to accomplish his part of what remains to be suffered in his own flesh of the sufferings of Christ for his body the Church. It is the objective nature of the sacramental life itself which requires, at the same time as it establishes, the subjectivism of the ascetical life. Each Christian, in his turn, following a way which is necessarily and rigorously 'monastic' in the etymological sense, that is, in which he must go forward alone and stripped of everything, to meet Christ alone, stripped, emptied of himself, in the embrace of the Cross, must re-live 'the mystery', that is 'the Christ in you, the hope of glory'. And it is not for himself alone, for his individual salvation, that this is necessary. The Church only possesses her life which is collective, single and catholic, in the measure in which each of her members hears the individual call of Christ to renounce all things, to take up his cross and to follow him. Consequently, only the man pledged to the monastic path, that is the path of voluntary self-stripping, which is the condition and measure of our putting on Christ, is among those living cells for the want of which the Body of Christ, numbed by a sort of arterio-sclerosis, would cease to grow and thus cease to live.

Just as Christ, in the tragic isolation of the Cross, prepared and brought about the blessed reconciliation of all things, both among themselves and with God, so the monk, in the isolation of his indispensable vocation, is the principal craftsman of the 'great mystery' of unity, 'so that we shall all meet each other in the fullness of Christ, who has come to the perfect stature of his manhood'—*Unus Christus amans seipsum.*

8

VII

AD PATREM

ADOLF VON HARNACK, the greatest theologian of liberal Protestantism, when summing up his entire religious thought in his book on the *Essence of Christianity*, declared that for him the Fatherhood of God *was* the essence of Christianity. In the dim, rationalized, merely natural sense in which he understood it, the phrase conveys no more than a banality without hope: namely, a vague confidence in a vague divine goodness. But if we reset it in its right context at the heart of Christian dogma understood in its whole depth and fullness, it does effectively show us the centre and very foundations of it.

The whole Gospel can be summed up as revealing at one and the same time these two fundamental truths: God is eternally Father; he is *the* Father—and he has willed, at the end of time, to become *our* Father.

God is Father because his life is concerned solely with one thing: engendering an eternal Son, loving him and receiving his love in the procession of the Spirit. God has willed to become our Father, and thus has sent his Son, his only-begotten Son, that we may all be adopted in him, forming his body, living in his own Spirit.

In the end it is this twofold truth that we must come to recognize. It is in it that all the considerations that we have been following must be summed up and unified in a single intuitive perspective which, as it goes back along many channels to its one single source, contains all the substance of it.

To Mary Magdalen who wanted to take hold of the risen Lord as if to keep him on earth among his followers, Christ said: 'Do not cling to me thus; I have not yet gone up to my Father's side. Return to my brethren and tell them this; I am going up to him who is my Father and your Father, who is my God and your God.'[1] Shortly before he had said to his followers: 'It was from the Father I came out, when I entered the world, and now I am leaving the world, and going on my

[1] John 20. 17.

way to the Father.'[1] It might be said that his whole work is to take us along with him in this return.

Referring to Christ and to ourselves, the first Epistle of St Peter says: 'Till then you had been like sheep going astray, now you have been brought back to him your shepherd who keeps watch over your souls.'[2] And of the Father and of Christ we read again in the Epistle to the Hebrews: '. . . God, the author of peace, who has raised our Lord Jesus Christ from the dead.'[3] This gathering up by Christ of creatures who have strayed far from their origin, and this return of Christ himself from the depths of Sheol to the bosom of the Father, where he will carry with him the lost sheep of our world, is placed by St Thomas in that part of the *Summa* which concerns salvation, just as he referred everything concerning creation to the diffusion of life coming from the Father.

Earlier Plotinus had formed a vision of God that traced all things back to a general emanation from the One, and then to a reintegration of all things in him. But here we are in no sense concerned either with a degradation of the divinity, or with a reabsorption of the world in its source. We are concerned with a gift, with a gratuitous giving which is willing even to risk frustration; and this gift elicits a return of love which, far from abolishing the gift, consummates it. For to have gone out to seek and save that which was lost and to have thus poured forth his own love even into the hearts of ungrateful and rebellious creatures, is God's final and ultimate gift.

At the beginning of these considerations we said that it was necessary to represent cosmic life as the beating of an immense heart through which the same *Agape* courses, first poured out in paternal love, then gathered up in filial love. The divine life is but the expansion in eternity of the love that flows out from the Father and returns to him who is its source. The son, we said, is the 'product', even before being the object, of that eternal love which constitutes the life of God and which remains undivided through all the multiplicity of the infinitely rich process of eternal generation that, for all that, is not divided. For the Son, loving the Father as he is loved by him, is only relation to the Father. Thus the whole Godhead, communicating itself from the Father in the generation of the Son, is brought back to the Father as to its source through the procession of the Spirit. The latter is the substantial love in which the Father and the Son are one at the term of the trinitarian life as they were one at its source.

[1] John 16. 28.   [2] 1 Pet. 2. 25.   [3] Heb. 13. 20.

That source, indeed, is the Father from whom everything proceeds. And it is to the Father that the Son who proceeds from him returns in the procession of the Spirit, since in this procession he is at one with the Father to such an extent as not to be distinguishable from him.

The final procession by which the infinite circle of the life of the Trinity is closed has no other principle than the Father, although the Son is fully associated with him, the Son on whom the Spirit rests eternally, to such an extent that the Father and the Son are, as it were, one single principle of the unique Spirit. Consequently in God himself *Agape* appears inseparably as the principle of distinction and unity, of the rich source which communicates life and of the communion which gathers it together again. And as this communication comes down from the Father, so this communion goes back to him. Thus everywhere, at the starting-point as at the return, it is from him alone, to him alone, that everything flows and is brought back. The Trinity is but the unfolding of what is contained in the Father, and the vital movement which circulates throughout it tends only to him from whom it emanates.

What takes place in the world is but the image and, as it were, projection of what takes place in God. To the recapitulation of the Trinity in him from whom it proceeds, corresponds the return to the Father 'from whom all fatherhood in heaven and earth is named'. Let us return for the last time to this vision of the universe and of the movement which animates it, which we outlined at the beginning. From the invisible Father as his perfect image the only-begotten Son proceeds eternally. From the Son in his turn the Image is multiplied in the mirror of the angelic creation. The spiritual cosmos refracts, as it were through the prism of nothingness, the pure light directly emanating from the Father. Then the material world, as a final echo, gathers up and fixes in its inanimate image the last vestige, on the borderland of non-being, of primordial spirit.

Then, following the original law of creation, the created spirit brings back the world of sense to the Word, its divine exemplar. The world of spirits is thereby reassembled and shares in the intelligible cosmos which is the Son, in whom all wisdom is contained in an incorruptible unity. Finally in the Word, the Spirit who proceeds from the Father brings back to him, with the only-begotten Son, the countless children of God who sang in chorus on the morning of creation and by whose act of thanksgiving every other creature was led back to him.

This primary law, in virtue of which creation is animated by the very Spirit of God, is so deeply inscribed in its being that the sin of disobedience and the fall have not succeeded in frustrating it. Like a dam that merely makes the water rise without arresting its flow, original sin simply brought about this second creation, even more marvellous than the first, which, of itself, returns to the Father instead of coming down from him.

In the world of sense which the pure spirits attempted to enslave to their service instead of leading towards God, the call from on high has raised man up—man, spirit born of flesh. From the same nature that had been seduced by the delusion of self-glorification suggested by Satan's trickery, the breath of divine life caused to be born the Man-God, the heavenly Adam, the Son of Man who rises on the clouds of heaven to meet the Ancient of Days. Thus, finally, in spite of all, the Son reunites the innumerable children of God, divided by sin, into a single body, that is his own. At the end of time when all things have been submitted to him, he himself will hand back the Kingdom to the Father, so that God will be all in all.

The sole significance of the Cross of Christ is to make clear the way for this return. And Christian life, monastic life, wherever it is to be found purified and freed from all the parasitic movements which slow up or hinder its impetus, is wholly concentrated on taking this course. Its sole aim is to accomplish the reintegration of all things in God who is their source, whither they are meant to be brought by the recapitulation of the Trinity in the Father.

There is still to be added, at the end of these progressive developments which unfold and repeat the same theme on different planes, that which forms its mysterious unity. The Thomist theology of the divine missions shows with the utmost clarity how, for a person of the Holy Trinity, to be sent by the Father to creatures and to proceed eternally from him, is one and the same thing. The mission of the Son as Redeemer of the world, as the one who reunites creation disintegrated by sin, the reconciler of men with God, seems to us something other than his eternal generation. In fact, in the final truth of things, there is there only one single reality. From all eternity, in engendering his Son, by the very act by which he engenders him, the Father destines him for the Cross. Even more, for God for whom time does not exist, the eternal Son, in being born from the bosom of the Father, produces, almost as part of his own eternal birth, the generation of the new creature. The creature is born, in time, and destined to share in the glory of the Only-begotten, by virtue of the Cross to which, eternally, he surrenders himself. But for him, to receive the glory inherited from the eternal Father and to give it to the innumerable brethren among whom he is the first-born, is but one and the same act.

Similarly, the sending of the Holy Spirit into the hearts which he joins with the sacred Heart of the Son made man, is substantially one with his timeless procession. Eternally he proceeds as Gift of the Father's love, resting on the Son and returning to the Father; and in this eternal procession his temporal procession is enfolded. For the overflowing of divine love upon creatures, and their final return to that love, are caught up as it were in the ebb and flow of love by which the Son is reunited to the Father and all is eternally consummated in him from whom all eternally emanates. But this participation adds nothing that was not there from all eternity.

All life, all light, is then only the light of this personal glory of the Father which is his Son, and the life of that personal love of the Father and the Son which is the Spirit. The world, history, are filled only with that which fills eternity, namely that unchanging movement which, in the other two persons, comes down from the Father and goes back to him. *Abyssus abyssum invocat in voce cataractarum tuarum* . . .

If all this is true, if indeed it is, as we have said, the supreme truth on which everything in Christianity hangs, the consequence will immediately be evident: a religion in which the eye of faith is fixed and immobilized by something other than the primary source, the final term: the invisible Father—will remain a Christianity which has something lacking to it. We must go even further and say that so long as we have not reached the source, we have failed to attain to what is essential.

Modern forms of spirituality, held fast as they are by what is of the senses and therefore purely human in the Gospel, tend to make us forget this. And they tend at the same time to make us misunderstand the meaning of the Incarnation, which is the justification of what there is effectively human, and therefore of the senses, in the religion of Jesus Christ.

Let us not be in any sense afraid to say that an adoration of Christ which primarily saw in him and adored the man, our brother, and which consequently was incapable of reaching up to the Father through the Son, would be a false adoration. To say this, far from withdrawing anything from the love and boundless veneration which the holy humanity of the Saviour should arouse, gives to this veneration and love that without which such sentiments would lose their meaning. No one has loved Christ more or better, nor with a more

human love than St Bernard. But no one has warned us more care-
fully against the tendency to cling to what he does not fear to call a
carnal love of the Saviour.

We shall only in fact be able to love and adore the humanity of
Christ as it should be loved and adored, if we know it 'according to
the Spirit' and not 'according to the flesh'. In other words, the view
we must have of it, if we are to venerate it as it should be venerated,
is the view of faith. It is the view which never regards that humanity
as if it subsisted in itself, but always as subsisting in the person of the
eternal Son. But this Person, in his turn, remains unknown to us so
long as his subsistence is not recognized precisely as that of a relation,
of a living reference to the Father.

In a word, Christianity cannot be reduced to what has been called
'Jesus-ism': an adoration of Jesus which fails to see the Christ in him,
that is, the Anointed of the Father, and which thereby would rob him
of his glory while claiming to honour him. As the Son in his humanity
is the perfect adorer of the Father and in his divinity is only relation
to the Father, we cannot adore him in reality—and not as a mere idol
of our imagination—without striving to see his divinity through his
humanity, and, through his own divine Person, eventually getting
back to that of the Father.

'To adore the Father', such is the final meaning of this worship in
spirit and in truth which he who is the very Truth of God came to
establish upon earth. But could we not perhaps apply to the Father,
just as much as to the Spirit, the saying of St Paul about the 'unknown
God'? So far as we think of the matter at all, is not his image one of
those most degraded for us by an enfeebled religious imagination?

The Father is not the 'Good God' of the simple folk, a pale anthropomorphic divinity, conceived of merely as the inexhaustible source
of a characterless benignity. The Father is the abysmal mystery in
which faith empties itself and in which it is lost as in the ocean of the
Godhead. The Father, to use the magnificent expression of St Irenæus,
is the invisible God. As he is the source of all that is and of the Godhead
itself, we cannot attain him directly. He sends the other divine Persons
to us. He embraces us by the Son and the Spirit, as if by his two sacred
hands, infinitely holy and venerable. But the Father himself, no one
could send: he is the 'Origin'. No one can see him, unless it be the Son in
whom he reveals himself to us, as he reveals himself in him to himself.

It is to him that the liturgical expressions of infinite majesty apply:
Domine Sancte, Pater omnipotens, æterne Deus. He is the holy Lord, the

almighty Father, eternal God. Certainly such expressions also apply to the Son and the Spirit, but only in so far as the Son and the Spirit are related to the Father. To the Father they belong absolutely. However categorical Holy Scripture, ancient tradition or the liturgy may be as to the full and real Godhead of Christ and of the Paraclete, when they say 'God', adding nothing more, it is always the Father who is meant. It is to him that all doxologies refer, through the Son, in the Holy Spirit. It is he who is properly speaking the God who dwells in light inaccessible.

To him are applied in a supreme degree the terms of Source, Origin, Root, of the Godhead as of everything which proceeds from it. In going back to him, we plunge into the ineffable. In reaching him we leave far behind all that the mind can conceive. Not only all our imaginations but all our concepts vanish at his approach. In him are opened those bottomless depths of what Eckhart called the 'Deity', transcendent to all that we can say or think of God, even were we to use the sublimest words, symbols and truths of revelation. All that remains to us is the cry of the Seraphim who, with veiled faces, sang unceasingly: 'Holy, Holy, Holy . . .'

Yet it is no less essential to maintain that the 'Unutterable' is identical with the Father of our Lord Jesus Christ. It is the Ineffable God himself whom we meet, or rather who comes to us, in the outpouring of eternal love in the Trinity, in the overflow of that same love in creation and redemption. To call God Father, to say that the Father is God absolutely, is tantamount to saying that the whole astounding, crushing immensity of the Godhead, on the one hand, and the communication of infinite generosity which revelation unfolds to us, on the other, are one and the same. It is there that the mystery really lies. It consists in perfect identification between the Absolute and Love, an identification which we cannot understand, but which we must accept on faith before contemplating it for all eternity in the bosom of the divine glory. The Reality which surpasses all qualification, and the limitless generosity of the *Agape*, which, in Christ, takes us, ourselves and our nothingness, for its object; to adore God as the Father is to discover in a living experience that there are not two things there but only one, or rather not a thing but a Person, Yahwe, the living God, the Father of Christ, our Father.

Until we have grasped that, we have not grasped the centre and vital heart of the faith. For, just as we have understood nothing of God so long as we have not understood that he is love, so we have understood nothing of the divine love which the Gospel reveals to us, so long as we have not grasped in the chiaroscuro of faith that this love is one with the grandeur, the purity, the terrible sanctity of Yahwe. And that is precisely the revelation of the Father: the Absolute animated by Love, Love magnified by the Absolute.

We are quite mistaken when we think the name 'father' connotes only the human notion of divine love, leaving out everything that suggests his grandeur, his infinite distance from mortals. The word 'father', in all the wealth of its ancient associations, was, properly speaking, much more religious. For the ancient Romans, the father was not only the *genitor*, he who is quite close to us for he knows of what we are made—the father was equally and simultaneously the showing forth of the *numen*, the august manifestation of the divine power in humanity. Kings were fathers, and so were the greatest of the gods, in the sense that they were sacred persons.

In attaching to the divine fatherhood the idea of an unlimited love for men, Christianity has in no way abandoned these fundamental associations of the name of father; rather it has orchestrated them up to their limits and beyond. For it is the very fact that he 'who dwells in light inaccessible' has 'so loved the world that he gave his only-begotten Son, that who so believeth in him should not perish but should have eternal life'—it is the fact of this unheard-of union of apparent opposites, unthinkable to the natural man, that properly constitutes the great revelation of Love which is at the same time the great revelation of God. The fact that it is the Sovereign, the Pure, the Inaccessible, who loves and who loves us to this extent—this alone can give us the measure of the *Agape*.

In actual fact, to use Huxley's apt expression, so biting underneath its quiet humour—when we say that God is father, we are too much inclined merely to think of him as grandfather. That is to say that we tend to remember only his kindliness and think that we are enhancing that quality by emptying it of anything that can make demands upon us. But, even at a human level, true love, love which is really virile and creative, is not that which consents to everything, but rather that which demands as much as it gives. It is the love of a father bringing up a child and not that of a grandfather who only spoils it. *A fortiori* God cannot be Love, in any sense that is not ultimately derisory, if God is not primarily God.

Thus the grandeur of the Father's Love which the Son has revealed to us and which the Spirit has spread abroad in our hearts is such only because it in no wise diminishes the Father. On the contrary it is we who are lifted up to him by it.

The Father, indeed, has manifested his love for us in that he has sent us two paracletes to search for us, find us and bring us back to him. The title of Paraclete, which Christ attributed to himself before making it over as it were to the Spirit, throws wonderful light on the mystery of our adoption, that is, of the extension of the divine Fatherhood even to us.

The usual translation of Paraclete considerably weakens its meaning. The word 'Comforter', which presupposes the general idea of an access of strength, going beyond simple 'consolation', the healing of wounded powers, is better but remains inadequate. In point of fact, the Paraclete plays a double rôle whose elements moreover cannot be separated. Like an advocate who is at once the counsellor and guardian of his client, and at the same time supports, encourages and strengthens him, he represents him effectively before the judge or sovereign. Thus, mandated by and supplied with an authority coming from the sovereign power, he raises up to his lord those to whom he was sent.

It is in this sense that 'we have a Paraclete with the Father, Jesus Christ the righteous, who is himself the propitiation for our sins, and not only for ours, but for those of the whole world.'[1] What such a declaration expresses is that, despite all that could hinder our access to the Father, all barriers have been broken down, all distance bridged, in the very Person whom he had sent to us and who has returned to him. That is why the same Father with whom he who is the first Paraclete dwells henceforth, 'always living to intercede in our favour', sent into our own hearts the other Paraclete.

But the Spirit, the 'other Paraclete' whom the Father has sent us at the request of the first, does more, in dwelling in our hearts, than merely console and comfort us. At the same time that he gives 'testimony to our spirit that we are the children of God, co-heirs with Christ', he 'intercedes in us with unutterable groanings'. For, as the Apostle exclaims, of ourselves we do not even know what we should ask for. But it is the Spirit in us who enables us to enter into the supreme mystery and cry to God 'Abba', that is, 'Father', putting into this single word the whole prayer of faith which assimilates us to the Uniquely Loved Son and gives us the right to share in his celestial inheritance.

The mystery, in short, is this: that the Father of the Only-begotten has made him 'first-born among many brethren'. Not only has he

---

[1] 1 John 2. 1 (D).

willed him from all eternity 'first-born of the whole creation', destined
to fill the infinite void with the infinite fullness of the Only-begotten
but he has further willed that, at the end of time, he should appear as
'the first-born among the dead'. This means that in 'bringing back
from among the dead the great shepherd of the sheep', he has willed
to confer the grace of adoption on the very world that came forth
from sin.

Having accomplished the purification of sin in his own blood, the
only-begotten Son, lifted up from the earth, thus returns to heaven
drawing after him innumerable prodigal sons. It was the Father
himself who in him came down to them without leaving his heavenly
throne. Again in him we return to the Father, to our Father's house,
to the bosom of the Father to which we are gathered by the embrace
of the arms that were stretched out in pain upon the Cross. Christ,
having come down to us through the flesh taken from the blessed
Virgin, has returned to the Father 'through the veil of his flesh',
through the Cross. Eternal Word, the divine praise of the Father from
all eternity, he has become in time the high-priest of mankind. He
appears as the author and priestly executor of the 'eucharist of blood'
through which creatures, in spite of sin, can have access to the incorruptible radiance of the divine glory. Far from being jealous of us, the
Only-begotten thus remains for us, prodigals without number as we
are, our intercessor and forerunner with the Father, as is shown in the
Epistle to the Hebrews. It is in this attitude and this function, presag-
ing, preparing and already consummating our meeting with the
Father, that he stands henceforward in the heavenly sanctuary where
we follow him by faith.

On earth the eucharist which we celebrate is one with Christ's
unique sacrifice, perpetually offered on the heavenly altar. It is thus
nothing other than our presentation to the Father—our ascent to the
Father, in Christ, through the Cross. In that sacrifice it is revealed here
and now that in Jesus Christ we are not only called, but are, children
of God. Celebrating it, assimilated to and incorporated in Christ
through the Spirit, we thus adore the Father, we go to the Father, we
live, like the Son, *Ad Patrem*.

*   *   *

Finally, if the monk achieves the fullness of Christian life, it is because
he lives the fullness of adoption. He has become to the fullest extent
the child of the heavenly Father because he has fully abandoned the

cares and anxieties of earth. Having ceased to labour for merely corruptible nourishment 'the heavenly Father feeds him'. His poverty is the condition of his accession to the inheritance of Christ. He has ceased to be a slave in the kingdom of Mammon and has become a king's son in the kingdom of heaven.

But above all he has heard the call, 'Be ye perfect as your heavenly Father is perfect.' By breaking the bonds which attached him to earth he has renounced a life divided between heaven and earth, and has thus allowed himself to be drawn by the Son who has returned on high, to that holy dwelling-place where Christ himself has only gone to prepare a place for us.

For the monk is simply the 'pilgrim', 'traveller', who was in quest of the 'heavenly country'. He is the last in the great cloud of witnesses of the faith, the first of whom was Abraham who 'believed' God and 'it was imputed to him for justice', and with him the whole company of them finally enters into the great rest, the final Sabbath where the Patriarchs were not able to enter before us. He too has heard and faithfully responded to the call: 'Go, leave thy country and thy father's house and go into the land that I shall give thee.' He is the son of that Mother who has forgotten her own earthly parents but who now finds herself Mother of the very children of God. And he finally recognizes that this Mother is no longer any earthly Jerusalem, soiled with the filth of sin, but the Holy City, the Jerusalem which is on high, 'the one who cometh down from God, decked as a bride adorned for her Husband'. Washed in the water of baptism, without spot or ageing wrinkle brought on by sin, plunged anew into the eternal fountain, immaculate, she has come down as a Mother in the Blessed Virgin and now returns in him as the Bride in the Church. Clothed with the very light of God and the Lamb, she rises from the desert of monastic life like a cloud of incense, amidst the glad cries of Alleluia.

The search of the whole of mankind achieves finality in the monk, in the Christian who here below has no longer any abiding city, but who awaits the one whose foundations are eternal. Seeking God, and God alone, as he does, he finds in Christ the radiant fullness after which all other men have been groping in obscurity. The source that whispers to our hearts 'Come to the Father', has welled forth in him. No longer having any love for earthly things, since his *Eros*, his earthly love, has been crucified, divine Love, *Agape*, bears him away in rapture *in sinu Patris*.

PART TWO

PRACTICE

DETACHMENT: THE STRIPPING OF SELF

MONASTIC life is dominated by the vision of a goal to be attained and it is this that gives it its full significance. It is a search for God, for God such as he reveals himself to us, that is, he himself seeking us, in his Word, in the Gospel of Jesus Christ.

But the striving which this vision arouses in us is circumscribed within a very concrete reality. It presupposes an evaluation of the whole of human conditioning, of mankind such as it actually is here and now. Without the vision of faith, such an evaluation would be merely discouraging. Even supposing that it might none the less be capable of eliciting a certain asceticism (as the example of Buddhism shows), such asceticism would be soulless. Conversely, for want of correlating the contemplation of the great realities of the faith with a clear perception of man's present condition, the mysticism which animated such asceticism would remain merely an intellectual vision. If we have understood how vital this mysticism is, that it engages the whole of one's being, we shall also understand that to reach that point and not to continue would be a fatal aberration.

Moreover, it is necessary clearly to understand that monastic practice must not be imposed on the theory of monastic life from outside. Because of what we have just said, because of the living character of the theory, the practice grows from it. The stage in the theory at which the practice arises spontaneously is also the central point of the theory itself. We referred to this briefly in the chapter entitled 'Death and New Life'. This expression which we have endeavoured to examine under all its facets is all-embracing: 'No one can see God unless he die.' The monk is the man who longs to see God because God himself calls him to his vision. But, as we have said, the monk is also the man who has recognized that he cannot meet God except in the embrace of the cross with its shedding of blood. If he failed to recognize this fact, his desire would lack all reality. He would fail to understand what we really are, we who are called to such high destiny.

Consequently, he would be unable to find the way which leads from our natural condition of lowliness to this supernatural height.

This way, once again, is the *via crucis*. It is because the monk knows this that he is a monk. The study of monastic practice will thus come to be a study of the concrete form which the application of our Saviour's saying: 'If any man will be my disciple, let him deny himself, take up his cross and follow me', must assume.

*   *   *

In fact, if we approach monastic life from the external side and the detail of its practice only, it is certainly the detachment, the stripping of self which cannot fail to strike us primarily. The monk is one who renounces, who renounces himself. He is to be distinguished from others, precisely because he has abandoned the life of others.

Yet, and therein the really initial, fundamental importance of the theory is at once clearly shown: whatever be the importance, capital in itself, of detachment in the life of the monk, such detachment apart from what prompts it would remain totally ineffective. Sought apart from the aim it must have, and which can only come to it from the theory we have outlined, it would remain completely useless and might easily become harmful in setting itself false aims, of which the taking of itself as an end would not be the least fallacious. For the monk does not renounce himself, nor does he renounce anything, for the mere sake of renouncing. That is, his renunciation implies no condemnation. All that moves him is a preference. In that consists the distinctive characteristic of all *Christian* asceticism. If this trait be lacking, there is no ascetic practice, from the most elementary to the most heroic, that can be qualified as Christian.

The monk does not condemn the creatures he renounces, since it is for their Creator that he renounces them, that is, for him who has made them and made them in such a way that they are all an image or at least a vestige of himself. Thus the monk does not abandon them because he thinks them bad. On the contrary, he abandons them because he knows they are good, but has learnt to discover in this very goodness the image or vestige of perfect Goodness. It may be said that when the Christian ascetic has heard God speaking to him through creation, creatures themselves say to him, when he would perhaps be tempted to allow his admiration to stop short at created things: 'Why do you call me good? One alone is good . . .'

It should be noted how closely the Christian idea of asceticism is linked to the idea of sacrifice, so much so that it is ultimately indistinguishable from it. Now to detach oneself from bad or harmful objects has never been to make a sacrifice. The worth of the sacrifice, on the contrary, is obviously to be measured by the intrinsic value of what it sacrifices. To renounce sin is in no sense to make a sacrifice. Modern formulas of devotion permeated with sentimentalism are in danger of misleading us completely in urging us to make a sacrifice to God of all our miseries and infirmities. In reality, when we use such expressions, we are playing with words. It is doubtless true that the man who suffers, the man who is finding things beyond endurance, should learn to draw the matter of sacrifice from his condition itself. But the sacrifice will not be in his suffering nor in his exhaustion. On the contrary, it will be made up of the strength and health that he might have had or that he might recover and which he abandons to God if such is his good pleasure.

Any other way of understanding sacrifice or renunciation fundamentally vitiates the very idea of it. We only sacrifice, we only renounce through homage to God's infinite goodness, explicit homage in the case of sacrifice, at least implicit in the case of renunciation. Now what makes us recognize this goodness as infinite and therefore divine in one or the other case, is the fact that all other values, *however real they be*, appear as nothing in comparison. One therefore behaves in regard to them all as if they were so in fact in the sight of the One who has taken us for himself wholly and without any division. Consequently, from the moment that the value abandoned seems to us doubtful or disputable in itself, the homage is so too, to the same degree. The God to whom we only sacrifice what we believe to be bad may well appear as relatively better, but he is no longer *the* best, absolutely speaking. It is tantamount to saying that we no longer truly consider him, in act, as being God. Sacrifice or renunciation thereby lose all properly religious significance.

Very far, then, from true monastic detachment being obtainable by a pure and simple contempt of the world, as one might be led to suppose by too many treatises on asceticism permeated with neoplatonist thought, there will be no genuine monastic renunciation unless it is preceded and as it were sustained by an effective esteem of creation.

A great abbot formerly used to say, when he suspected a postulant of aspiring to the cloister simply through fear of life: 'My child, have you ever been in love?' If the young candidate for asceticism hastened

9

to answer: 'Oh no! never, Father!' the abbot would retort ironically: 'How then do you think you can love the Creator if you have not even been capable of loving a creature?' It will easily be understood that there is nothing in common between this dialogue and the romantic idea of Don Juan becoming a monk through despair of love. On the contrary, far from falling back on the Creator, for want of having been able to enjoy the creature at one's pleasure, it is a matter of understanding that all that a creature could give us or draw from us is no longer anything where the Creator is concerned.

The monk, to repeat—and this is permanently true—is one who seeks God, neither more nor less. He is detached from all simply that he may be held back by nothing in his flight, in his course towards the One. That is, of course, why he will detach himself particularly, perhaps, from what he recognizes as most valuable. For it is precisely that which would be most liable to hinder him, to immobilize him, whereas what he is aiming at is liberation from all fetters. His sole aim is to plunge, to fall ceaselessly and, above all, unfettered, into the abyss of infinity.

When this primary truth has been understood, there is no longer any fear of going too far in meeting the demands of asceticism. And, in fact, it must be said that what Christian asceticism demands of us is not only detachment but the stripping of self. There is in fact a difference in meaning between these two words which it is important to make clear. What it comes to is that we have not only to renounce the created things which surround us, but over and above this we must renounce ourselves.

Moreover, the two things are linked together. And in the last resort it is the necessity for self-stripping which explains the necessity of detachment. It is because it is necessary primarily to renounce ourselves that it is necessary to be detached from the rest.

In fact, when we have said what has been said above of the essential goodness to be recognized in everything we renounce in creation for the Creator, we might be tempted to be surprised that it should be necessary to renounce such things at all. If, as we have affirmed, all things are only images or vestiges of God, should they not naturally be completely transparent as between him and us, between us and him?

Ought we not to find God through and in his work? Why is it necessary thus to turn aside from it? Or, rather, why is it necessary to break through it with an incision heroic indeed, but which inflicts a wound on the work and bruises us with it? The reason lies in sin. Sin has vitiated our relations with things by vitiating the natural attitude of our soul, thought, will. Turned in upon ourselves by the deepest tendency of our being, instead of tending directly to God, we relate everything to ourselves instead of referring all to him. That is why in order to find him again, it is essential to strip ourselves of ourselves. And it is to strip ourselves of ourselves that it is finally necessary to detach ourselves from everything created—from all that, since it is finite, can be possessed by us—in order to find at length the only Infinite being that we cannot snatch at in our egoism, the only being whom we can know only by giving ourselves to him.

Things would not form a screen between us and God, creatures would not hide the Creator from us instead of speaking to us of him, if, of ourselves, we who are made directly in the Creator's image had not a tendency to reflect upon them, instead of rediscovering in them their model and our own. And that is also why the most heroic detachment would be of no use at all without the stripping of self. If, having deprived ourselves of everything, we were to remain masters and lords of ourselves over the ruins of the external universe, our pride, in other words our sin, would simply be at its height. It would have become really diabolical. But our personal being is of course so closely linked with that of the world into which, through our body, we plunge with all the fibres of our being, that the stripping of our ego must take place concurrently with detachment from the world, from that world which all too easily brings us satiety, satisfying our desire to relate everything to ourselves.

All this is a warning to us of the depth at which the effort at ascetic detachment must aim. It is to be free in the search for God that the monk must detach, must strip himself. But, as we see, for him it is not only a matter of safeguarding his liberty. It is a matter of conquering it. He has not only to guard himself against attaching his heart to what he might meet along the way which is leading him to the Sole-begotten. He has, at the outset, to detach his heart, to detach it from himself— which is the most difficult of all detachments, for it presupposes, properly speaking, a division which cuts into the living flesh. It is necessary literally to be cut in two, to sever this *liaison* which our inveterate habit, or rather, which our moral and spiritual heredity has established between our self as loving and our self as loved. It is necessary to straighten the incurving road which, through all things, leads us from ourselves to ourselves, so that it may finally come to lead us from ourselves to God. Yet, to repeat, that can no longer be done, not only without a piercing through of the world, but without an essential rending of ourselves, of our heart which has become set in a kind of encrustation which has formed upon it.

And, always, it is essential to remember that all effort in this direction would serve no purpose, worse still, would become simply harmful, if, forgetting that it is solely a matter of rediscovering the infinite value of God, we turned in making it to deny our own value or that of the world. What is required is to lose everything, in so far as it is ours, or rather in so far as it is possessed—in the strongest meaning of the word—by the deadly power of egoism and pride, to find it all again in the service of the life-giving power of Love.

*   *   *

The monk renounces ownership. That is he abandons the possession of material goods. No longer can any single created thing be his, nor any of the objects of human industry.

Other men labour and toil to acquire their share in the divine work. They labour themselves, not only to carve out there a sphere which shall be theirs, but to set on it, as it were, the seal of their possession by incorporating into it something of their mind and heart. The monk will labour indeed more than all, but without expecting any reward of that order. Not only does he renounce any idea of making his own any portion whatever of creation, he refuses to attribute anything to himself of that on which he could imprint the tangible tokens of his work. His hands refuse to clutch at anything of that which comes within their reach. They will no longer even retain what they have been able to fashion themselves, to impregnate with the best of the intelligence and will that move them.

Far, however, from despising anything of this world where God has placed man, as the choicest plant in the garden which the divine hands have planted, the monk recognizes everywhere in it the imprint of those sacred hands. How could he be tempted to depreciate these things from which he detaches himself? The Word to whom his ears are continually attuned reveals to him with unparalleled fullness and delicacy the supernatural poetry of the whole of nature and of each of its elements. The Liturgy which he serves blesses and consecrates them. Even supposing that he had of himself no awareness of the aroma of God which rests upon all his works, the liturgical and biblical cosmos in which he moves would cause him to be penetrated with God's fragrance in an all-powerful sweetness. The cosmic poetry of a Claudel and his exultant optimism is only a reflection or an outflow of the spiritual joy with which the psalter names and evokes each created thing to draw from it praise of its Creator. In the measure in which the monk participates in Christ in the restored purity of primitive creation, he rediscovers the beauty of each single thing as he rediscovers that it is only a trace of God. But this beauty is powerless now to arrest and hold his gaze, just as that in which it inheres can offer him no abiding place, no repose that he would accept. What he seeks is the source of life, not the channels by which that life streams towards him. From now onwards it seems to him that to stop short at such channels would be tantamount to obstructing or muddying them. It is not that he cannot love all that his hands touch, all that his eyes see, it is not that he does not love all this, but in such created good his love desires more than the things themselves and it can no longer cleave to them.

For him, the work by which God in some sort completes his own work through man, has taken on, so to speak, the fullness of its redemptive meaning. But the works which are the fruit of his hands cannot absorb him wholly any more than can those of the kindred but lower creation. The most personal work which he can supply in this world, that which will demand of him the best of what he has within him, no longer aims at any appropriation of the world. It now aims solely at continually breaking through the crust, the shell in which his presence in this world would tend to enclose him, that he may restore to the created things which are a kind of prolongation of himself the transparency through which he himself will pass to God. His work in the world is in no sense the construction of a dwelling-place, even were it a passing tent, but rather the boring of a route continually threatened with obstruction, along which it is necessary that he escape to the only home that can hold him for its own: the Eternal.

The monk renounces the family. In embracing complete chastity, it is not only the most gripping of earthly joys in fact that he denies himself; it is, even more, a society which is yet the very image of the society of heaven. In the union of man and woman, his faith shows him the predestined image of Christ and the Church. In family life, and more particularly in fatherhood, it is the very image of the divine paternity, source of the life of the Trinity, that he renounces.

He renounces because he wants not the image, but the substance. It is not that he fails to appreciate the beauty, the sanctity there is in the fruitful union of bodies in which the heart gives itself and is enriched. It is because he fears that this beauty, this participated sanctity, may hold

him back from immediate access to, from entering wholly into, the fullness which they call to mind. It is because he wants Christ and Christ
alone to live in him, that here and now God himself may be all in all.

Finally the monk renounces himself. Obedience deprives him of
his own selfhood. He knows, however, better than anyone else, for
he has heard and listened to the call of God, that this selfhood is willed
by God, loved by God, as if it were unique, irreplaceable. He knows
that nothing, no creature, either earthly, infernal, or heavenly, will be
able to separate him from the love with which God loves him in Jesus
Christ. He knows that it is for him that Jesus Christ delivered himself,
that it is he whom God loves, as if he were alone in the universe. 'I have
shed *that* drop of my blood for thee.'

But he does not want this ego in its present and passing form to be
able to interpose itself between 'what we shall be' and 'that which has
not yet been manifested'. Beyond his present ego, he aims at rediscovering the idea that God had formed of him from all eternity, such
as He bears it within himself. In comparison with this ideal which God
entertains in his regard, all the reality of his earthly and sensitive ego
grows pale and vanishes like a star in the light of day.

In all his renouncements then, the monk tends only to fullness of
being. He knows that what he is abandoning is not bad; on the contrary, he knows that all of it God called 'good' after making it with
his own hands. But it is the very Goodness of the Creator which he is
seeking after. All he shuns in creatures is the partial and the passing, in
order to attain to the total and the immutable. It is not through fear
or through disgust at living in it that he leaves the world. It is because
all that makes life attractive there has awakened in him an attraction
to a higher life.

More precisely, it is not even for a limitless good that he is leaving a
limited good. It is for a Person, for the One of whom all other beings,
all other persons, even his own which is at the root of all he does, of
all he is, speak to him henceforward. And he can no longer bear that
anything, that anyone, that his own person should at the same time
hide this Unique Being whom all that reveals to him.

*　　*　　*

From what has been said, it must follow that the only meaning of
the renouncements that are at the root of monastic life is thereby to
escape from all that which makes the soul rigid, which might ossify it
in its quest for God. There immediately follows from this that the

abandonments comprised in the monastic vows have no value unless they remain perpetually actual. They become a pure vanity if practice renews in fact bonds which have been severed in principle.

It is here we come up against routine, inseparable from one's establishment in monastic life as in a stable and permanent condition. What would it profit us to have left all things if, in detail, we were to take back in fact what we had once left?

Yet that human condition of life which is ours after monastic profession just as much as before means that we are in continual temptation to fall into such a state. If in principle we are dead to the world, yet we remain in the world after profession as before, we use the world, we continue to frequent the children of the world, and still less can we escape from ourselves.

Life here below cannot be pursued without a certain appropriation of objects in fact, whatever may be the situation in theory. All that we have at our disposal for the future, even if it should be a stylus or tablets, says St Benedict, is no longer ours and must no longer be considered by us or by anyone as ours. This does not prevent our using it, or the fact that we cannot use it in any way substantially different from the use that would be made of it by a real owner. Whence comes the continual menace, the inevitable danger of what St Benedict calls the vice of ownership. In our external, and, above all, perhaps, in our internal behaviour, the tendency to use that which is no longer ours, since nothing is ours now, as if something were still ours, is so strong!

The books which are at our disposal, the familiar objects which we use, the very obedience which has been given to us, with the tools it presupposes, are so many occasions for us to re-form in act the mentality of owners which we have virtually shed once for all. Let us add that however poor and however few are the objects which hold us, the danger of our concentrating on them a power of attachment which people of the world, distracted by the multitude and diversity of their goods, would perhaps not pour out upon their wealth, is all too real. If we are not ceaselessly on the alert and continually on the defensive against this danger, our monastic profession will be nothing but a snare. It can even become a much more formidable trap, because a much more subtle one, than the clinging to worldly possessions.

What would it serve to have pretended to oneself to leave all things, if our attachment was in the end to be merely exacerbated by the fewness and precariousness of our holds on the world?

Similarly we cannot shun all worldly society. For us in a sense the monastery necessarily replaces the family. It is inevitable, too, that there affections and spontaneous sympathies should more or less correspond to what would have been the heart's affection in the society of the family. But if all this is not controlled, if the tendency, never wholly extinguished, narrowly to particularize our life in some earthly companionship, even were it the most purified of friendships, is given free rein, what, once more, will it profit us to have renounced marriage and the ties of fatherhood? And even supposing that there were no danger of all this, if our attachment to the monastic society itself, in its ensemble, becomes naturalized, if this society becomes our true home and our resting-place, and not just the dynamic conjunction of efforts orientated to the 'Jerusalem on high, who alone is our mother', —what use is it to us to have entered its ranks?

It was to help us to march unfalteringly, and now it is that which is paralysing us. From the moment we think of the cenobitic community, of its establishment, of its temporal labours, of its particular and limited ends, in the same way that a father of a family would think of such things as they affected his household, our entering the monastery has lost all meaning.

This tightening, this hardening of our views on the monastic life is too natural a tendency for one ever to be able to overcome it. Yet if one abandons oneself to it, one has thereby killed the justification of such a life. If of ourselves we carnalize the institution which was to spiritualize us, what have we still to hope for from it?

It should be remembered that the setting up of an earthly home by way of marriage, in spite of all the inertia, the danger of which it brings with it, is holy in itself and a means of sanctification, even if it be indirect. But settling down in the paradoxical society of the monastic *cœnobium* is a pure non-sense. For such a society only exists to help us, by community of fervour, not to settle down at all.

Even obedience can become a trap in an atmosphere pervaded by routine. Confidence in a superior that is too human, by liberating us from the effort, so often painful and trying, that a particular responsibility requires, does not then give us in exchange deliverance from our selfish ego. It is from its worries that it frees us; not from its state of being rooted in itself. It can on the contrary even help such a state, however unlooked for such a result may be. When we interpret obedience itself as a simple discharge from responsibilities, as does happen—and any merely routine habit of obeying contributes to this— the way which leads to such a condition is swift and easy.

Without going too far, how crafty our ego is to obey materially, by accommodating and adapting itself superficially to the demands expressed, even anticipating them, but in such a way that we only have the eagerness to obey because, practically, there is no longer any means of prescribing for ourselves anything but what we desire. However far-seeing the authority of a superior may be in what it prescribes, when it comes up against this false suppleness, all the more dangerous for being ingenuous, unconscious of itself, the good of obedience is killed in embryo.

Someone who during the course of the last war witnessed the German occupation in Belgium and in France observed with a certain humour the very different reactions of the two peoples in the face of the occupant's injunctions. If a notice of any kind was posted up by the Kommandantur, the French, as soon as they had taken note of it, recriminated loudly, protesting that they would not conform. Then, even if they did so grumbling, they conformed. The Belgians, on the other hand, massed in silence in front of the placards bearing the order or prohibition. They peaceably commented on them among themselves in order to grasp their exact portent. Then they carried out the letter of the injunctions punctiliously . . . but in such a way as to paralyse the effect intended, even were it by the very literalness of their obedience.

It is exactly the same with the reactions of many monks when confronted with the wishes of their superiors. Those whom superiors find most difficult are not always the ones who seem to have the most difficulty in submitting. They are rather those who almost forestall the injunction, but in such a way that they always make the point of it ineffective, in one way or another. While never refusing to obey, at bottom they manage never to do anything except what they want. This is a strange variation on the parable of the two sons: the one who says no and then does his father's will; the one who says yes, but who then evades the issue. Anyone who thought such a situation uncommon in monasteries would be mistaken.

In a general way the danger of familiarity in the monastic life is perhaps that one bends oneself too easily to its constraints. Yet they have no other significance for us than to disturb and incommode the old man in us, in his settled condition, in his ease, in his comfortable curling up around himself. But he is singularly artful in finding comfort in situations which one would imagine the least favourable to rest and relaxation. Even if he needs some time for this, he will always succeed, if not watched, in carving out a comfortable niche for himself and in falling back into his invincible torpor.

That is why it is absolutely fundamental, in the pursuit of the monastic life, not to see it primarily as a state, but as a race, a race in which, to use the expression of Gregory of Nyssa which we quoted at the beginning of this book, the course to be run is a course that has no end. According to the exhortation and example of St Antony, the monk should not measure virtue by the time spent in retirement from the world, but by desire and resolution. 'He himself did not call to mind the time already spent but, day after day, as if he were just beginning asceticism, he forced himself to progress, repeating to himself continually the saying of St Paul: "Forgetting the things that are behind and reaching forward towards that which is before, I run straight to the mark"' (Philippians 3. 14 [D]).[1] In order thus continually to keep himself alert, the monk has only to bring back to his mind constantly the consideration of which we have already seen the truth when discussing chastity, but which has a general bearing. None of his three fundamental renouncements rejects anything positively bad. They are realities which are good in themselves, realities which, frankly accepted, could be positively sanctifying. The monk, however, has left them behind once for all, has denied himself their normal use, in order not to be weighed down by anything heavy in his course towards God. But, if he now returns to them by devious paths, if he returns to them without admitting it to himself, he loses everything. He loses the good of the renunciations and he cannot regain the good of their positive acceptance, since he has rejected such a possibility once and for all. Nothing is more lamentable then, because nothing is more false, than the life of the monk whose daily practice secretly gives the lie to the initial principles of monastic life. What will it serve to have cast off the bonds that were ours by right, in order to load ourselves with unjustifiable attachments? The latter would become all the more paralysing as we found ourselves unable frankly to recognize them. The monk who gets to that stage is truly the man whom one devil has left only to go back again with seven other devils much worse than himself.

The man of the world can make the goods he possesses, the work which becomes his as he creates it, serve his progress towards God. The monk can no longer do so, for in striving to regain one or other of these things, he is denying the fundamental vow of his life.

[1] *Vita Antonii*, 7; P. G., Vol. 26, col. 853 A.

The man who is married in Christ, the father of a family, can, through his human affections, raise himself to the love of God. The monk cannot do this, for his *ersatz* of marital or fatherly affection is nothing more than pure and simple infidelity to the divine love that is constraining him.

The man who remains his own master can ordain his own progress towards God. The monk who strives to become his own master anew is merely trying to reject the yoke of the servitude of Christ. It is the greatness of the monk's vocation that it has brought him up against the choice of all or nothing. For him there is no middle way between sacrilege and sanctity. What he has refused once and for all is precisely the possibility of half-measures. Let him always remember this. Let him remember at the same time that liberty, the total liberty to follow Christ, to seek God, is the good beyond price which he has paid for by this refusal. How could he allow himself to surrender it again, merely to haggle over the payment he has already agreed to and which now is beyond compensation? What a blessed necessity he is in of preserving this liberty once he has purchased it! Let him only remember that there is no other means of preserving it than to continue to conquer it unceasingly.

II

PRAYER

WHAT is the road thrown open by detachment and the stripping of self to those seeking God, if it is not prayer? God has called us, has sought us out, by a Word which has touched our heart. It is in speaking to him as he has spoken to us, in words in which the heart moves with the lips, that we respond to him and seek him in our turn. Thus the monk is essentially a man of prayer.

Prayer is his proper task. If no common human task, although he might be called upon by circumstances to accomplish some such work, should be considered by him as *his* task, it is because prayer is and remains *his* work. If the other labours which he can perform do not turn into prayer, if they take on for him another meaning than that of, so to speak, forming a framework for his prayer, the monk has denied his vocation.

Prayer is his work, but it is also his rest. Obviously the monk's life is a hard one. And perhaps what is hardest about it is the constant presence of these fundamental renunciations on which we have meditated: the renouncement of earthly possessions, of earthly affections, of his own will. If the monk does not want to be tempted to seek shameful and unlawful compensations for these renouncements, one way alone is open to him, and it is precisely to force himself to engage in it with all his being that he has finally blocked up all other ways. This way, which leads him forward to the heights, all horizontal issues being closed to him, is prayer. In prayer, he will breathe the supernatural atmosphere which will purify him, which will relieve him from all his weariness, from the weight of the flesh, from the *acedia* of the lonely soul who complains of having left men without having found God. Prayer will continually reanimate, refresh, renew the strength which has been used up in a rhythm accelerated by the perpetual tension in which those who have renounced once for all the imperfect for the perfect, live.

More than his work or his rest, prayer is quite simply the monk's life. His life does not take the search for God as one occupation among

others. It is identified with this search. That is to say, his life is no
longer anything but prayer—prayer is his life.

Other religious have special hours set aside for mental prayer. In
recent times, it was thought that such a period should also be assigned
to monks. This was not perhaps a mistake, for the dissipation of the
modern world is so general that it even threatens the recollection of the
cloister. Thus it is not a bad thing that there should be a time of special
concentration with a view to prayer. But that cannot signify that outside that particular hour, the monk would not have to practise mental
prayer. It means, on the contrary, that he must do everything possible,
so that the remainder of his time is effectively occupied by prayer. To
the centrifugal forces which are always there beneath the surface, the
special hour of mental prayer should provide a counterpoise. But the
monk's time of mental prayer is his whole day. He is set apart, in the
Church, precisely for conversation with God.

In the body of Christ, priests are like the hands, destined to produce
sacred actions. Monks are like the lips. It is through them that the voice
of the Bride is unceasingly heard by the Bridegroom. They perpetuate
the presence of Christ among us as intercessor, to use the magnificent
expression of the Epistle to the Hebrews, *Semper vivens ad interpellandum
pro nobis*: 'Always living to make intercession for us'.

Thus everything indeed in the monk's life is aimed at enabling him
to attain to the fullness of prayer. His solitude is assured, so that he may
have only God with him. Silence is imposed upon him in order that
any cause of distraction may be removed. The vacuum thus effected
by these two great negative monastic practices will be filled by two
positive practices: the *lectio divina* and the Office. The one will enable
the divine voice, which first invited us, to be heard. The other will
link up with it the response which the voice expects from us and itself
elicits from us.

The monk should be perpetually aware of the privileged situation
which is his. The world, unlike the monastery, is merely an organization of 'diversion' in Pascal's meaning of the term. It seems only made
to provoke an absence: the absence of God and the parallel absence of
our deepest and truest self. It interposes between us and God a reality
which is merely skin-deep, but in the curious detail of which the mind
wanders and flounders. It thus loses him whom it was to seek, and also
loses itself; for it is not only the divine absence which the world brings
about for man—but even the forgetfulness of this absence. It distracts
us from the void it creates in us. It fills it up deceptively with a

cancerous proliferation of activities which stifle the life they seem to
dilate. The life of the world indeed, and of the modern, industrialized,
'americanized' world, is precisely, to use the words of one of Claudel's
characters, 'a total absence of interior life'.

The monk's privilege, which cuts him off from this parasitical life
and gives him at the same time the possibility of a personal life and a
life with God, brings with it a duty. Or rather this privilege *is* his duty.
He who can seek God in a way that others cannot, ought to do so
for them. The monastery, in the world of man, is like a window opening to admit the 'Sun of spirits'. If this window is darkened or closed,
the whole of mankind suffers thereby. It is not only in praying for his
brethren's intentions that the monk is valuable to his brethren, indeed
is irreplaceable: it is simply because he prays. His most contemplative
prayer, that which is most absorbed in God, is both an essential
function of humanity and one which the monk is perhaps the only one
to fulfil well. If he fails to fulfil it, no one will do so in his place. The
absence of this activity which nothing can replace would signify the
asphyxia of the mystical body.

Thus if the monk jealously safeguards the two initial conditions of
his life of prayer already mentioned—solitude and silence—this is not
an insistence on selfish luxury on his part. It is an imperious necessity
incumbent upon him if he is to fulfil his purpose in life. The task for
which he is responsible in the Church, for the Church, is to pray, to
pray without ceasing and to the utmost of his capacity. To attempt
this without remaining in solitude and silence would be to mock the
world. It would be simultaneously to contract an enagagement and to
put oneself in circumstances rendering its fulfilment impossible.

When this elementary truth has been understood, any fallacious
argument which would dispense the monk from solitude falls to the
ground. Before everything, it is necessary to know what one wants.
If the monk wants to be a monk, if he really believes that that is his
fundamental vocation, no 'apostolic' concern—if we use that term in
its modern sense of 'activism', rather than in its ancient meaning—
can supply him with a plausible pretext for avoiding that which makes
the monk a monk. The monk is called by that name because he is a
solitary: *monos* means alone. If he gives up being a solitary, he gives up
being a monk.

Let us put things quite plainly. One must choose either one thing or
the other: either we really believe that the monk, in so far as he is a
man of prayer, performs an irreplaceable function in the Church, or

we do not believe it. If we believe it, there can no longer be any 'need of souls' which can justify a desertion of his mission. This does not mean that charity cannot demand that the monk at certain moments and under certain conditions perform a clerical task. But it will certainly mean that he cannot be an 'apostle' in the modern sense of the word, for that would mean that he would thereby cease to be a monk. On the contrary, he cannot become a true apostle except by being *primarily* a monk. The apostolate must not intervene in his life in the sense of bringing the performance of his task of being a monk to a temporary standstill. It must rather be the crowning of that task.

We have seen that spiritual fatherhood appeared to the Christians of ancient times as the natural flowering of a successful monastic life. This idea clearly shows us how the apostolate can, and how it cannot, be combined with this life. If one were looking for an image which would sum up the all-important distinction to be retained here, it might be said that the taking up again of contact with the world, if and when charity demands it, must always be done by an eventual progression *beyond* solitude, and not by a regression from it. In other words, the monk will only be able to return to the world and to do a certain good to it in the measure in which he has previously drawn from solitude all it can give him. Then he will be capable of taking his solitude with him, and his leaving it physically for an hour or so will matter little. Otherwise, an ill-prepared apostolate will in no sense be able to compensate the dead loss of a solitude which has been destroyed.

All this amounts to saying that the monastic apostolate would be mere show to the extent that it permeated the soul of the monk with the world once more, instead of permeating the world with the monk's new master, the Spirit. The fact that this truth is so difficult for many of our contemporaries to accept, merely shows how much we have lost the sense of the things of the Spirit. The gibe to be found in the apophthegms of the Fathers is well known: the two kinds of persons whom the monk must flee more than all others, it is said humorously are bishops and women. The meaning of the remark is clear. There is nothing and no one of whom the monk must beware more than of those who want to make him serve the world and those who would like to make him love the world, without taking account of his fundamental duty: to seek God. Once the basis of one's life has been lost to sight, with all one built upon it obviously crumbling, then it is futile to rely on this basis for justification of a negligence so fundamentally ruinous. What more stupid than to pretend to hang up a precious and delicate object by a nail, if to do so we begin by pulling the nail out of its hole?

If this is the case with what might appear *a priori* the best claims to dispensation from monastic solitude, what of the others? A monk who willingly accepts, much more so one who seeks, occasions to go out of the monastery, thereby denies his vocation. For the monastery, because it is the place of his solitude, is the place of his vocation. A monk out of the monastery will always be a fish out of water. This is, or should be, so obvious that one would be ashamed to stress it.

For instance, it is certainly not superfluous to recall that the monastery itself, if it is a society, is only a society of solitaries, and, moreover, a society which has no other purpose than to pursue in common the striving after solitude. It is not that the life of society cannot be sanctified in itself. It is sanctified in the Christian family. But if the monk has renounced the family, he has renounced that real but imperfect means of sanctification to be found in the life of Christian society, for the more perfect means of solitary life. If the monastery becomes simply another family for him, we have fallen back into those unacknowledged compensations, into those *ersatz* of what one has renounced, which imply the total failure of monastic life. To repeat, the monk now no longer has the legitimate satisfaction of a natural tendency; nor, further, the supernatural advantage that he could draw from his sacrifice. Thus he has nothing at all but a life in which everything is on a false basis. The simple acceptance of God's gifts would have been better than a rejection of them which is not only sterile but inevitably vitiated.

The cenobitical state is not an end in itself. The most ancient monastic tradition is unanimous on this point. St Benedict adheres to it without hesitation. For him the cœnobium is the school of solitude and nothing more.[1] Consequently a cenobite with exclusively domestic virtues can be a type of kindly, pious bachelor: but that gives him no title to bear the name of monk. We should hesitate to say that it would have been better for him to accept marriage, with the sacrifices inherent in fatherhood than to lead this life which has the tranquillity of celibacy without its heroism. It is necessary to repeat over and over again: when we say monk, we mean solitary. He who is not truly a solitary and does not desire to be so, is no monk and does not desire monastic life.

What distinguishes monastic society from that of the family is that its centre of gravity is not within itself. It is in the life of the society

---

[1] *Rule*, Chaps. 1 and 73.

which they have set up that the Christian couple will find God. They can do so without both becoming tainted with egoism because it is essential to their society to be fruitful, and thereby to be drawn away from themselves. But a society closed to the human plane, as monastic society is, is only justifiable by an immediate opening on to the divine plane. It is with a view to that plane that it is organized. But it will certainly not discover it otherwise than by obtaining solitude for its own members and by preparing them for it. Monastic society is not a home which binds us to the earth in sanctifying it. It is by contrast an army on the march which is to snatch us away from earth, to sanctify us in God, the one alone with the One. If we have not understood this, it would be better to remain in the world. For there are two ways of finding God: the indirect way of union with creatures, the direct way of renunciation of creatures. Between the two there are only the forms of sin, ineffably sad, because ineffably sterile. There is nothing more deplorable than a religious existence which has renounced the human love that could have been sanctified, without renouncing the earthly attachments that fetter divine love. There are no more illusory sacrifices than such offerings of withered fruits.

Such considerations are in no sense intended to exclude the idea that the monastic community can (and should) in a certain sense become the monk's family. We shall say something later (p. 195) as to how, in the common celebration of the Eucharist and the Office, the monastic community becomes a prefiguration and even an inauguration of the heavenly family. It is in this sense also that the idea, so strongly put forward by St Basil, of the monastic family considered as a community of charity has a permanent value. But all this presupposes that a completely supernatural notion of the foundation and nature of this society is kept in mind. When this has been understood, the solitude towards which the cœnobium leads us of itself, no longer seems an oppression but an expansion. Then, its material observance, far from being grudgingly kept or manœuvred round in this way and that, is spontaneously prolonged in a spiritual realization which knows no limit.

Necessary as the support of material solitude is to the monk indeed, it would be deprived of all significance if it did not lead him on to spiritual solitude. What would it serve to have left the world materially, if he were to remain completely absorbed in it by thought?

How vital it is to watch over what I should call the 'escapes' from solitude! I refer to the many occasions which are necessarily offered to us to desert it spiritually, even when we may scrupulously observe the material reality. What is the good of fleeing from world to cloister if we allow the world to introduce itself and rejoin us there?

Correspondence is the first of these outlets. There, too, in our own eyes the pretext of charity so easily covers the insatiable curiosity of the mind, which is rebellious at the idea of remaining alone with itself. The echoes of the world are no less harmful to monastic life than the direct sound of its noise. *A fortiori* it profits nothing to have renounced the world's tasks if we retain its preoccupations. I know of enclosed nuns more than a thousand kilometres away from Paris who are so well informed about what goes on in the world that they find flats in the capital for their friends, who cannot succeed in so doing by their own efforts. The altruism which they display in this form is assuredly not the end for which they were enclosed.

What is true of correspondence is equally true of newspapers or the radio. We have heard the story of the traveller in ancient Egypt who disembarked on an island where two solitaries had been enclosed from time immemorial. Hardly had he set foot there when they ran up to him and asked: 'How's the world going on?' It was really not worth the trouble of cutting themselves off from things to that extent, if it was only to remain, or to become, involved in them to such an amazing extent. For it is a fact that the people of the world easily become blasé about what is going on there. But if religious do not crush interest in temporal things of their own accord, it is quite certain that the little food they give it will excite it all the more. In such cases the remedy is worse than the disease. When one thinks that there are cloisters where the monks are set against one another through politics— a thing which was known as long ago as the Byzantine period, but which assuredly did not disappear with it—one wonders what use such people still are!

There is a final category of worldly preoccupations which is none the less apt to paralyse the effect of material solitude—intellectual preoccupations. We shall discuss, and that fully, the normal place occupied in monastic life by intellectual work and, a deeper question, the natural bond between monastic prayer and a certain form of culture. All this does not militate against the fact that the monastery is not a 'thinking shop'. To make of one's solitude the means, not of a truly spiritual life, but of an intellectual life, is one of the subtlest ways of adulterating it. The cloister is not an ivory tower all ready made for the 'sages' of this world. To think so, or to behave as if one thought so, is perhaps the last but also the most insidious of the forms of vulgarity which threaten the monastic militia. If the monasteries have legitimately played, and are to continue to play, the rôle of centres of enlightenment of the Christian intelligence, they will only do so on condition that they remain at the apex of the Church on earth. But the latter is certainly not engaged in scientific research, but in the quest of the 'God of all knowledge'; which is not at all the same thing. If we forget this, there again we shall lose both the good proper to the monastic life, and the good proper to a Christian life of research set in the world. A monastery in the forefront (and it would inevitably get lost in the fog) of those who are known as, or who call themselves, Catholic intellectuals—there is no place where we may be more certain that the *adæquatio rei et intellectus* would halt on both feet. Incapable of enlightening a world to which it no longer belongs on problems that cannot be understood if one has not had experience of them, and equally incapable of diffusing there the uncreated light, it will be nothing more than a lamp extinguished under the bushel, asphyxiated by its own smoke.

Yet the exercise of intelligence is essential to the monk, since it is essential to the prayer of faith. But it must be said that intellectual exercise that does not, for him, end in love, no longer has any meaning. For it is no longer a source of light: it is a screen between him and *the* source, the 'Sun of minds'.

*   *   *

In order that the search after, and continual safeguarding of solitude may not be a sterile and wearisome task, it must of course be inspired by love: by the love of the One who is not seen, and who cannot be seen, here below, with the eyes of the mind alone any more than with those of the body. Newman has this admirable sentence: 'Saint Peter makes it almost a definition of a Christian that he loves Him whom he has not seen.' To how great an extent should this be true of the monk, and what significance it gives to the solitude he is pursuing! It is of such a solitude, if of any, that it can be true to say by faith *Nunquam minus solus quam cum solus*: 'Never less alone than when alone'.[1]

It seems that in our world, more and more carried away by amusement, Christians themselves, monks themselves, experience some difficulty in really giving effect to such words and thoughts. In all sincerity, no doubt, but deceiving themselves in a very curious manner, how many religious there are to-day who think, or who are inclined

---

[1] Theophrastes, quoted by St Jerome, *Adversus Jovinianum*, I, 47.

to think, that a life of solitude with God is an evasion of the claims of charity. It seems to them that an ideal of this kind has only filtered in through a perversion of Christianity. For such 'mystical' ideas to spread, they think, it must have been contaminated by the contemplative ideal of Hellenism. A Christianity whose ideal is the anchoretic life, would no longer—to hear such people speak—be Christianity but disguised neo-platonism. For St Paul's idea of charity, for his 'apostolic' zeal, such people would substitute the frigid *Solus cum Solo* of Plotinus.

In actual fact, what we really ought to ask ourselves, is whether those who have come to think in this way, far from having, like St Augustine, left neo-platonism behind to attain the Gospel, are not quite simply falling back below the level attained by the supreme efforts of pre-Christian systems of spirituality. A very acute and far-seeing analytical writer of our times, the late Anglican bishop Kirk, made a remark which many of us would do well to meditate on. Passing in review numerous historical studies of Protestant inspiration which oppose to the mystical tendency what they call the prophetic tendency, identifying this with an activist current, he pointed out that the descriptions given of the latter, from the moment the contrast is maintained, end by being only disguised descriptions of primitive religion. As soon as we scratch the surface, we discover there simply the idea of a god whose value is that of a source of energy, to be captured and exploited for the benefit of mankind. But the idea of the personal God, whose worth is in himself, and who is worth infinitely more than all the rest, is absent.

It is impossible to recover this idea, or rather this reality which is yet the heart of the Gospel, without returning to the *Solus cum Solo* of Plotinus, even if this means giving it a significance which Plotinus scarcely glimpsed, or did not glimpse at all. Again, the least one can say is that the institution which, in him, galvanizes dying Hellenism and obscurely raises it, was aroused, as one of the most learned scholars who have interpreted his thought recognized, by aspirations more akin to the Bible than to the *Phædo*.[1] To reject this is thus not to reject a possible paganization of the Gospel, on the contrary it is to reject the most fundamental innovation which the soul of antiquity sensed in the announcement of the divine Word.

For it is in short a matter of continually returning to the all-important thought of Martin Buber that we recalled at the beginning. Is it some thing or Some One whom we are seeking when we seek God?

[1] E. Bréhier, *La Philosophie de Plotin* (Paris, 1928), pp. 7–8.

If it is Some One there is no other means of finding him than to listen to him and respond. But neither is there any means of hearing him if we have not begun by silencing the voices which smother or confuse his voice.

*   *   *

And that is another reason why solitude would not be sufficient to find God if it were not accompanied by silence. We are speaking now of the silence we impose on ourselves, the other being presupposed by solitude. But we shall understand how much this personal silence matters too, as soon as we have understood this certain fact: among the voices which prevent us from hearing the divine voice, the most deafening is perhaps our own. Dialogue is killed at its source if one of the interlocutors, and at that the one who can at most do nothing more than reply, persists in refusing to keep silence.

Solitude preserves us from invasion by the world. What benefit will it be to us if we continually go out from ourselves?

To be in some way effective, silence, like solitude, must, as the first step, be observed as well as possible physically. We must always beware of the modern tendency to 'spiritualize' observances unduly. So often it tends in fact only to evaporate them! It must always be borne in mind that monasticism, with its initial exodus from the world, either presupposes the necessity of a material basis for asceticism, or it has no longer any *raison d'être*. 'Benedictine silence', said a disillusioned monk, 'consists in being silent when one has no wish to speak . . .' Just as a healthy liberty, particularly on such a delicate point, is necessary to asceticism, so it is important that this liberty should not dissipate the spontaneity it protects.

It would be scarcely less dangerous, moreover, to think that to effect true asceticism it would be sufficient to strengthen its material demands. The necessities of cenobitical life mean that where perpetual vocal silence is imposed, signs have had to be allowed. But the temptation (and also the facility) of finding in signs, once one has become accustomed to them, an even more irresistible possibility of escaping from real silence, is very great. Monks in communities where the rule is not so strictly interpreted, and who consequently have not this compensating factor, will keep absolute silence, at least in the recognized places: oratory, refectory, chapter-room, or else after Compline. Monks who are more rigid in principle will be able, thanks to the signs, to get round the rule everywhere.

Without going so far as certain Carthusians who prefer to sing out of tune in choir rather than to have chant practices which would disturb the silence, every monk should constantly remind himself that there is scarcely any treasure which it is more foolish to squander than silence. The oriental liturgy, on which the monastic imprint is so marked, is full of prayers against the spirit of vain chatter.

Why this insistence? Once more, because nothing kills the life of prayer more surely than the spontaneous movement of the soul trying to escape from itself. Now that is precisely the motive power behind the chatterer. The man who cannot remain alone is distracted from colloquy with God by others. The man who cannot be silent is distracted from it by himself. Entertained, carried away by the flood of his own thoughts, he drifts about haphazard instead of coming back to the source. How could he recollect his soul to go to God, as he must, without reservation, if he himself offers it continual enticement to escape? Above all, how can he enter within himself to find God there, who is always present by grace in the fine point of the soul in which the divine image adheres to its own model, if he is always absent from himself?

As was the case with solitude, such remarks imply that the material silence, necessary as a basis, will be worthless if it does not develop into an interior silence. Mastery over our thoughts must go hand in hand with mastery over our words, for it is on control of thought that control of word depends. The first gives its meaning to the second.

The monk, then, should not allow himself to be absorbed by his different tasks and occupations. He must ceaselessly, without rigidity, but without weakness, refuse to listen to the distracting thoughts they arouse. Above all, he must not allow himself to be absorbed by himself. This is obviously the major temptation of solitaries and it increases in the measure in which they are truly solitaries. Like Montaigne, no longer having anything else with which to distract ourselves, we think about ourselves continually, we examine ourselves, we enjoy ourselves, we turn in upon ourselves.[1] When we have got to that stage it can be said that the soul is rotting away. In these conditions, even the exercises most directly ordained to spiritual progress, like examination of conscience, have an adverse effect. Referring everything to ourselves, enclosing everything in ourselves, we embitter and sterilize everything.

It would, moreover, be a fallacy to believe that to palliate this defect it is sufficient to offset it by certain altruistic practices, such as detailed

[1] Cf. *L'Essai XVII* of Book II, p. 644 (ed. A. Thibaudet).

intercession. The root of the evil is deeper than that. By stopping short at that point one would be in danger of having a life in mosaic as it were, divided between a stifling narcissism and a dust sprinkled with good intentions. Such organized distraction would keep us from entering into our inner selves without necessarily drawing us out of ourselves by true charity. The Carthusians, conscious as they are of their function as intercessors, generally refuse to accept any particular intention. Without going so far as that, we must always remember that it is the purity of the vertical movement towards God which will increase charity in us, both in regard to our brethren and in regard to the Father. The sheer quantitative multiplication of horizontal pre-occupations is rather in danger of putting us back once more in the dissipation of the world of sin, from which above all we must pull ourselves away. We should remember the saying of Origen: *Ubi peccatum, ibi multitudo.* The spiritual life grows larger and deeper not in proportion to the number of its objects, but, on the contrary, to their simplification, provided that the latter is carried out on the proper plane, on the supernatural plane alone: in God, who transcends the one and the multiple. The final snare which it is important to avoid, is to confuse anxiety about our needs, even be they our loftiest spiritual or altruistic needs, with the search for God. Many apophthegms of the Fathers amount to saying that the monk who still knows he is praying has not yet begun to pray as he should. It must be understood that what is all-important is not the knowing *what* one is praying for, but *whom* one is praying to. Is prayer a true dialogue or is it not?—we must always come back to that.

That is why, finally, concern for interior silence which is the ultimate condition of true prayer, must not become a scruple—all too frequent a case, be it said. The war against distractions must not itself come to be a major distraction, much more harmful than all the others. That would be the case once we came to think that the words or thoughts of the prayer, whether it be vocal or mental prayer, form the ultimate centre where our whole attention must be fixed.

In saying this, we certainly do not intend to adopt the naïveness of Thomassin, in his *Treatise on the Divine Office.* Answering the Protestant objection that the Church sometimes gives the Office to be recited by people who do not understand much Latin, the excellent Oratorian retorted: 'So much the better: at least the meaning of the words will not distract *them* from prayer!' Such an answer implies a radically false notion of the natural relationship between vocal and mental prayer, a notion, alas, far too widely spread among people of to-day. Without any of these false, artificial contrasts, it is rather a matter of realizing what corresponds to an accurate psychology of speech. Contemporary investigations into this matter have convinced us of the error which must be imputed to the analyses of the grammarians. A sentence, for the mind which utters it, is not formed by the accumulation of the separate meanings of the different words which compose it. It is the global meaning which takes hold of the words and organizes them in accordance with living logic, without any parcelling out, whereas the analytical logic of the grammar books is an autopsy rather than a synthesis. Such should be the case with our prayer. Across the necessary multiplicity of words and ideas, as heart speaking to heart, our prayer must tend to the ineffable communication of the one to the One: beyond the exchange of words, to the exchange of looks, where we rediscover at a single glance all that we have said to each other, and realize all that we are unable to say.

*   *   *

Thus from the meaning which can be traced through the intricacies of these successive eliminations, we can perhaps glimpse the object which is going to fill the void reserved by silence and solitude. This object is God alone, but the God of Jesus Christ. That is, he is no mere anthropomorphic reality, nothing that image or concept can embrace: he is the God of faith, the God revealed and at the same time the hidden God. In other words, mystery. Not just any mystery—but the mystery of the God-Trinity. Again, not an abstract, theoretical view of the Trinity: but the revelation in Jesus Christ. Thus finally it is the Mystery of Jesus. So many points which are interlinked, so many steps that our meditation must follow in sequence.

It is perhaps for want of understanding that silence and solitude should develop in us the sense of mystery, which finally leads to the sense of God, that we understand so little their imperious necessity. Mystery irks our minds, which are more than ever loquacious and volatile. For nothing is so much lacking to them as the sense of respect, of the unmeasured respect which the holy demands. Without this respect, without this religious awe, the sacred itself fades away. This awe is the atmosphere out of which it could not live in us. This means that so long as it refuses mystery, so long as it is not orientated upon mystery, our prayer will remain empty of God. Every kind of idol can claim it. God, the true God, will be absent from it.

We only come near to him in the measure in which he whom we seek is the Wholly Other, the Unknown, the Unknowable, who has nothing in common either with the beings of our world or the thoughts of our heart. But how, then, is he to be sought, since we do not know him, since he is the One whom man has never seen? He attracts to himself, the answer is, precisely those whom a sure instinct attracts towards the depths of solitude and silence, an instinct which derives in them from something beyond themselves. We do not know him before having found him, because it is he who seeks us, let us remember, when we think we are seeking him. When we are journeying towards him, he is the invisible centre of the whirlwind in which all beings who are not him, and ourselves with them, seem to be swallowed up and lost. And it is indeed a kind of dizziness which draws us to him: but a strange dizziness, in which, at the heart of our fear, of a fear to which no other can be compared, lies a kind of attraction, even more un-paralleled. *Mysterium tremendum*, but also *mysterium fascinosum* say Rudolf Otto's admirable analyses of the holy, which we have already mentioned.

The psalms, as we shall shortly see, are the monk's prayer *par excellence,* principally because they are full of this attitude. There are no religious songs which breathe such an impression of the dread majesty of the God whose existence by comparison overwhelms all others. Likewise there are no hymns shot through with so deep an appeal of the soul towards this God, by so intimate and, antici-pating, so exulting a conviction of the nearness to himself to which he calls us.

The paradoxical mystery of the *Rex tremendæ majestatis*, who is also *Deus cordis mei et Rex meus*, is opened to us, rather than, properly speak-ing, discovered, in the revelation of the Trinity. It is not that this revelation makes us understand the mystery: to say so is meaningless. It is rather that it causes us to enter into it. Yahwe, the God who has no house made by men's hands in which he can dwell, is nevertheless present *with* Israel in the shining cloud of his Shekinah into which Moses has entered. By the breath of the Spirit which inspired his prophets, he will be present *in* them. In the Christian, the heart of man becomes the temple of the Spirit. Henceforward, adopted by God, man lives with the Son, he lives with the mystical body. In the word made flesh, the Shekinah of light and life, the Wisdom which made the worlds dwells with us. Thus the Father, the Holy Lord, the almighty Father, the eternal God, becomes our Father.

In the *lectio divina*, the Father speaks to us through the Son. In the Divine Office the Spirit himself who had shed abroad his love in our hearts answers the Father through us, that is, to repeat, through the Son, for he and we are henceforth one. Between these two practices stretches the monk's whole life of prayer. It ebbs and flows from *lectio* to Office and from Office to *lectio*. It is continual meditation on the divine Word by which the Mystery has been revealed to us without losing anything of its inaccessible grandeur. It is the constant taking up again of the divine Praise in which the Word chants, in words which are his own, the Spirit's own canticle. Enough has been said to show that the place of the monk's prayer, at the same time as it is silence and solitude, is Jesus Christ. Certain gnostics called him the 'Word emanating from silence'. We can appropriate the term for ourselves. All this immense effort of detachment from creatures and himself which the monk imposes upon himself, has no other purpose but to leave room for Christ, for Christ speaking to us of God, for Christ speaking in us to God, which is the whole of Christian prayer.

St John Climacus tells us that the thought of Christ should be as continual in us as respiration. The name of Jesus, inseparable from our breathing, will alone enable us to find the meaning of solitude with God.[1] In such expressions we have in embryo all the hesychastic mystery which was that of ancient monasticism.

The ἡσυχία, the perfect pacifying of body and spirit—such is the first objective to which the monk's silent solitude should tend. In this silence and perfect absence of disturbance, the ancients advise him to quieten eventually even the rhythm of his breathing. When he has reached this point, let him murmur, as he slowly inhales each breath of pure air: 'Lord Jesus, Son of the living God! . . .', then, breathing out the vitiated air of his body: '. . . Be merciful to me a sinner'. In this prayer indefinitely repeated, the rhythm of which will come to harmonize with the very rhythm of the monk's physical life, all is contained. Adoration of the Father as the living God, the God who alone possesses in himself the Spirit of life, is there made by the adoring recognition of the Sovereignty of Jesus. The humility of the creature, of the sinner, but also filial confidence, are therein renewed unceasingly.

Gradually prayer will become even more simplified, but with a simplification which has nothing in common with abstraction. For the vision of faith will be concentrated more and more purely on the

[1] P. G., Vol. LXXXVIII, col. 1112 C.

unique fullness of life which is JESUS, and finally the monk will find nothing more to say but this one Name, charged with all his love, or rather with all the love of God spread abroad in his heart by the Spirit.[1]

[1] On all this see the admirable *Centuries* of St Maxim the Confessor, P. G., Vol. XC, col. 1421, 1424, 1441. For a brief, but very suggestive commentary, cf. M. Viller, *Spiritualité des premiers siècles chrétiens* (Paris, 1930), pp. 174 ff. The most moving *Récits d'un pélerin russe*, published in *Irenikon* in 1928, show to what extent this traditional monastic devotion remained alive in the Russian people, not so long ago. The Western rosary, recited calmly but with deep fervour, tends precisely towards the same simplification of prayer and life, all gathered up in Christ by his Mother.

III

PENANCE AND MORTIFICATION

WE have spoken of the ties which renunciation must sever if the monk is to seek God effectively. We have mentioned the obstacles which solitude and silence must thrust aside if the meeting with God is to take place. Such reminders indicate by implication the reason for which God has to be *sought*, although his presence pervades everything he has made: namely, sin. If it were not for sin, everything would speak to us of God. The love of creatures would lead us to the love of God. And if any religion is unthinkable without an offering of all one has, of all one is, such an offering would never need to take the form of immolation for its accomplishment. If it were not for sin the purest human happiness would of itself as it were lead us to supernatural happiness.

The implications, however, are not sufficient. It is essential to realize that monastic life is not only conditioned by sin and its necessary reparation, that sin does not merely give it certain particular features, even fundamental features, but that sin is its *raison d'être*. Monastic life is reparation for sin.

But sin is not repaired merely by compensation of its consequences. It is not simply a matter of correcting the initial disorder it has caused in the course of human life. Yet to believe this, to act as if one believed it, is the spontaneous, almost inevitable tendency of Christians to-day. Whatever we do or say in this connection, we always give the impression that sin is merely an inertia to be overcome, a natural inertia, which the fall has at most accentuated. So long as we remain at that point, we have not even begun to glimpse the real state of affairs.

Our failure to acquire a true notion of sin comes from our being hardened to all true sense of the sacred. Where the sense of God has been lost, how should the sense of the offence against God be preserved? But this is no less an impoverishment of our humanity than a forgetfulness of that which surpassed it. If for us sin is reduced to a vague force of inertia, we not only lose sight of its supernatural character, we even forget its human character. We no longer see that we are concerned with an act in which our conscience is engaged, a drama in which our person is at stake. The state that results from this thus appears to us as a simple misfortune, completely external to the deepest part of our being, and concerning which all that is necessary is to mitigate the consequences. But the true situation is that there is a fault to be expiated. Precautions, even heroic, or prescriptions, even supernaturally prudent, will not repair it. Under the first heading fall the fundamental renunciations of monastic life, and under the second solitude and silence, so long as they have not been explicitly linked with a personal conversion: with penance. Thus we are now brought to investigate the reality that we have to classify under the name of penance and its relation with all there is mortifying in monastic life.

* * *

Monastic life, we have been saying, is not only conditioned by sin. It is directly in function of sin.

On this point the Greek Fathers have developed a detailed teaching, too little known to-day. It seems to have found its most lucid explanation in the writings of St Maxim the Confessor.[1] According to him, after sin, and for its reparation, two ways were opened to humanity. The one was the indirect way of the family. By prolonging the human race beyond the death of its sinful progenitors, the family holds a possibility of redemption and conversion for mankind. The other was the direct way of chastity consecrated to God, and this way alone directly engages in the creation of the new man, by its renunciation of the extension of the old creation of fallen man. In the first way fallen man is saved from the death of his species and therefore left with the hope of future redemption. In the second, fallen man is made to die, but by this 'dying' he is created anew.

The ascetic, consequently, is of the ranks of the violent who are not content with enlarging the field in which the Kingdom can be set up when it comes, but want to make that kingdom come down upon earth *to-day*. After that, it matters little that history comes to an end: it had no other significance than to reach that point.

These two ways, think the Fathers in general, are each wide of the mark of what would have been the 'natural' way of approach to God

[1] Père von Balthasar, in his *Liturgie cosmique, Maxime le Confesseur* (Paris, 1947), pp. 127 ff., has fully perceived the importance of this thought. But confused by a naturalist view of the sanctity of marriage, such as our contemporaries understand it, he does not succeed in grasping its permanent value.

if it had not been for sin. Then human society, existing under a form quite different from those under which we know it, would have been sanctified in itself. But sin now leaves only these two possibilities: either a human society which will reserve the possibility of sanctification by extending the human race; or else a sanctification actually carried out in the sacrifice of posterity. It is by no means purposeless to develop such considerations at the beginning of a meditation on penance. All too easily, as soon as we arrive at this notion and want, as is indeed essential, to say more about it than we have done up to the present, our modern minds revolt. It seems to them so obvious that we are being driven to something against nature. To this invincible prejudice of our contemporaries, it must be answered that the life which by-passes penance is no more natural than that which engages in it. If he who 'crucifies his flesh with its concupiscences' is beyond nature, he who 'nourishes his own flesh and loves it' does not follow nature to any greater extent. Human 'nature', that is man such as God would have willed him to be without sin, is not even a thing of the past: it is a possibility which has never been realized and which will never be realized. Now man can only vegetate below that to which God calls him, looking forward, however, if he remains in the line of the divine commandments, to a better future, or else respond immediately to the divine call by burning his boats. Both ways are possible. Marriage is holy, in this sense, as St Paul says, of 'the begetting of children'. But penitent virginity is holier, through the immediate and total consecration that it alone effects. The choice must be made. In actual fact, one who has chosen the indirect, imperfect way may very well be able to live there more perfectly than another who has chosen the direct way. But each of the two ways remains what it is, and it is wholly useless and unreal to imagine a way which would combine the satisfactions of the one and the generosity of the other. As the proverb says: 'One cannot have one's cake and eat it.'

* * *

What, then, is penance, properly speaking, and how is the mortification it implies necessary for the flowering of eternal life?

To the first question it must be answered that penance is what St John the Baptist, the solitary *par excellence*, the monk's ideal as the ancients termed him, was the first to preach under the name of μετάνοια. What it is necessary to put under this heading is best expressed by the word 'conversion'. And that is why in St Benedict's realist and far-seeing view, what he calls the *conversio morum* is the first principle of the way of penance which the monk must follow.

Conversion is etymologically a change of direction. Since the fall, mankind has been following a certain line. Conversion breaks with this line to follow another. More deeply, as the etymology shows us once more, the μετάνοια will be a change of heart, but a change of heart so radical that it demands a complete break with the past. The development of the new man along the new way presupposes that the old man is already dead.

It is obvious that penance thus defined, even if, once again, it is not against nature properly speaking, is certainly supernatural. If it had not its mystical foundation in the sacramental union with Christ crucified, by baptism and the eucharist, penance would be merely suicide.

We have said this with sufficient insistence and in enough detail to be dispensed from returning to the subject. It is now the moment rather to speak of the counterpart. Mystical union with Christ in its mystery of life-giving death would remain a pure chimæra if it were not translated into terms of everyday reality. 'To mortify the members who are upon earth', 'to treat one's body hardly and keep it under subjection', 'to die daily', such are some of the very realist formulas in which St Paul expresses this truth. We must now examine their application to monastic life.

These expressions of St Paul make it sufficiently clear that the asceticism of penance means something more than to break attachments or to sweep aside obstacles. If we were contented with that, we should not go further than an abandonment of the superfluous for the essential. But penance includes more: a privation of the necessary. Otherwise, the use of the term 'mortification' would be sheer hyperbole. But such is not the case. What the *conversio morum* requires of us is a real death, the adoption of the traditional practices of the life of penance in the place of the practices of the life of satisfaction which leaves sin unrepaired.

The monk indeed is primarily someone who deprives himself. And there is no privation in the strict sense until it affects the necessary. We shall understand this perfectly if we consider what the material privations which lie at the root of monastic life are.

They presuppose that the life we call natural, if it is not bad in itself, in its substance, for this was created by God, is in any case bad in its actual exercise, for which we are responsible. But there is no means of separating one from the other, except in the abstract. In the concrete, if one wants to reform the actual exercise of it, the substance must be mortally wounded. Such a dying, let us never forget, will of course only be effective if it is sustained by faith. But that does not mean that it will be the less real for that. For faith is a first real mortification which involves all the others: is it not the renouncement of the visible for the invisible? of the present for the future?

The monk first of all suffers deprivation in his food. It should be clearly understood that this is not simply the purely psychological asceticism to which present-day people are inclined to reduce mortifications of this kind. It is not only, it is not directly, the mortification of taste at which the early monks aimed. For that frugality would have sufficed. What they were counteracting was the principal end of feeding: repletion, satiety. The kind of sense of well-being which follows, I will not say an excessive meal, but a good meal, a meal which we should be tempted to classify as normal, as natural, is the experience against which their asceticism in food was aimed. Either this means nothing, or it means that it was precisely the satisfaction of nature which they refused. And that is precisely what the word 'mortification' should mean, unless it is an exaggerated, pointless expression.

It is the same for comfort. The early monks set such store by an ascetic practice which they called 'chamœonia', from a Greek word which means 'to sleep on the ground'. In their opinion the body ought never to consent to a reciprocal adaptation between itself and the world. It should be forced to remain in the world as a thing out of place there, never at ease.

Finally, the monks of earlier times insisted before all else, perhaps, on the privation which seems to us the most against nature: that of sleep. They wanted the soul not to accept, or never to accept willingly, this kind of daily burial in the body, which yet constitutes the relaxation, repose, refreshment which are most indispensable to a balanced life.

It is useless to juggle with these fundamental facts of monastic tradition. They do not presuppose the ideal of an asceticism which would be simply a hygiene of the soul. They rather presuppose what one would be tempted to call a morbid effort. And, once more, if the word 'mortification' has a meaning, it is difficult to understand how the reality it designates could avoid producing this impression.

This is not to say that the most far-seeing advocates of hygiene are not themselves inclined to sense the rightness of the instinct which drives monks in this direction. Galen noted long ago that 'one must always rise from table with a slight appetite'. Nearer to our own times Carrel has shown by what harm to our faculty of adaptation, and therefore to our vitality, the pleasures of comfort are paid for. Such remarks in themselves, however, rather than permitting asceticism to be brought back to the reassuring sphere of a 'life in conformity with nature', would make us suspect the unreality of such a notion. The nature of present-day man is a nature which has been vitiated. If we do not wound it, it wounds itself: that is what we learn from such observations. They enable us to guess that the folly of asceticism will perhaps be the only true wisdom, but they do not tell us why. Only the vision of faith can do that. It should be noted that the three essential mortifications, in food, in comfort, in sleep, are aimed at the same thing under different forms. They attack peaceful and satisfying accommodation, installation and enjoyment in this world. Why then is it so important that the monk, the monk who seeks God, should refuse himself what, to repeat, seems so natural?

The only possible answer is that this appearance is an illusion. It is an illusion, because what seems an elementary right of man is so no longer. Merely to live, to use this world as if it were made for us (a fact which the Word of God is yet the first to declare to us as true), we can do this no longer, we have no longer the right to do so. To recognize that is the basis of penance. But we never really recognize it unless we have experienced it in fact. To enjoy the goods of this world in tranquillity presupposes a good conscience *vis-à-vis* the world's Creator. It is no longer possible for us to have this good conscience. To abandon ourselves to the sanest earthly enjoyments, even if we should use them in the most moderate fashion, would be to entertain a misunderstanding, the most harmful of illusions. The contentment and tranquillity which are the normal consequences of the satisfaction of the elemental needs, would allow us to live in a false security. The peace in which this satisfaction would establish us would be a deceptive peace. Actually, it would merely be a numbing of the conscience, a slipping down into a false earthly paradise which is no longer possible for us.

The final reason for which the monk here below must shun all rest, all sense of permanence, all accommodation, is that the first thing to do in order to discover God afresh is to recognize oneself as a sinner. Now a sinner who behaves and feels in regard to God as if he were perfectly at home is a sinner who has not even begun to be aware of his situation. *A fortiori* for him there is no question of reparation: he no longer even glimpses the necessity for it.

On the other hand, the repentant sinner, on the way to becoming an effectively penitent sinner, is the man who, like the Prodigal, says to the Father: 'Father, I have sinned against heaven and before thee. I am no more worthy to be called thy son. Treat me as one of thy hired servants. . . .'

The first effect of mortification must be to entertain such a spirit in us, for the want of which the monk's life would lack all genuineness. Monastic tradition has defined this spirit by the word 'compunction'. The degrees of humility to which St Benedict relates the whole spirituality of his rule merely detail its progressive deepening. It is a matter in short of establishing and maintaining oneself in the fundamental reflection that our life starts out with an error, with a fault. It must then be put right again (that is where the μετάνοια comes in) by a regret, by reparation. The principle can be none other than the acceptance of suffering as the only really *natural* law of our life on the bases on which we have ourselves established it. A discord, a fundamental disharmony with the design of God, that is what St Paul calls 'the law of our members', that is the law which our vitiated nature has formed for itself. To take account of this, to realize the necessary opposition between this 'law' and the divine law, is the whole principle of penance. But so long as we live in the illusion of a possible agreement between our existence and the general order of creation, there will be no means of our acquiring this awareness of the true position which, alas, is ours. Whence the necessary link between penance and mortification. Mortification will make us experience, not by intelligence alone, but in the experience of daily life, which alone is convincing in this connection, that we are unworthy of the most elementary gifts of God. Once accepted and willed by us, it will not be a mere abstract, inert recognition of this fact. It will bring us to put ourselves in our true place, the only place where grace can find us and raise us up.

It might be asked here if this development and systematic maintenance of the painful sense of a fundamental discord between us and God is not opposed to the pursuit of the ἡσυχία, of the deep security of a life of union with him which we have given as the objective of prayer. Not at all. Newman, in one of those formulas, as supple as they are strong, of which he has the secret, shatters such a confusion. To be at ease, he tells us, is to be unsafe. We might express it in other words: to be at ease is to put oneself outside true peace. The prayer of Jesus of which we have spoken, which should lead us to perfect repose in him, derives its support on the contrary from an act of humility which becomes progressively deeper. Each aspiration which raises us towards him whom we call 'Lord Jesus, Son of the Living God! . . .' in an adoration which becomes increasingly more serene, presupposes the progressively deeper abasement and prostration of the 'Be merciful to me a sinner! . . .'

Far, then, from there being any contradiction between them, we must realize the necessary interaction between true prayer and true penance. Our prayer will only be what it ought to be in the measure in which we feel within us the need of grace. But we shall only experience this in the measure in which we are penitent. Conversely, our penance will only be generous, and, above all, will only be effective, in the measure in which grace itself opens the eyes of our heart as to what we are without it. And that can only be obtained by prayer.

We shall return to this last idea. For the moment, bearing in mind the preceding considerations, we must, now that we can do so to good purpose, set forth the demands of penance in detail. It is obvious that the three great penitential practices: the privation of food, comfort and sleep, cannot be applied without a wise discretion. Therein lies, indeed, the primary justification of the cenobitical life. Monks have come to live together, under the authority of a superior, to combine emulation in penance with the necessary moderation demanded by the perpetual presence among us of a judge who is objective, because independent.

But to say this is tantamount to saying that discretion, moderation in the use of penance, is the first business of the superior or director. The monk puts himself into their hands to reassure himself in this respect. But what *he* must seek within the shelter of this safeguard, that which is his own personal affair, from which no initiative of another can dispense him, is the performance of penance that shall be as real and as generous as possible. As soon as the superior has to stir up a monk in this direction instead of restraining him, it means that the monk is no longer *really* seeking God. From then onwards, all he can do to help him along will be of no more value than encouragements addressed to a dead body. The sinews, the indispensable driving force of the quest for God, are the personal striving for a mortification as generous as possible.

We must not let ourselves become the dupes of a false humanism born of the Renaissance, which is the implicit denial of all monasticism presupposes. Except in the case of a very special call, one must not indeed destroy one's health, at the risk of destroying in oneself the means to all progress, to all conscious and voluntary effort. But care for one's health must not be allowed to become dominant in the monk. More generally, his aim cannot be a harmonious equilibrium of soul and body, such as the 'Christian' humanists have been proposing since the sixteenth century.

In the first place the monk knows that such an equilibrium is a chimæra. One cannot believe in it without failing to recognize the conditions created for human life by sin. 'The Spirit in us striveth against the flesh and the flesh against the Spirit.' Obviously that does not signify, as we have already said, that soul and body are irreconcilable enemies. But it does signify, at any rate in the present life, that the soul must, still using St Paul's expression, 'treat the body hardly and keep it in subjection'.

This is not to say that the monk does not also aim at a certain equilibrium. But such an equilibrium is the eschatological equilibrium of the resurrection and the only way of attaining to it is the cross. Any other equilibrium, were it possible of achievement, which it is not, would in the eyes of the monk be a pure and simple falling from grace. Thus he shuns repose and settling down as sheer paralysis which will impede the flight which is to bear him towards God. That such a flight is necessarily painful is what becomes increasingly apparent. But the pain is one which wrenches us away from a fatal paralysis. Thus, as we have already said, monasticism is the only true humanism: the only one which integrally and permanently saves the whole man. But that is because it is a humanism which is definitely eschatological. In this respect there is no doubt at all that it will always appear unhealthy to those who confuse health with accommodation, at least apparent, with the present world.

*   *   *

The effect of this penitential asceticism must finally be to put us before God in the state of men who know that they have no longer any right to what they have, however little that may be. And it is not a matter of merely inculcating this idea in us. We must go further than mere psychology. This is moreover the final reason for which the monastic tradition has always considered a purely spiritual asceticism as radically insufficient. This situation of ours must be given effect to concretely: it is not sufficient to consider ourselves as poor, we must be so in fact.

Let us be quite clear that if Christ has not thought it possible to relieve our wretchedness except by taking all its reality upon himself, it would be most unlikely that we should be able to free ourselves from it at a lesser cost. We here discover why the poor take up such an all-pervading place in the religion of Israel. After the preaching of the great prophets and in particular of Jeremias, after the experience of the exile and the dispersion, the religious conscience of the Jews recognized that the only man who might be acceptable to God was the poor: not only the man who tries to give himself the feelings of a poor man, but he who accepts to be so and wills to be so. There is no other means of placing oneself in the presence of God where his grace must find us to touch us.

The servant of Yahwe of the great prophecies of Isaias is the poor man *par excellence*: he is the needy, the outcast, the one of whom men make no account and whom it has pleased God to break by suffering. The psalms which bring us closest to the Gospel are merely the prayer of this ideal poor man. Finally among the Evangelists, St Luke was to be distinguished by the insistence with which he stressed the poverty both necessary and necessarily realist, of him who wills to become a child of God and to return to the Kingdom of the Father. In St Luke, Christ does not content himself with saying: 'Blessed are the poor *in spirit*'. He says: 'Blessed are the poor', quite simply, and, to close the door upon any loophole, he adds: 'Cursed are the rich'.

The Fathers had a very strong sense of this central demand of the divine word which the Gospel was to develop to its fullest extent. In their eyes, the fact that the prayer of the monks was the psalter implied that they were in fact the poor, for the psalter is merely the prayer of the poor, just as the Gospel of the beatitudes is addressed only to the poor. Let us listen, rather, to the terms in which a great spiritual writer of the French school has summed up their doctrine, and primarily that of St Augustine:

> The poor who often accompany us when we go to church, or who, by a providence which St John Chrysostom has remarked upon, are sitting at the gates of the temple where our prayer is made, ought to make us remember our condition by theirs and teach us to pray in the way in which they pray. For Scripture never wearies of repeating to us that God hears only the prayer of the poor. The psalms seem intended only to instruct us in this truth; and we cannot meditate upon it too much, or examine its consequences and full extent too thoroughly.

The princes have been despised and the poor man has been succoured in his indigence. The proud have been rejected, and the humble man has been enlightened. The poor man is a beggar who attributes nothing to himself, who expects all from the mercy of God, who cries every day at his master's gate, who knocks that it may be opened to him, who is completely naked and trembling with cold, who asks for some clothing, who keeps his eyes lowered, looking on the ground, and who strikes his breast. It is this beggar, this poor man, this humble heart whom God sustains with mighty help. This poor man is a multitude of families; this poor man is a multitude of peoples, a multitude of Churches. He is also a single Church, a single people, a single family. What instruction is hidden under these figures! What depths!

It is indeed a great mystery that the whole Church should be merely one poor man, and that all the saints make up only a single poor man, who alone is heard.[1]

Again, as Duguet adds, it is necessary that we should see this poverty as a poverty of guilt. The humility which must be ours is not merely that of the creature who recognizes that he possesses nothing that he has not received. It is the humility of the sinner who knows that he has profaned the first grace, that of creation, and that the grace of redemption not only is not due to him, but ought, if God were merely just, to be refused him. The monk is primarily the man who realizes this state of sin in which all men are, but which other men do not accept and do not recognize. In order that he may recognize it, he must get out of the abstract. His personal penance must make him confess his personal sins and accept their just consequences. For to recognize oneself as a sinner, so long as we take refuge behind the universality of sin to evade personal responsibility for it, is perfectly futile. It is necessary that an act, that a series of acts take hold of and mark our whole life, obliging us to shoulder sin no longer as a general anonymous fault, but as our own. The progressive cultivation of humility of St Benedict has no other aim. Thus it gives meaning to all the monk's mortifications. The latter oblige him to say, with all the conviction that reality demands of us, but which will not be obtained without an effective and voluntary humiliation: 'Thou art the man.'

Yet the detailed recognition of all his faults on the part of the monk

---

[1] L. Duguet, *Traité sur la prière publique* (7e ed., Paris, 1713), pp. 142 and ff. The phrases in *italics* are a series of quotations from the *Enarratio in Psalm. 106* of St Augustine.

would not be sufficient, if it were only as faults or errors that he admitted them to himself or to men, his brethren. He must come to the point of acknowledging them to God precisely as sins: 'I have sinned *against heaven and before thee* . . .', there is no effective confession so long as one has not arrived at that point. And it is indeed to this that the withdrawal of all that comes to us from God tends: to place us not in the condition of just *any* needy men, but of sinners: 'I am no more worthy to be called thy son. . . .'

We are here brought back to the necessary interaction of prayer, the prayer of faith, and of penance. One only recognizes oneself as a sinner before God, in that relationship with God which is founded on faith in Jesus Christ, in considering the Cross, viewed first of all as the great, personal reproach which God addresses to each one of us. Yet the Cross of Jesus will not pierce our heart unless it becomes our cross. It is not sufficient to look at the cross to understand its meaning: it is necessary to stretch oneself out upon it.

Perhaps we are catching a glimpse at last of the supernatural depth of this war upon natural satisfaction which constitutes the penitential asceticism that we have described. In the state of mankind to-day it may be said that all intense consciousness of things is necessarily painful. It is a well-known fact that the most finely sensitive natures are those whose hearts are perpetually torn. Conversely, earthly happiness, the most natural and healthy human happiness, undeniably tends to a numbing of consciousness. The satisfaction of alimentary or sexual needs is spontaneously prolonged in sleep. Sleep is the beatitude towards which all earthly satisfactions converge. The romantic confusion between love, death and the poetic ecstasy of a purely earthly mysticism is singularly enlightening. The peace towards which humanity tends, to flee from the pain which is always hard upon it, is finally the peace of non-being. Happiness is only a narcotic.

On the other hand, monastic asceticism tends to awaken at any cost the invincibly somnolent being, fallen man. It deprives him of sleep, which yet seems to him, and indeed is, his fundamental need. It deprives him of the relaxation of the comfort in which he would forget the painful nature of the contact between him and the world, such as they now stand towards one another. It deprives him of the repletion which would satisfy his physical desires by extinguishing them. In all these ways it keeps him both alert and in suffering. But this physical suffering which it inflicts upon him is only the pointer to the disharmony which is his as a sinner. It brings him back then to the only awareness which is not more or less a dream, but which is truly actual and total awareness.

In this awareness only, in this consciousness incapable of rest, of appeasement, he finds himself before God, there just where he is, if he still can be said to be: in his sin. He thus finds himself where God seeks him, where God finds him in Jesus Christ: in Jesus Christ made sin and malediction to save sinners, of whom the monk at last recognizes himself as the chief.

When this point has been reached, we shall perhaps understand St Jerome's saying that the task of the monk, in contrast to that of the priest, is not to preach but to weep. We shall also understand the importance given by the mysticism of early times to the gift of tears. The Roman Missal has preserved for us a prayer *pro petitione lacrimarum*. We cannot do better than quote it as summing up the traditional teaching that we hope we have succeeded in synthesizing:

> *Omnipotens et mitissime Deus, qui sitienti populo fontem viventis aquæ de petra produxisti: educ de cordis nostri duritia lacrimas compunctionis; ut peccata nostra plangere valeamus, remissionemque eorum, te miserante, mereamur accipere.*[1]

It is indeed for those who are thirsting that God, the God who is all-powerful and yet full of sweetness, makes the source of living water to gush forth. Those who are satiated with the goods of this world could not drink from it. To those alone it is offered whose heart of stone has been struck by the rod of the divine chastisements. Without the tears of compunction, the heart of flesh which God looks for in the new mankind could not be re-created in us. But to him who weeps for his sins, their forgiveness is offered through the divine grace whose first gift is the shedding of such tears.

Penance, finally, should make over to us the fruits of the Cross. But it cannot do so except by nailing us to the Cross. The crushed Heart of the man-God by whom the sanctifying and reconciling Spirit is spread abroad in mankind cannot communicate these fruits except to hearts which are themselves broken. It was our sins that crushed the Heart of the Just One; how can we expect him to wash us from them if our own heart refuses to pass through the same trial? It would be futile for us to

---

[1] Almighty and most merciful God, who didst bring forth a fountain of living water from the rock for thy thirsting people; bring forth from the hardness of our heart tears of compunction; that we may be worthy to mourn for our sins and deserve, by thy mercy, to receive their forgiveness.

rest upon the love of God that Christ has manifested to us if we were to forget that this Love is only known to us as crucified Love. But it was our offences, once more, which crucified him. Could we really give back love for love, or rather could God's own love come into us, without our offering ourselves, spontaneously, to the Cross?

To offer oneself to the Cross, however, in no sense means to take delight in suffering. Of us as of Christ it must be able to be said: 'To win his prize of blessedness he endured the cross and made light of its shame.'[1] It is not, for that would be the acme of unhealthy masochism with which true asceticism has nothing in common, that we ought to seek or expect some *dulcor lacrymarum*, some pleasure taken in the tears themselves. It is that, through the Cross, through the Cross illumined by faith, through our cross merging with that of Christ, we come to the only true joy. Beyond the Cross, beyond all crosses, in that blessed eternity where 'there will be no more death, or mourning, or cries of distress, no more sorrow',[2] extends the region of the joy which is lasting, that which is not as the world gives, but that, too, which the world cannot take away. But already here on earth, now, under the Cross, if the Cross is truly the great experience of faith, this joy hidden from the world radiates in the penitent heart. Then uniting himself beforehand with Christ in glory, as he has already united himself to him in his passion, the penitent can make his own prayer of the holy and just One before the Cross, 'Father, the time has come: give glory now to thy Son, that thy Son may give the glory to thee. . . .'[3]

[1] Heb. 12. 2.   [2] Apoc. 21. 4.   [3] John 17. 1.

IV

WORK

'MAN is neither angel nor beast,' said Pascal, 'and the catastrophe is that he who tries to play the angel becomes a beast.' This remark would be directly applicable to a monk who had not been awakened to an intense awareness of his present condition, which has to be his starting-point in his search for God, by an asceticism based on reality.

The supernatural, eschatological view which should be that of genuine monasticism has sometimes degenerated into a vision lacking reality. In the monasticism of early times, a veritable sect sprang up, that of the euchites, who refused all earthly occupations on the pretext of devoting themselves exclusively to prayer. We should be wrong, too, in thinking that the danger of illusion no longer exists for monks who practise mortification strictly. Work, work which brings out the sweat on one's brow is, according to Scripture, the primary mortification of sinful mankind. An asceticism which neglected the basic mortification, which no man can escape from, to devise and invent all sorts of mortifications of its own making, which would then fall into the category of pure artifice, would not be particularly realist. It should be observed that temptations of this kind do seem to threaten monastic institutes periodically. Byzantine and Cluniac monasteries have both fallen into decadence by way of idleness. When a monastery is founded, the first monks are generally overwhelmed by material tasks and long for the day when their life will be sufficiently organized to ensure them the leisure of contemplation. But when the time comes when community life is stabilized, it is very rare that one does not exceed the measure, that one does not yield to the idea that one would have a much more fruitful life on the spiritual plane by no longer allowing oneself to be distracted by earthly tasks, the necessity for which has disappeared. And, to judge from history, the result is always the same: without being able to determine the precise moment at which the error took concrete shape, we slide from the *otium contemplationis* to a pious slothfulness which has no longer anything in common with the former.

From this time onwards, the monastery is everything but a monastery. It may still keep up a decorous outward life for a certain time. It has now ceased to walk in the way of the divine commandments. It is no longer the school of divine service. It is at most a house of retreat for sluggards who have given up the pursuit of the quest for God. Against this insidious aberration, the most treacherous of the menaces which hang over the development of a monastic community, it is essential ceaselessly to recall the common teaching of all the great monastic legislators: work, hard and laborious work, is itself an ascetic practice. It is the most indispensable of ascetic practices because it is, let us repeat, the most fundamental.

St Paul tells us this; St Pachomius, St Basil, St Benedict, following the first hermits like St Antony, repeat it: 'He who is not willing to work, should not eat.' The monk must work, and first of all work manually: because he cannot escape from the world, renounce the world, mortify his own flesh to the extent of no longer eating, no longer being clothed, no longer having a roof over his head. It would, then, be scandalous that, continuing to enjoy these things as other men do, he should not provide them for himself as other men indeed are obliged to do. If in a certain sense the monk shuns and should shun the world, it is its joys that he flees from. But for him there can be no question of escaping from its tasks. More than any other Christian the monk should repeat to himself the word of Christ, 'I am come not to be ministered unto but to minister'.

It is not even sufficient to say of the monk that he ought not to seek to escape from the tasks of other men. It is essential to add that he ought not even to shun their cares, at least certain of the gravest and most legitimate of them. I remember one day having seen a company of religious go by in a little village of the Ile de France. A child, surprised at their strange dress, asked its mother, who was standing on the doorstep of the house, in my hearing, who they were. I shall never forget her reply. There was no animosity in the tone, but a sadness which was all the more impressive. 'Don't worry about them, my dear,' she said to the child, 'they are happy all right; they have no wife, no children, no cares . . .'

It does not seem to me that any more serious accusation can be made against religious. Nothing could continue to make their withdrawal from the world lawful if such withdrawal in fact freed them from the great preoccupations willed by God, which are both the trial and the honour of their brothers in humanity. If the monk has no longer to experience these cares for himself, as he obviously has not, charity must lead him to bear those of others as if they were his own. The very fact that he has reduced his own needs ought to make him free to practise fraternal charity without restriction. Other men can be dispensed in some measure from troubling about strangers, because they have to trouble about their own family. The monk has not this excuse.

And here as in the case of mortification we must repeat: charity, before claiming to be spiritual, must begin by being corporeal. The monk who claims to love the souls of men, his brethren, and who is deaf, indifferent or ignorant in the face of their most absorbing cares, mocks the world. At ease in this respect for his own account, if such ease makes him blind to the difficulties of others, it only imprisons him in selfishness.

In a more general way it is important to realize that a monastic society, present in the midst of human society, must never be or appear to be parasitical. Even on the material plane, or let us say at least on the terrestrial plane (we shall clarify this distinction presently), it is essential that the monk produce for mankind around him more than he asks from them. Monasteries who have forgotten this, who have come to live only on the largesse of lay people, have, once more, all fallen into irremediable decadence by this means. But if this were so at periods when the faith, since it was widespread, meant that all men admitted that the spiritual aid given by the monastery to the city largely dispensed it from other obligations, what is to be said to-day? In a world where hardly anyone is now capable of understanding such reasoning, how can parasitical monks avoid giving scandal? The situation is all the more serious by reason of the fact that the modern worker has such a strong sense of the universal duty of production. The effect of a monastic society which spent without producing correlatively, would to-day be that of a veritable canker.

It is considerations of this kind which explain the liberality with which Benedictine hospitality was always practised. Such considerations, too, enable us to understand that monks, at other times, have been able to carry out the task of civilization which we have referred to, without thereby in any way losing sight of their principal, indeed their sole objective. Obviously monks who taught their neighbours to make corn grow where there were thickets or swamps gave back generously in practical and effective charity what the world might have lent them for their terrestrial installation.

In saying all this we are not for one moment forgetting what we have so much stressed: that *the* task of the monk is prayer. But prayer, if it is not to become hypocritical, cannot dispense the monk from terrestrial solidarity with mankind. Once again, since he enjoys this solidarity, for him there can be no question of simply remaining a receiver. To him the fact that his proper task is prayer should, on the contrary, mean that he profits by the solidarity we are speaking of so little, that it is easier for him than for anyone else to compensate, and more than compensate, by what he contributes to the common treasure, what he draws from it. The life of St Antony shows him redoubling his work, and at the same time redoubling his fraternal charity, in proportion as he reduces his own necessities.

If we think again of the saying of Christ we referred to just now, 'The son of man has come to minister and not to be ministered unto', it should be obvious that on no consideration could monks be dispensed from work that is properly servile. All that which, since it is done for us by others, presupposes in others a dependence in our regard, or, *a fortiori*, a degradation, the monk should do for himself. And, obviously, just as he owes it to himself to refuse to allow others to perform such tasks for him, so he should be prompt to perform them for others. That is indeed why even those communities who have lay brothers have maintained the custom that all the fathers should in turn serve at table. The idea of a monk having servants seems so patent an absurdity that it has only to be mentioned to become untenable.

Does this mean that the monk must also necessarily perform all the non-servile material tasks which his existence requires? Is it necessary that he should produce his own food, make his own clothes, etc.? It does not seem so. In this connection the monk is in the same position as the other members of human society. A certain division of tasks accompanied by a mutual exchange of the contributions of each, is indispensable. If the monk accomplishes intellectual work which earns his keep, he can in some measure be dispensed from non-servile manual work. But in every form of manual work there is also an element of salutary humiliation which is not so immediately apparent in the work of the mind, and which makes it desirable that every monk, from time to time, should toil at labours which bring out the sweat on his brow. In one way or another, what is valid for the monastery as a whole is valid for each of its members: each one must give back to the earthly city what he exacts from it and even more, in the way of what is costly and painful to nature.

* * *

After all this, there remains the fact that the monk's work, inasmuch as he is thereby producing an earthly thing, must always take a secondary place in his life. That is not *his* work. It is not the task which sets him apart among men. He must, while he works as he should work, maintain in himself a necessary detachment in regard to the work performed. Even when he works at an earthly task, the monk must always have his eyes on the heavenly building. All Christians, of course, should do this. But for them the pursuit of the final end can remain more or less mediate. For the monk it cannot cease to be immediate.

It was said of old that the monk should not be given a task which would weigh down his mind. He should not be made, it was said, to hew stones all day long. He could not acquit himself of such a task and at the same time continue to think of God as was his duty. But he can weave baskets, for that leaves the mind sufficiently free to apply itself to prayer at the same time.

In short, the monk should only labour for the earthly city, however well he may labour there, as a guest who does not feel he is in his own home. He is all the more scrupulous about paying his share of the reckoning, but he is not attached to this temporary lodging, or to anything of what he should leave there to pay his debt. All that will be destroyed. He knows this and wills to be the man who now works only at a work that is eternal, even while he collaborates temporarily in another task. Even when he lends a hand to the earthly city, what he does is done solely to build up the heavenly city, and primarily to make of himself a well-polished stone in it.

It is perhaps in this double exigency more than anywhere else that the incomparable ascetic value of monastic work is found. On the one hand the monk must toil and labour more generously than anyone. But at the same time it is essential to refuse, break, cut off, all attachment to what one does materially, in an earthly connection. No one should put more conscientiousness into what he does than the monk, for since his whole life is consecrated to God, all that occupies him becomes sacred. But, rightly, what he does on this plane must no longer be measured by its value on that plane alone. That is not his work; it is only a necessary side issue of it, which has its meaning outside itself.

There is, however, one task widely entrusted to Western monks to-day, which seems to set special problems. It is the task of the priest. Since the Middle Ages, and particularly in more recent times, monks have been called to the priesthood in large numbers. Consequently, monasteries themselves are often to be found collectively engaged in apostolic tasks, in which even those monks who are not priests may find themselves more or less involved.

One might be tempted to think that this is precisely where the internal opposition we have just analysed in monastic work would be resolved. This would be a serious error never made by those of early times. On the contrary, we have only to read St John Chrysostom's *De Sacerdote*, or, if you prefer, the correspondence and poems of St Gregory Nazianzen to discover how acute the conflict created by a priestly vocation superimposed upon a monastic vocation, appeared to them. For it is, in fact, the conflict mentioned above, carried to the maximum of tension.

To understand this, it is enough to recall what was said at the beginning of the second part of this book, on the principle of Christian asceticism and particularly of renouncement. We are still concerned with a preference for the absolute, not a condemnation of the relative. Consequently, as we added, the more precious the reality in question, the more necessary its abandonment may prove, and the more painful. Of course the end of priestly work in regard to others is linked with the end the monk pursues himself. Thus *a priori* it would seem to be merely a communication through charity of what the monk has himself received. In cases where in point of fact it comes to be only that, the priestly work will become as it were the natural expansion of the monastic work. But it would be naïve or pretentious to think that the situation on the concrete plane can always be so simple.

In effect the task of the priest is primarily incorporated and particularized in detailed, local responsibilities, the care involved in which enters into inevitable conflict with the *unum necessarium* that is the monk's objective. Then such responsibilities themselves will demand of him activities which are much more difficult to reconcile with the exigencies proper to his life than the activities emanating from a task which is simply material, or even intellectual. And to all this it is pointless to reply that any priestly task is prompted by a requirement of charity and that the exercise of this charity will compensate in the monk for the imperfection of his spiritual exercises which it will have occasioned. To say this is to forget that the monk has only adopted his exercises because they seemed to him necessary, in his particular case, for the realization of perfect charity. It serves no purpose, then, to promise him a compensation in that which he was in point of fact seeking, and at the same time withdraw from him the means of attaining it, without giving him other equivalent means in their place.

And what is more, what the monk was seeking to avoid in avoiding the life of marriage, was not so much merely human affections as the particularization of charity in them. But it is precisely this particularization that the priest finds. And it is at this point that we see to what extremes the conflict between the immediate end of the task and the end which the ascetic pursues in working, is pushed, far from being suppressed, when the task in question is a priestly one. In this task the very price of the work to be pursued in the souls which are entrusted to him, requires of the priest a gift of self of unparalleled depth. The priest must literally make himself all things to all men. But the monk must detach himself from all things and all men. Is there indeed a solution possible?

Solution there certainly is, but it cannot be found in perfection except in the realization of that spiritual fatherhood whose incomparable importance for the monastic mentality of early times we have mentioned. In other words, whereas the priesthood obliges the monk to leave the framework of the monastery and liberate himself at least from some of its demands, it is essential that the monk, if he is to give himself to priestly tasks without danger to his vocation and without remorse, should have reached perfection in the essential of his monastic task. It is essential for him to have reached, by the way of monastic practices faithfully observed, the stage of spiritual fatherhood which will enable him to deliver to others what he has received, without losing it himself in so doing.

But such self-expression always presupposes that the monk will not see in his priesthood an excuse for abandoning half-way that which makes a monk of him. On the contrary, it is essential that he should see therein the necessity of pursuing to its utmost limits, at an accelerated rhythm, the development which monastic life alone, accepted with all its demands, can ensure him. Unless it is to be simply the shipwreck of monastic life, the conferring of the priesthood must be an invitation of fresh urgency to forestall ordinary men in the path of Christian perfection. Thus interpreted, it is comprehensible that in the East the priesthood is often given to monks called 'Megaloschemes', or 'monks of the great-habit', that is, to those who are considered to have perfected their monastic development, as the supreme consecration of the gift of spiritual fatherhood correlative to such a stage. For the monks of the West, who generally receive it much too soon nowadays, the priesthood should remain, not a dispensation leading away from monastic obligations, but a higher exigency, of the maximum urgency and completeness, of their realization. If the Church entrusts the priesthood to monks *qua* monks, it is certainly not because she thereby wants to dispense them from being monks. It is that she is asking of them to be monks with the maximum of generosity, convinced that there is no more efficacious way for them to make themselves worthy of a state known as 'acquired perfection' than to borrow and follow faithfully the path of 'perfection to be acquired'.

V

LECTIO DIVINA

Aʟʟ the practices we have examined up to the present tend in different ways to form in us a well of humility which grace must fill. It now remains for us to discover by what ways grace itself comes to those who are expecting it and who prepare themselves to receive it.

If grace, as we have repeated so frequently, is primarily a Word spoken to us by God, and afterwards the new creation that the Word is to bring about in our heart, then the unprecedented place which the rule of St Benedict gives to the divine Word can be understood. There is certainly no monastic practice on which the holy patriarch so much insisted as on *reading*. The final chapter of the rule (the 73rd), completed by the 42nd, tells us precisely in what this reading consists: it is the reading of the Holy Scriptures, commented by the Fathers, and more particularly by the lives and sayings of the first monks, such as, for instance, those cited by Cassian.

It might be said that such reading is *the* monastic practice. It should be for the monk what the *Exercises* are for the Jesuit, methodical mental prayer for the Sulpician, contemplative prayer for the Carmelite, and so on. . . . Over and over again surprise has been expressed that the rule does not speak of mental prayer: the reason is, in all early monastic literature, 'reading' comprises all we put under the heading of mental prayer and much besides.

Nothing is more remarkable than the all-pervading, absorbing place of the divine Word in the life of the early monks. It was in the liturgical reading of the Gospel that St Antony came to understand his vocation. Again it was the words of Scripture that prompted all the steps he took and inspired the whole of his spirituality. It was the same for the very first monks in Egypt: they are depicted for us as always having the Scriptures in their hands, never ceasing to meditate upon them, having them spontaneously on their lips when they come to formulate their own teaching. The Cappadocian Fathers, who were the first to introduce an element of intellectual culture into monastic life, far from truncating anything of the primacy of Scripture in so doing, gave it heightened relief. Works of Origen, St Basil and St Gregory were to compose the Philocalia, a real treasure of all that the learned thought of the great Alexandrine could bring to the understanding of the Bible. The medieval monks did not depart by one iota from the path thus traced out. The recent research of Dom Jean Leclerc has shown to what extent they remained immersed in Scripture. The prayers of John of Fécamp are merely a patchwork of the Scriptures showing so perfect an assimilation of the Bible that it is impossible to distinguish what is spontaneous from what is the work of memory. The same can be said of the Byzantine monks who were contemporaries of the Cappadocians. The research in iconography of J. D. Stefanescu has revealed to what extent the frescoes of Mount Athos are impregnated with meditations that are wholly Biblical. Again in our own times, a contemporary observer, Dom Theodore Belphaire, has shown as the most salient feature of the spirituality of Mount Athos, a constant use of Scripture; and familiarity with its most minute details is to be found among monks of the holy mountain who are sometimes without any other education.

In order to be able to understand how this 'reading' has acquired, or retained, such an importance in monastic spirituality, it must be remembered that 'reading', in the tradition to which we refer, has not all the meaning that we ordinarily give to the word. It would be wrong to believe that the difference is solely in the subject: the Word of God and what relates to it. It lies also in the one who reads. One does not read, in the sense of the *lectio divina*, as we usually read, that is, in order to have read. One reads for the act of reading. Such reading may be likened to a conversation with a friend, which is enjoyed for its own sake and not simply for what we learn from it.

First and foremost all ideas of utility, even of apostolic utility, must be removed from this reading. We are not reading to retain an idea or a formula which will be useful for future occasions. The *lectio* may be compared to intellectual culture: it is of value not for what we learn from it but through what it makes us become. It is, however, true that this disinterestedness from the reading cannot be understood if we abstract from its subject. It is, on the contrary, a keen awareness of the subject that gives it this characteristic, and it sustains this awareness in return. The important point is to understand why the *lectio* is called *divina*. It is because the Bible, as the monks of early times were well aware, is not a book like other books. Origen has here spoken the decisive word. The Bible is a world, a cosmos of unlimited riches with a living unity. It is a world of spiritual meanings, a new creation, interior to the first creation and renewing that creation's significance.

For the Bible is the Word of God, which means the Word who created the world, and who now desires to create it anew. In the world darkened by sin, deprived of its power to express the design of the love of the living God, this Word has been brought back progressively by the prophets. In Christ it receives total expression. The apostles communicate it in its unity and totality. The Bible is merely the document of this expression, in history, of the re-creating Word, which re-echoes within the confines of creation, taking it up and fashioning it once more.

We must indeed realize that the humanity of an individual man is not made up merely of his flesh and his soul. . . . His words, like his thoughts, are an integral part of it. Thus the words of Christ are an essential element of his sacred humanity. If it can be said that the Sacred Heart incarnates the Son of God more particularly as redeeming Love, it can equally well be said that the Bible is his incarnation as the Word. And here the words of the Gospels must not be separated from those of the prophets or of the apostles. In the former, the divine Word, sole-begotten Son of God, has stooped down to our level. In the latter that Word remains actual through the Church who is the body, and whose doctors are the lips of Christ. Thus to understand the Bible is to understand Christ, just as to be ignorant of the Bible, to use St Jerome's forceful expression, is to be ignorant of Christ.

To succeed in thus understanding the Bible effectively, and to develop in regard to it the reactions which such comprehension implies, it is essential to understand that it is a history, an incomparable history indeed. This history is that of the people of God, of the *qahal*, of the *ecclesia*, that is, of the assembly convened by the Word of God and gradually assuming a shape both human and divine under the breath of the living Word. Primarily the Word is addressed to the dismembered multitude scattered by sin. It then operates a purification and progressive segregation there. The line of Abraham is set apart. The people of Israel is brought away from Egypt. Among that carnal nation a 'remnant', which will be the Israel according to the Spirit, is gradually detached by the tribulations of the exile. Finally this 'remnant', on the Cross on which Christ dies, is reduced to the one and only faithful 'Servant'.

As the creative history of the people of God had led them from the manifold to the one, so now it was to move from the one to universal fulfilment. For universality will be grasped in the embrace of the 'One', that is, the only-begotten Son of God, without any fresh breaking of the holy unity of the body of Christ, gradually drawn, under the inspiration of the re-creating Word, from the chaotic multitude that made up the old race of Adam. In Christ drawing all things to himself after his 'lifting up', the scattered children of God will be gathered up and assembled into a single body, until we all meet to form one single, perfect Man, who has now reached the eternal perfection of his adult age.

Once we have seen this design as a whole, a design which is also God's plan working itself out through the mystery of the Cross, our understanding of Scripture becomes clear, and it can become the whole of our meditation. It at once follows from this, indeed, that Scripture unfolds itself on three planes. These planes are not indeed parallel, it should rather be said that they engender one another. The first is the plane of the history of Israel. The second is the plane of the history of Christ. The third is the plane of the history of the Church being built up by our own history. On these three planes the reality with which we are concerned is the same; the people of God, that is the new creation raised up within the old, to restore and perfect it. Consequently everything in the Bible relates to us. For it all tends to produce Christ and his mystery, and within the Mystery of Christ the all-powerful gravitation of divine grace irresistibly draws us.

When this has been understood, the sterile discussions between partisans of the literal and partisans of the spiritual exegesis become pointless. The letter of the Scripture, on condition that it be taken in its full comprehensive unity instead of piece-meal, is nothing more than this movement, this *élan*, this creation which from the people draws Christ and in Christ renews the multitude that we form. Thus we come to understand that the whole Bible is threaded through with great themes the final application of which refers wholly to us in Christ. It is of such themes that the meditation nourished by the *lectio divina* must take hold.

The first theme is redemption, the buying back. In an initial phase, it is the theme of the Jewish Passover, the people bought back from Egyptian slavery by the mighty hand and outstretched arm of Yahwe. Moving in more spiritual direction through the teaching of the prophets, and particularly of those who were to undergo and express the experience of the purification of Israel by innocent suffering, this

It is only possible where the Word finds a soul who listens, and anticipates creative obedience. This means that it is only possible where life
is organized on the mortifying bases of work and penance in unceasing
prayer. For us and our reception of the Word, the case should be what
it was for the humanity of Christ, in whom the Word became incarnate.
As the incarnation of the Word was a consecration of Christ for sacrifice, so the descent of the Word into our heart must bruise it. And as
Christ was not led to sacrifice by external force and in spite of himself,
but by the most spontaneous movement of his heart, so the listener to
the Word must lend his hand to the crushing of his heart of stone,
without which the heart of flesh of the new and eternal covenant will
never be re-created within him.

Let us endeavour to set out clearly all the essential points comprised
in what we have just been saying.

The *lectio divina* is in the first place work. It is in no sense an idle reading that one pursues effortlessly, as one can follow a play. It demands
an effort, an effort in which we bring all our human resources to bear in
order to understand this communication which God has made to us
expressly in our human medium. All that we should bring into play to
understand a literary creation which is human and nothing more,
must obviously be set in motion, as far as our resources allow, for the
understanding of the Word of God. It is a culture the development of
which, without being sought for its own sake, must be a spontaneous
fruit of monastic life and of the meditation which forms the centre of
it. This culture is that of the pre-scholastic, or more generally, monastic,
Middle Ages, as it was that of St Augustine following on Origen. The
culture to which we refer is disinterested, like all true culture. But its
disinterestedness is in no sense that of a decadent intellectual enjoyment
which would take itself for its own end. It is that of an understanding
of the divine Word, cultivated for its own sake, evoking and utilizing
for its own ends all the resources of human experience and reflection.
Arising from the *lectio divina*, of which it is really only the extension,
it is to this same *lectio*, to the most perfect realization of it possible, that
this culture as a whole tends. If its invariable type is conveyed by its
definition, its forms are capable of infinite variety. The movement and
effort which inspire it should, of course, suffice to put us on our guard
against any temptation to archæological reconstruction of the Augustinian or Cluniac culture. Since we are seeking to understand the Scripture as those of early times understood it, we must apply all our
resources to it, as they applied all theirs.

Consequently, it would be an absurdity to think that we should repeat what the Fathers did, when they read the Scriptures, thus artificially producing more or less poor imitations of their own interpretations. It is essential, on the contrary, that we should draw from historical and critical methods all the responsibilities that our own age provides us with, as they in their era profited by the philology which they knew and practised. Without entering into, and above all, without losing ourselves among the technicalities of modern exegetical research, it would be unpardonable on our part to neglect what it gives us, not only by its detailed results, but by its general attitude in regard to the texts and problems it sets forth, in the measure in which all this contributes to a better understanding of the Bible. St Augustine, St Jerome, still more Origen, if they had had within reach all the possibilities we have, would have profited from them to an extent far beyond that with which the majority of us content ourselves. But it is obvious that that is only a point of departure—the point of departure necessary for a contact as wide, and, if I may say so, as close as possible to the objective reality of the Scriptures. This must form the basis and support for contemplation, which always looks to the spiritual sense.

After what we have said above, it will be understood that the spiritual sense of which we are now speaking must never be a luxurious fantasy merely clinging to a realism which is flat and without depth. The authentic spiritual sense, coming from a true understanding of the Fathers themselves and not from a slavish imitation of their procedure, to say nothing of their weaknesses, is a different thing altogether. It is the rediscovery of that movement of enrichment, by going beyond the fundamental themes and transposing them, that we have recognized as being the movement both of Biblical history and of the progress of scriptural revelation. We must lay ourselves open to the great gesture of God who is coming back once more into a world which has strayed far from him, and we must allow ourselves to become interpenetrated by this thought, to the extent of becoming actors in our turn, or rather of allowing the sole actor to accomplish his own plan in us himself. We have to be initiated through the whole of the Scriptures into the unique mystery of Christ and his Cross, of the Christ in us who is the hope of glory. We have to enter into the way and above all, into the deep inspiration of the Wisdom which is not the wisdom of man but of God, the whole design of which equates with his immensity and is a venture of God's grace in pursuit of us.

It should be abundantly clear that the discovery of this mystery, the entry into this wisdom, cannot be a purely intellectual matter. The mystery is essentially sacramental. It renews in us that of which it speaks to us. There can, then, be no question of understanding it without at the same time lending ourselves as the material of its creative work. Origen distinguishes several categories among the readers of the Word. There are first of all those who listen to it with pleasure, but merely as if it were music that delights for the moment, without really making a permanent impression. Then there are those who drink it in like rich wine and whom it intoxicates with a holy fervour. But the only genuine *auditores verbi* are those who become, whom the Word itself by its own power makes, *factores verbi*. In other words they are those whom this Word, which is ever the Word of the Cross, bruises in their turn. They are those who go down to the wine-press with the divine vintager of the mystic vine and who concur in this crushing of themselves as the necessary condition of their rebirth and of that of their brethren. To them they will become bearers of the Word only if they have themselves first of all been touched and marked with its imprint of fire.

Nothing of this will come about so long as the reading has not become personal. And once more we come back to the natural and in some sort necessary harmony between the *lectio divina* and monastic life. Let us recall that the vocation of Antony, and that of innumerable other monks after him, came to him in a word from the Gospel which he heard and obeyed, as if it were a word addressed to himself, in the full force of its significance and demands. Similarly it is essential that the Word should find in us a heart ready to apply it. It is necessary that we should always read it, persuaded that for us, for each one of us at every moment of our lives, it is indissolubly woven of demands and promises. As we read, we must unceasingly say to ourselves: 'What is it asking of me? What is it offering me?' And this must not and cannot be done in the abstract. Important as it is that we should enter into the meaning of Scripture, it is just as important that it should enter into us. This demands an opening of ourselves, a conscious and living attention of the whole of our being that cannot be effected except by a pondering over and assimilation of the Word which will bring all the detail of our existence, all the depths of our being and recesses of our heart into life-giving contact with it.

There we find the inexhaustible domain of the moral applications of Scripture to which the ancients so rightly attached importance. This is the final product of the elaboration and assimilation of our reading without which the letter would miss its aim, through not having really come face to face in its full reality with the living truth that the Word sought to convey. But such applications will only be fruitful, they will only avoid falling back into hollow artificiality, if they remain guided by a twofold concern for realism, a realism of the great theological vision of the mystery, and a realism of our own living attention, opening to its revelation and light. This is the place to point out again how closely the two condition one another. For of the mystery of Christ and his Cross in the Scriptures, one can assuredly say what St Augustine said of the mystery of the Eucharist: 'It is the mystery of ourselves which is present here. Christ only lived his life in order to live it over again in us, and we have not really begun to live until we have begun to live again in Christ, to live again in his mystery.'

Thus the necessary presence of our mind and heart in the *lectio* brings us to the final point, certainly the most important, the one which might in a certain measure make up for the deficiency of all the others.

It is essential that the reading be performed in faith. What this means, in short, is, that in reading the Scriptures we must always adhere to the living and active certainty that God himself is personally present in his Word, present each time it touches the heart of man. It remains Word, Word addressed to our persons and re-creating them, because it eternally remains the personal Word of the Father. Each time we read it, we ought to be convinced that God is there uttering it to us, with all his love, all his power, all his gifts and all his demands upon us. Thus the reading must finally be resolved into a perpetual and increasingly direct meeting between him and us. And when it has reached that point, and it is at that and nothing else that it aims, we shall have passed from reading to the purest and highest content of mysticism.

The conclusion, if it is necessary to formulate one after what we have just said, will link up with what we said at the beginning. The reading will only bring about such an interior development in us if it really makes us enter into the Bible as into a world. The monk is the one who has left this world to rejoin the world to come. The divine Word alone can bring that world to him. But it will only bring it to him if he allows himself to be wholly absorbed by it. And that obviously demands that in the monastic life the *lectio divina* is not just one exercise among others, the occupation assigned to certain particular hours. It is essential that this reading should become an assiduous reading, assiduous to the extent and in such a way that the monk literally immerses him-self and lives in it, without departing from it again. The thoughts of God must be substituted for his own thoughts, the feelings of God for his feelings, and he must come to acquire this 'mentality of Christ' of which St Paul speaks. The faith in the Word will so to speak close the windows which open upon the present world and from that time onwards the monk will live in the eternal future.

VI

THE 'OPUS DEI'

S T Benedict tells us in Chapter 43 of the Rule: *Nihil operi Dei praeponatur*, 'Nothing must be put before the work of God'. Obviously the divine office must be at the centre of the monk's life. But how are we to understand this? We have already spoken of the medieval charters which declare that monks are *propter chorum fundati*. If we interpret this as meaning that their proper function is to provide for the celebration of the office, we are, as we have said, mistaken. For monks have no other end than to seek God, by the ways of this life of contemplation and penance we are attempting to describe.

What *is* true, of course, is that the divine office is both the pre-eminent means to, and an anticipated realization of, that end.

It is the means because it engages the monk in prayer. The office is actually the monk's *schola orationis*. It is the anticipated realization of this end, because the ecclesiastical, and more especially the monastic, choir figures the collective and perfect praise of which heaven alone will bring the full realization.

The interaction between these two aspects is moreover obvious. It is because the choir initiates us into the life of heaven that it prepares us for it, and it is because it prepares us for it effectively that it already resembles it.

But what constitutes the essence of the divine office? Still to-day in the West, as everywhere in the beginning, its essence is the psalmody, that is the recitation, or rather the singing, of the psalms. The importance given to this practice by the early Christians cannot be over-emphasized. Although it is more or less common to all the Christians of early times, its systematic and increasingly perfect performance stood out from the beginning as one of the essential features of monasticism. The education of Eustochium by Paula in preparation for the monastic life is dominated by an initiation into psalmody. Cassian, from his visitation of the monasteries of Egypt, formed the idea that the training of monks in prayer and their training in the knowledge and recitation of the psalms were one and the same thing. He has an admirable expression to describe their material knowledge of the psalter and their adherence to its words: he maintains that, when they recite it, they appear to be not so much reciting as improvising. The connection between the psalmody thus understood and practised and the *lectio divina* as we have explained it, is obvious. In the long lessons of Matins, the office takes up the *lectio divina* again. It is extended or recalled in the little chapters of the other hours. In the psalmody man responds to the Word of God received in the *lectio*. Only, what constitutes the unique value of this response is that it is elicited by the divine Word himself. Or rather: it is itself divine speech. For if it is true that God alone can speak properly of God, one could equally well say that God alone can speak to God. It is the Holy Spirit alone, St Paul tells us, who can teach us to speak to God as we ought. But in what words would the Spirit have us express ourselves, if not in those he has himself dictated for this purpose?

It can thus be said that if the monk's fundamental exercise is to listen to the Word of God in the *lectio divina*, his final exercise will be to learn to make response to God in the psalmody. *Lectio* and psalmody are, as it were, his breathing in and out, the diastole and systole of the heart created in him anew by the Spirit.

Thus we can understand in what sense it can be said, with Cassian and all the monks of early times, that the monk's education in the life of mental prayer will go hand in hand with his assimilation of the psalms; the monk must devote all his efforts to penetrating the letter of them, in order to acquire the spirit. The study of the psalter, the initiation into a psalmody which comes from the heart, is one of the monk's great tasks.

It is indeed a task. For the psalter cannot be understood, much less practised, without an effort. But one cannot refuse to make this effort without thereby refusing to be a monk, except to outward appearances. In this respect no prayer, no devotion which we might judge less difficult could dispense us from the labour necessary if the psalmody is to become *our* devotion, as is essential. Nothing can replace it. Nothing can deprive it of its place.

It is essential, in the first place, that the monk should know the psalms, and above all know them in the letter. We cannot rush headlong into psalmody, and if people so frequently complain of not being able to enter into it at all, it is simply and solely because they do not seem seriously to consider any other way of approaching it. The monks of early times, whose memory had not been impaired like ours by the abundance of books and the facility of writing, usually knew the psalms by heart. Many monasteries have at least retained the practice of singing the Little Hours and Compline without a book. In so doing they are doubtless carrying out the intention of the holy legislator of the monks of the West, since he wished Compline to be said without lights and expressly arranged the Little Hours in such a manner that they could be said outside choir, which at that time practically meant saying them from memory.

If not only knowledge but material familiarity with the psalms is desirable, despite the danger of routine, the reason is that we shall only *pray* them if we bring to them an interest which is wholly free from curiosity. For those who say them, indeed, they will only be prayers when, like the monks of Cassian, they become aware that they can find in them the response to their own needs. This presupposes an habitual attention to the deep understanding of the sentiments they express, a thing which precludes the fascination of discovery and the unknown. What we have just explained indicates sufficiently clearly that the material knowledge of the psalter would serve no purpose if it did not provide the basis for a deep and appreciative understanding of its meaning. All we have said about the reading of Scripture in general applies here too with quite a special urgency.

It is essential primarily that the monk as far as possible should arrive at a perfect historical knowledge of the meaning of the words which he repeats as his own. The structure which rests upon misunderstandings and misinterpretations is always a precarious one, the value of which remains very doubtful. But here, more than anywhere, since he has to make all that is said his own, material understanding, far from excluding spiritual understanding, should contribute to foster it. We have sufficiently explained how this could come about, to make it unnecessary to revert to the matter. The important thing is, beginning with a historical understanding which is sufficiently deep and synthetic, to see all that we read in the perspective of Christ and the Church, considered as the fulfilment of the Old Testament. To help us to do this, certain patristic commentaries are indispensable. In the first rank must be instanced the *Enarrationes in Psalmos* of St Augustine. What we have quoted from them in connection with the psalm *Quemadmodum* is sufficient proof and explanation of what we affirm. He who reads and meditates on these commentaries and other patristic writings of the same kind will learn to recite the psalms as his own prayers, through learning to recite them in the body of Christ as the very prayer of

Christ. In a more precise way, using even the resources of contemporary exegesis, what will help us most effectively to make the prayer of the psalms our own, is an inventory of and meditation on the great themes of their prayer. As in the meditation of all other scriptural themes, it is always essential, in connection with each one of them, that Israel should lead us to Christ, and that from Christ, through our incorporation into him, should come the application to ourselves.

It is essential to begin by recognizing and entering deeply into the meaning of two great dynamic themes which inspire the whole of the psalms and which make their prayer action.

The first of these themes is that of struggle. In mentioning this we at once touch upon the major obstacle which so often prevents our contemporaries from giving a true assent to the prayer of the psalms. They seem to them, with the exception of a few verses, prayers which are definitely out of date for Christians. The curses, the cries of hatred, or even the warlike atmosphere which we breathe in them are surely in irreconcilable antagonism to the Gospel revelation of charity.

If, however, the Church, as she does in her unanimous tradition, presents the psalter to us as a Christian prayer, as the prayer of Christ in his mystical body, we must grant that this supposition must contain one or several misunderstandings.

The first is to believe that the *Agape*, that the life of charity revealed in the Gospel, removes the conflict from the world in which we have to live. To believe this is one of the almost unsurmountable tendencies of the modern mind; but the Cross, the reality of the Cross with all its bloodshed, is a permanent challenge to such a tendency.

The Cross of Christ also releases the kernel of truth contained in the error we are considering. It does this by showing more eloquently than any explanation how much the painful sense of conflict, inherent in any human religion which is at all deep, is both confirmed and transformed by the Gospel. What must be hated, what must be cursed, what it is essential to struggle against without any possible compromise, is not 'flesh and blood', to quote St Paul. That is, the long battle-cry which the psalms constitute should not now be uttered by man against man. On this point the protest of modern Christians made unhappy by the psalter is justified. Here the New Testament invites us to a definite superseding of the Old. But here as elsewhere, the superseding must be a transposition and not a pure and simple abandonment. If it is no longer a struggle of man against man that must be waged, this does not mean that there is no longer any struggle. It means that the struggle must be waged against a mysterious enemy who is both transcendent to mankind in general—which forbids us to identify him with any of our brethren—and interior to each one of us—which obliges us to apply to ourselves the most terrible words in the psalter.

Once this necessary transposition has been effected, it seems truer for the new Israel that it was for Israel in the flesh, that our life on earth from beginning to end is one mighty conflict. Thus the psalms, precisely because they are the most perfect poetical expression of a battle-cry, must remain the chant of the Church militant. And in a special manner they must be the chant of monks, for it is true, as we have sufficiently emphasized, that the fully conscious and deliberate struggle against the devil is the deepest characteristic of monastic life.

The second dynamic theme which runs through and underlines the whole psalter is what we may call the desire for a theophany, for the manifestation of God.

Obviously, this theme is closely linked with the first, from the very beginning. In the thick of the battle, Israel calls upon Yahwe as his almighty help. He alone, by appearing in the midst of the conflict, can put the adversary to flight.

The innumerable allusions in the psalter to the exodus, to the intervening of the column of fire and smoke to protect Israel from the pursuit of the Egyptians and to crush Pharaoh's army, are references to the same idea. It may be said that it was from this event that this notion took shape for the thought of Israel.

But, reciprocally, the final significance of this conflict which the New Testament, far from suppressing, reveals to us as impregnated with a vastness and depth at first unsuspected, is eventually to overthrow the obstacles which separate us from God, which prevent us from seeing him. There is a power, in us and above us, which hinders us from finding God, as he himself calls us to seek him. The Cross of Christ signifies that the Word himself who called us, must have been rent by this obstacle. Our struggle and the divine theophany are only the two complementary aspects of the cosmic mystery which finds its unity in Christ. To see God, 'to contemplate the King in his beauty', 'Oh that thou wouldst rend the heavens and come down'—that is the desire, that is the cry that the divine Word who has come down to us wishes to draw from us. There is not a psalm which is not penetrated either directly or indirectly with this cry, with this desire. If the monk's whole existence hangs on the Quest for God, and if, as we were saying in the early pages of this book, it is God who finds us rather than we who find him in this quest, it is obvious that on this ground also the psalms are the peculiar, special monastic prayer.

The two great dynamic themes which we have emphasized pursue their counterpoint around three static themes closely connected among themselves: we may term them, the theme of Christ, the theme of the people, the theme of the new creation.

The psalms are occupied by a series of personalities whose features can be found again and composed anew in the figure of Christ. Just as four different evangelists were necessary to throw into relief for us the unique figure who surpasses all human categories, so this providential convergence of the figures of Jewish hopes was necessary to prepare the revelation of the personal mystery 'in whom are buried all the treasures of wisdom and knowledge'. It is by going over these different facets of the same hope, one after another, that we can best meditate upon its transcendent fulfilment.

The Messias, the King anointed by God, like another David, to found upon earth the kingdom which will be one with the divine kingdom—as this was the initial formula of the hope of Israel, so it is the final formula of the Christian faith. Psalms like the 2nd or 109th (Hebrew 110th) present the Messias to us under his first aspect of conqueror. He is, primarily, the one who wages, and who wages to their conclusion, the wars of Yahwe, that is, for us, the cosmic and hypercosmic conflict which fills history and the conclusion of which history will come to fruition in the blessed eternity where God will finally be all in all. Thereby, he is also the Judge as the 71st (Hebrew 72nd) psalm describes him: the one to whom Yahwe has handed over his Day, the one who will finally sort the good grain from the cockle, putting an end to the conflict of the intermingled forces of good and evil by the final elimination of the forces of evil.

But already in the 109th psalm appears, conferring a supraterrestrial nature upon this royalty, the priestly character, a mysterious priesthood, like that of Melchisedech directly emanating from God. It is in such perspectives that the sacrificial psalms, closely linked with the idea of the victory of the chosen King of God, must be interpreted. Moreover, the ultimate meaning of sacrifice—the offering of oneself, willingly given without reserve, to God who speaks to and calls us—is shown in psalms such as the 49th or 50th (Hebrew 50th and 51st). The formula of sacrifice which the 39th psalm (Hebrew 40th) gives, could be taken over literally by the Epistle to the Hebrews: 'It is written of me in thy book that I shall do thy will: My God I agree to it and thy law is within my heart.' It should be noted that this is precisely the definition given by Jeremias of what the new alliance would be, the alliance which Ezechiel was to qualify as eternal.

Of such a sacrifice the Elect of God necessarily appears as victim as well as priest. For we have learned, from Christ dying in person, to apply to the Messias the psalms inspired by Isaias' theme of the Faithful Servant. The 21st psalm (Hebrew 22nd), that cry of anguish and of faith that is unconquerable in spite of all, uttered by Christ on the Cross, like the 68th (Hebrew 69th) that St Paul uses each time he speaks of the Cross of Christ, should become the privileged expression of our identification of Christ in the martyrdom of asceticism.

Just as the psalms properly termed Messianic throw their light over the whole of the royal psalms by showing to what depths the theme of the Son of David could be developed, so these psalms of the Suffering Servant throw light on all the psalms which treat of the just man suffering or persecuted, as they do also on all the penitential psalms. Never did cry of sorrow of more intense and tragic purity rise towards God than the lament of psalm 87 (Hebrew 88); it is the paradoxical prayer of the man who cries out to God that he feels himself abandoned by God himself. And what richer and more infinitely varied expression of the sense of sin could be found in the psalms than in those known as the penitential psalms (6, 31, 37, 50, 101, 129, 142 in the Vulgate; 6, 32, 38, 51, 102, 130, 143 in the Hebrew)? But human sorrow and repentance, so fully expressed in the words of the Jewish psalms, only discover light in the darkest depths of the abyss when they are taken up again in Christian prayer. Then, indeed, it is the Sole Just One suffering for all the people—he who knew no sin but was made sin and malediction to buy back those who are under the curse—who voices them in us. On those lips, lips which of ourselves we should never have supposed could utter them, these appeals of distress become words of all-powerful consolation.

With these last psalms, the mysterious solidarity which unites the King to his people invites us to move from the theme of the King to the theme of the people.

Whether we consider the great historical psalms, which promise ultimate deliverance by reminding us of the first interventions in creation by which God took in hand the history of man, or again the gradual psalms which nourished the sacred patriotism of Israel by raising it, even then, from the city built by men to the one which God will build—in either case the Church has in the psalter hymns in which her whole destiny is enshrined. The assembly of those who are sought and brought back from the four winds by the Word, the citadel where God himself is the safeguard of his own people, the sanctuary where he dwells with them for ever, and also the tabernacle where he makes pilgrimage with them from earth to heaven, none of the earthly aspects or heavenly perspectives is absent from the psalter.

Around the Church, around the people, the whole universe, created for the people, created anew in the final and definitive establishment of the people of God, eventually finds in the psalter—as it were, a third and last theme enveloping the other two—the theme of its evocation which is conformable to the views of faith upon the cosmos and its future. An instrument of praise, its strings muted by sin, but which the Day of Yahwe will cause to sound again, such is the universe revealed in the three great Lauds psalms, the 148th, 149th and 150th. The man who recites them, be he monk or simple Christian, in so doing becomes the cosmic priest, in the Word incarnate. These psalms inaugurate the eternal liturgy of the whole life of the universe, a life drained by human life, which in its turn is regenerated by the life of the Word made flesh; and it is this liturgy which will make of the cosmos once more the choir singing with the very voices of angels, such as it was on the morning of creation.

If we now try to gather together the thoughts which the psalter, organized around this twofold series of themes, elicits from the heart which recites them in the Spirit who dictated them, what do we find?

The deepest thought of all is certainly an insatiable longing for God. Whether we think of the references to the city-sanctuary suggested by the gradual psalms, the *Quemadmodum* with its recollections of thirst for God, the great vision of peace of the *Quam dilecta*, or the anguish of the *Super flumina Babylonis*, where could the soul in quest of God find a like yearning for his presence amid the exile of this world and this life?

But if this yearning is to be ours, it must be the yearning of the Prodigal Son. It must be the cry of contrite humility. And it is here, if anywhere, that the psalms seem irreplaceable and without parallel. More than all else they are the prayer of the poor, the prayer of the poor whom St Augustine describes as 'a multitude of families, a multitude of peoples, a multitude of Churches, and also one single Church, one single people, one single family, one single sheep'. The filial trust which Christian faith places at the root of this humble contrition can find no better expression than that which the author and finisher of the faith has chosen, to arouse this confidence in men's hearts. I refer to the image of the divine Shepherd of Psalm 22 (Hebrew 23): 'The Lord is my shepherd, how can I lack anything? He gives me a resting place where there is pasture, and leads me out by cool waters to make me live anew. . . .'

Finally, how can we better express and create in ourselves the eschatological expectation, the expectation of faith clinging to the hope of the Day of Yahwe, of the day when Christ will appear in glory and when his people will appear with him, better than by the words of the psalm of the Reign of Yahwe? Such an expectation already dissolves in praise, in that universal praise in which all things will join, according to the expression of Julian of Norwich, when all shall be well, because God shall be all in all. The final cry of the psalms *Cantate Domino* and *Dominus regnavit*, the psalms of the enthronement of Yahwe in his kingdom, is indeed the best refutation of the idea that the psalms could ever be surpassed in the present life; are they not already leading us to the morning of the day whose light never declines?

*   *   *

But the *opus Dei* does not merely place the psalms upon our lips haphazard. In accordance with primitive monastic tradition, it makes their recitation correspond with the different hours of the day. After what has just been said of the psalms taken in themselves, how easy it is to recapture their meaning, fresh each day, as it is conveyed by the hour at which we say them and the choice this hour has guided.

For the night vigils, the great historical psalms by their reminder of past prophecies fill the vigil with the faith which awaits the final morning. The expectation of the ultimate future is thus nourished on the fulfilment without repentance of the events in which God has already intervened and has, as it were, irrevocably pledged himself.

At dawn and at sunset, corresponding to the double sacrifice of perfumes, as a symbol of which we still offer incense at the *Benedictus* and *Magnificat*, the psalms of praise open and close the day in that which is the origin of creation as it will be its term, the glory of God alone, overflowing into the joy of creatures. At the Little Hours of Sunday and Monday, the great 118th (Hebrew 119th) psalm will fix our attention on a consideration of the law, that is, of the divine Word, meditated upon under all its manifold aspects. Or again, at the weekday Hours, the Gradual psalms, with their unceasing call to trusting faith, will ever make us rely upon God and upon him alone throughout the whole course of the day, at the beginning as at the end of all our actions and thoughts.

Finally in the evening the *In manus tuas* of the 4th, 90th (Hebrew 91st) and 133rd (Hebrew 134th) psalms will bring us back to the holy and venerable hands from which we came forth, to whose embrace the voice which cast us into being recalls and draws us.

*   *   *

How is the monk to assimilate the inexhaustible treasures of the prayer of the psalms? The first condition of so doing is of course to discover their incomparable beauty. If the Bible is a world, and if this world is only the everyday world brought into the perspective of the divine plan, the psalms fit into it as a microcosm which condenses all its beauty in the translucid crystal of their praise. The splendour of the psalms will guide the monk spontaneously and better than any laborious industry along the journey he must make from those beauties which are only a reflection to the beauties which are source, to the Beauty beyond compare of the one and only Source. Their literary beauty is inseparable from their spiritual beauty. The one is fused in the other like the scintillations of the dawn in the white radiance of the day.

Their light and their song must illumine and rejoice his whole life, as they filled the life of the early Christians, after filling the soul of the Messias. And for this to be so, he must begin by pouring his own life into them. He should elicit and express his most personal feelings when he takes the words of the psalms upon his lips. At the same time that it offers him medieval authors such as those brought to light again by Dom Jean Leclerq, the Christian renaissance can offer him infinitely attractive and convincing examples of this penetration of a soul by the thoughts of the Holy Spirit. We have only to mention, as a reminder, the admirable exercises which close the *Sancta Sophia* of the great English Benedictine, Dom Augustine Baker, or the delightful *Preces privatæ* of the Anglican Bishop Andrewes which Newman translated with so much love and fervour.

In return, with its rhythm in the divine office which is as wide as the world and the history which fills it, the prayer of the psalmody will take possession of him and teach him by inner experience those thoughts of God which have *not* entered into the heart of man. It will lead him, *fortiter suaviterque*, along those paths which he alone has traced out until his heart meets the pierced Heart of the God made man. It will lead him right on to this Heart, the centre and sun of all hearts, where the Spirit whispers to us unceasingly: *Veni ad Patrem*, and continually answers in ourselves: *Ecce venio!*

VII

THE MASS

THE whole of religion and at the same time the whole history of humanity is summed up in the Parable of the prodigal son. For the drama of the prodigal son who becomes aware that he has gone astray and is brought to ruin by his own fault, is the history of the religious awareness of man forestalled, as it were, by the divine Spirit in his prevenient grace. The more this awareness deepens, the more the desire of returning to the Father wells up in it. . . . A yearning and a painful desire: with what obstacles will not the return journey be strewn! And at the end, what sort of a welcome awaits the prodigal? Even if an irresistible confidence draws him to the Father whom he feels he has offended, as to one who none the less remains his only refuge, what will be their meeting now? And even if the Father is ready to forget all, how can he, unhappy, guilty child—unhappy only because he is guilty—ever after his fault feel at home in his Father's house? Yet it is better far for him to return to this roof, even were it to return there as a fugitive slave, than to remain in the eternal, universal exile which every other place represents from now onwards. We see him then heavy-hearted and yet trembling with hope, trudging once more along the steep and rocky path, which had seemed so easy to him as he descended it. . . . But he has hardly taken more than a few steps when he finds the Father running along the road, his arms flung wide open, having set out to meet him, and having set out when his prodigal son was still out of sight of all the others, and was not even thought to be making his way back towards the home he had formerly left. And the son can scarcely lisp the first words of the expression of sorrow and submission he had prepared:—'I have sinned against heaven and before thee, I am no more worthy to be called thy son . . .' Before he has been able to suggest being reduced to the rank of a mere servant, the Father has given his orders, which amount to treating the unworthy prodigal as if he were the Only, the Well-beloved Son. Let him be clad in costly apparel, let a ring be placed on his finger, let the fat cattle be killed for him, and let the house be filled with

lights and music. . . . Yes, for there is more joy before the angels
—and before God himself—for one sinner doing penance than for
ninety-nine just who need not penance.

The reconciliation is thus effected. But it is the one who has been
sinned against who bears all the cost of it. It is the Father who sur-
mounts the accumulated obstacles of which the son was afraid. It is
the Father who will pay the ineluctable reparation which, to the son,
appeared as impossible as he knew it to be essential. He despaired of
ever finding the place he had abandoned of his own initiative, again.
But the Father's limitless generosity was reserving an even better place
for him.

To repeat, the whole of the Gospel and of the religious life of saved
humanity is in this return to God. Suffering is not absent from it. It
could not be absent. But, however deep, however sharp the suffering
may be, it is transfigured by an unheard-of, an unhoped-for fact, which
transforms the whole situation. The fact is that God himself has come
to man, that man might be able to return to him. And what the parable
cannot express directly, for the mystery is too great, is this: that it is
likewise God who has first taken upon himself the suffering which
is to be gone through. In his sole-begotten, his faithful Son, he has
assumed it all for those who have been unfaithful, when they themselves were not thinking at all, or even troubling in any real sense,
about returning. Behind the cross of Christ, behind the cross on which
the arms of the only-begotten Son, of the only faithful Servant, are
stretched out and nailed, there are the very arms of the Father stretched
out to clasp to his heart his innumerable faithless children, enclosing
them in the open heart of his well-beloved Son which has been rent
by their faults. Such is the mystery of the Cross, the mystery of the
Father's love. For, St Paul tells us, it is in this that the Father has shown
the incomparable character of his love for us, that he delivered him
up to death for us when we were still wicked. . . .

The Redemption, the effecting of the world's salvation, is that the
Cross thus understood comes to pervade the world, to fill the history
of each individual man and that of all mankind. The Mass is there offering us the possibility of this extension of the Cross. The Mass is the
return to the Father in Christ, who has come to us on behalf of the
Father—who has come to us and returns to him, this time bearing us
in himself through the death of obedience.

As we have said from the beginning, the monk is one who lives
only for this return to the Father. That is why the monk's life is a

crucifixion; for, between God and sinful man, there is no other way than the one God himself has opened: the way of the Cross. But this crucifixion of the monk would be vain, would be merely sterile suicide, if it were not accomplished through a participation in Christ's own Cross. Such a participation can be accomplished through the Mass, and that is why the monk's *Suscipe* will only receive its significance when it is so to speak enfolded in the offertory of the Mass, as his charter of profession is in the altar cloth.

Thus the Mass must daily bring before us primarily the mystery of the divine Word who is seeking and calling us: therein lies the whole meaning of the Mass of the catechumens; then the mystery of the same divine Word who elicits from us the only response truly effective, that is, who crushes us to create us anew: therein lies the whole meaning of the eucharistic immolation at the centre of the Mass of the faithful. And both are there given to us in Christ: the appeal which touches us, the response which moves us and carries us over all obstacles to the very heart of the Father. For the Mass, finally, under all its aspects, is only the perpetual fulfilment of the apostle's words: 'Christ in you, the hope of glory'.

In every Word of God that the Church makes us listen to, but very specially in this reading, of exceptional solemnity, of the first phase of every Mass, we must ever hear the divine Voice calling us, as Antony, the father of monks, heard it in like circumstances, at the Gospel of the Mass. Each reading of the Gospel, each announcement of the Gospel in the eucharistic celebration, should cause to re-echo in us the voice which the martyr Ignatius of Antioch heard within himself saying 'Come to the Father'.

After this, each eucharistic consecration to which we unite ourselves, or which is effected through our own ministry, if the priesthood has crowned our monastic consecration, should appear to us as the culminating point of the word, of the Fiat, breathed by the divine Word into humanity itself, our humanity, in Christ. In this human word of total abandonment which only the divine Word of total giving has been able to engender, the new creation takes place. It takes place in the rending of the cross. It is, however, not only the new, but the eternal creation. For it is the reconciliation wrought, creation gathered up together and reunited to its Creator, the new and eternal covenant. What then is this indestructible alliance which is coincident with an immortal creation born in the death of the God made man? It is, the last prophets told us, the creation of a new heart in humanity:

the heart of flesh inserted in the place of the heart of stone of the old humanity of Adam, the pierced heart of Christ, of Christ opening his heart to all mankind that they may enter and establish themselves there for ever, as in the ark of the eternal covenant.

Despite its initial, fundamental aspect of immolation, the Mass understood in this way, as the realization at last of the return to God of prodigal humanity, which had strayed far from him, overflows and abounds with joy. It is in the Mass, that is, by participating in it and, by a lively faith, making it penetrate our whole life, that we understand how the liturgy can say that 'by the wood of the cross, joy has come to the world'. Seen in all its perspectives, which are indistinguishable from the perspectives of Christian hope, of that hope which has been the motive power of the monk's whole quest, we understand how the Mass is fundamentally eucharistic. It is in fact the 'giving of thanks' in the fullness of its meaning, that is a return ultimately exultant, and jubilant, a return to God *in hymnis et canticis* of all that had proceeded from him but had become lost far from him, *in terra longinqua*, as the Gospel says, *in regione dissimilitudinis*, according to the Fathers. In the chant of the Preface, its radiant centre, the Mass breaks out as the great praise in which man acts as universal priest, in the Word himself, the eternal high-priest of creation, in order finally to dedicate the whole world to God with himself. The joy which breaks out in this return is the joy which only Christ has been able to bring to the world, as he alone brought peace—the joy which is founded upon reconciliation with God. It is the joy of the created heart finally discovering anew the beauty of this world, of which he is appointed priest when he restores to it its splendour, leading it back to its source, in the flowing back of the *Agape*, of divine love finally returning to its home.

How greatly it is to be desired that Christianity should once more come to discover this primary meaning of the Mass: its theocentric meaning, and the reorientation of the whole of mankind, of the whole universe, towards its one true centre: this universal return, wrought in Christ crucified and ascended up to heaven; this resumption of all things in the immense flood of divine love, flowing back finally in filial love towards its source, the Father. There, once more, is to be found the only true joy, the only joy in which all things can find themselves again reunited and made immortal in an eternal spring, in that incomparable gladness which is found in giving rather than in receiving—the joy which is the great secret of God, the great mystery of Christ and of his Cross, of which the eucharistic song is the proclamation.

But the monk has been prepared for the recovery of this meaning as no one else has. For it is equally the meaning of his whole life, if it is true that his life is wholly inscribed within this unique pattern of return to the Father, of liberation from all that would hinder it or turn it aside. The monk, then, should feel himself drawn towards the eucharist as to his natural milieu. It actualizes for him the reality of faith on which his profession rests and the life that profession involves. Attuned to the eucharistic joy, he can and should give out to it a resonance which no discord mars: his whole soul should literally be fused in the eucharistic chant. And as the eucharist gives its supernatural substance to the act of donation in which his life is summed up, his life should in turn be a proclamation of the eucharist (the overflowing return in joy to the Father's home) down to its smallest details.

At the same time, and by the fact that it leads him back in Christ, through the Cross, to the Father, the Mass reintegrates man in the choir of the angels. When mankind is given the privilege of celebrating the eucharist, it is by that very fact reintegrated into that heavenly choir which the Apocalypse reveals to us in the invisible world. Let us remember that the immense flock of spiritual worlds gathered round the eternal Shepherd had never, during this evil interlude of the fall of the Prince of this world, of the fall of men with the world, ceased to chant the *Sanctus* of adoration around him. But the loss of even a single sheep among the hundred, left a gap which the ninety-nine others could not forget any more than the Shepherd himself. Once mankind celebrates the eucharist, once the Cross has thus produced its effect, the loss is made good. The joy of the angels overflows. The *gloria* of the angels of the Incarnation, glorifying, after the glory of God outside time, the new glory he has acquired by the reconciliation of the fallen world, is added to the hymn of the seraphim. And now our own voices mingle with those of the invisible powers, to declare in their turn: 'Holy, Holy, Holy, Lord God of hosts. Heaven and earth are full of thy glory.' To this is joined the hymn of victory 'Hosanna in the highest', and acclamation to him who has wrought the reconciliation, who is still the Same who comes down to us, and who also leads us to the Father: 'Blessed be he who cometh in the name of the Lord.'

Thus here and now in the eucharistic celebration, the monk will discover the fulfilment of his angelic vocation, of his vocation as man to be an angel of substitution. Here on earth, initiated into the canticle of the seraphim, he will be with them; snatched away from the shadows of this darkening world, his faith (the mighty faith which St Athanasius declared to be the monk's essential characteristic) will carry him back to the rediscovered morning of primitive creation when the sons of God sang in chorus. Here on earth, equally, the essentially choral, collective, ecclesiastical celebration of the Eucharist, will be accomplished for him in fullness in the monastery, which is his family and country, becoming in choir, around the altar, the Church of divine praise, the panegyris, the festal assembly, in which the Epistle to the Hebrews sees the figure of the eternal Church. Thus in the third place, the eucharist will appear to him as the realization already effected of the gathering up into a single body of the scattered children of God. In this assembly, in this eucharistic choir in which monastic life finds its highest religious expression through the glorification of the Lamb who is slain, the monk for his part will find the hundredfold promised even here below to those who have abandoned all human society for Christ. Seen through faith, attaining as it were its purpose in eucharistic communion, the society of praise into which the celebration will integrate him will be for him the continually renewed first-fruits of that fraternal communion in which all created affections are rediscovered and finally supernaturalized in the heart of the beatific vision.

The experience of the eucharistic community will become for him as it were the earthly initiation into the communion of saints. He now sees the monastery in the radiance of that showing forth of Christ which reunites in a common glory the company of the solitaries themselves, and thus he no longer has any difficulty in finding in his fraternity, sublimated to the plane of grace, the promise and dim outline even here and now of the universal reunion which will be consummated, once the separation of the sacrifice itself has been consummated, in eternity now regained.

Finally the Mass, food of immortality, will bring to his faith the only nourishment which can sustain it, the viaticum of which it is in perpetual need for this monastic life, essentially a pilgrim's way, 'seeking the city to come, that whose foundations are eternal, the heavenly Jerusalem, our Mother'. He will find in the heavenly manna, in the living and life-giving Bread come down from heaven, which is identical with the flesh of the Son of Man, both the full satisfaction of his expectation here on earth, and the renewal, the progressive deepening of the desire for eternal riches, which should continually move him and bear him with an ever swifter impulse towards the world to come.

Receiving under a veil pierced by the eyes of faith the very One whom he expects as reward in the fatherland, why should he not find in him the strength to be patient in this exile far from Jerusalem, which the present life constitutes for him? Indeed, will not the very veil which still hides and conceals from him the One whom it gives to him, arouse more than anything else this aspiration, this quest which must go on in him with increasing vehemence, which must cause him to transform the desert of his exile, into the path, painful to walk upon but blessed, of an exodus towards the Father? This last aspect, the eschatological aspect of the eucharist, is the one to which the monk should finally always return, not of course as to a static point of view, but precisely as to the perspective which ever eludes his grasp, which draws him on without respite towards infinity and does not allow him to rest on any earthly line of horizon. In this relentless march which his progress must consist of, the bread which satisfies, which restores and remakes—the eucharist, will principally be for him the bread which of itself creates hunger: nourishment which feeds *before all, desire.* In the presence of the eucharistic bread he should dwell continually on the last verse of the *Adoro te devote*:

> Jesu quem velatum nunc aspicio,
> Oro fiat illud quod tam sitio:
> Ut te revelata cernens facie
> Visu sim beatus tuæ gloriæ.

That is what he is aiming at, that is what gives its final meaning to his life. What is there to hinder him from tending with all his being towards the eternity where He, for whom his whole life has been a quest, is awaiting him, when all that now separates him from his goal is the impalpable thickness left by the divine wheat between sight and faith? Between the darkness of the faith in which he works, toils, suffers, sacrifices himself and dies, and the unfading brightness of the glory in which he will repose, rejoice, exult, triumph, live in him who is himself not only the source of light and life, but Life and Light themselves?

The monk's eucharist, then, should, like that of the first Christians in the Didache, always end in the cry of the seer in the Apocalypse: 'Come, Lord Jesus! Come quickly! Let this world pass and thy glory come!'

Then He whom he has already received in it, will answer in the deepest depths of his being: 'Behold I come quickly and my reward is with me. To him whom I shall find faithful, I will give a crown of glory and a seat near to my Father's throne. . . .' And the monk in his turn will respond, linking his eucharist with his daily life which is beginning anew, borrowing his words from the very Person with whom he identifies himself in his praise: '*Ecce venio* . . . Behold I come to do thy will. Teach me, O Lord, to do thy will, for thou art my God. Be it done unto me according to thy Word.'

CONCLUSION

WISDOM AND GNOSIS

Now that we have reached the end of this study, we cannot refrain from asking one question. Among the manifold ways open to human existence, what place falls to the way of monastic life? In relation to the effort of mankind which has continued over several thousand years to emerge from the chaos into which original sin cast it, where must Christian monasticism be situated?

In our Western world in which monasticism when it appeared did so within Christianity itself, the human effort to escape from primitive barbarism is concentrated in what is called philosophy.

Philosophy, according to Socrates, is the search for wisdom. Now we find the Fathers, after giving the title of *true* philosophy to Christianity in general, applying the term more especially to monastic life. They called it 'our philosophy', or again, the 'philosophical life'. It was a way of telling their contemporaries that only Christianity, and especially the white-hot Christianity of monastic life, could lead to the wisdom which was the object of their desires.

But what does the idea of 'Wisdom', in the search for which the whole of philosophy consisted, precisely represent? Where did the idea itself come from?

'Wisdom' seems to have arisen at the same time as the great organized nations, centralized by the royal power. It is found more or less simultaneously in Assyria and in Egypt, towards the close of the second millennium before Christ, under the protection of the throne. In Assyria it was the book of Ahikar, in Egypt the sayings of Amen-em-ope, the formulas of which even at that date offered so many striking analogies with those later to be found among the Sages of Israel. At this stage Wisdom is seen as an empirical art of governing men and hesitates to develop in the direction of a psychology of human activity in general, or in that of a simple prescription for success in life.

Its creators are the representatives of a new class. They seem to have arisen as the first consequence of the constitution of great empires, now substituted for tribal government in which the chief commanded with hardly any intermediaries. They are those who will be called 'the king's men'. As scribes entrusted with the arrangement and solution of affairs of an extent and complexity hitherto unknown, they probably invented writing for this purpose. Their importance for the effective exercise of authority would, by force of circumstances, very quickly bring them to be, if not its official holders, at least its depositories in fact. Placed between the inaccessible sovereign and the people in their crowds, rather between the hammer and the anvil, as it were, they had to confront problems unknown before their time. In order to equip themselves for this task, they invented besides writing, almost without realizing it, arithmetic, geography, history, and the elements of political economy. But more perhaps than by these rudimentary technical achievements, their success was conditioned by their experience of men, and their capacity for learning the art of managing them wisely. Early forming a caste, with the natural tendency of all castes to hand on their office to their successors, they very quickly concerned themselves with gathering together this accumulation of observations, prescriptions, reflections, in order to hand it on. Such was the first 'wisdom'. It has been compared, not without reason, to lessons given in a kind of School of political science by those long experienced in the ways of power to their great-nephews, anxious to enter the 'profession' after them.

With the royalty, the caste of functionaries now inseparable from it was transplanted to Israel, bringing to the Israelites the wisdom which was its prerogative. This explains the astonishingly down to earth flavour which characterizes the sapiential books in the Scriptures. It is simply the odour of the original soil. But it is sufficient to go back to the latter, to collections of sayings like those of Ahikar or Amen-em-ope, to note that in fact the transposition is nevertheless substantial.

Coming into Israel with the royalty, as it did, Wisdom, like the royalty itself, became saturated with the Israelite religion. This was all the more easy since wisdom had always been religious, though obviously after the manner in which religion was understood when it came into existence. Since the King of Egypt or Assyria was himself considered as a manifestation of the divinity, a correct religious practice was a fundamental duty of the 'king's men'. But at that time, neither in Assyria nor in Egypt, did that seriously imply a spiritualizing process of any magnitude. In Israel the matter was quite different.

As the history of Samuel and Saul shows, it was under the favour of an alliance with the prophets of Yahwe that royalty was able to implant itself there. The special development of Wisdom in Israel thus coincided in space and time with what is called deuteronomist religion, that is a tremendous effort, to which a king like Josias gave his support, to make the spirit of the great prophets pass into the life and institutions of Israel. To express this phase it is not sufficient to speak of concomitance. The development of wisdom and that of the deuteronomist legislators and historians move towards one another. There is such a close relationship between the formulas which are arrived at by both these movements, that one has the impression that the two streams mingle their waters and that the two schools exchange or intermingle their disciples. This juncture is of paramount importance. It may be said that its product was to be the first example of what we should call religious humanism. On the one side there was the gift of God, the transcendent revelation of the exigencies and promises of Yahwe. On the other, there was the greatest and most extensive human effort ever yet made, at least in the West, to come to full awareness of the data of human existence and to dominate them, thanks to an experience gathered and reflected upon maturity. A whole storehouse of concrete psychology, of thought in the process of being systematized but yet very close to reality, falls under the judgement of the divine Word. Conversely, the Word itself was welcomed by a humanity no longer now rough and improverished, but having grown out of adolescence into a full maturity, sometimes close, if not to senility, at least to a contemplative old age in which experience is set aside and decanted.

Thus it was no longer a childish faith but faith confirmed by the richest and most deeply assimilated of experiences which made the Sages of Israel say: 'The whole concern of man is to fear God and keep his commandments.' Reciprocally, the divine inspiration will allow the refined, already blasé Ecclesiastes to transpose the disillusion of his 'vanity of vanities' into a first outline of pure hope in God.

The most remarkable thing, which seems almost patently providential, was that when matters reached this point, the earthly justification which Wisdom retained in Israel, was removed. The exile, in bringing about the collapse of royalty, took away the *raison d'être* of the king's men. But the Wisdom which they had capitalized, which they had begun to recast in the crucible of the Spirit, was not for that reason to disappear.

Already imbued with the spirit of Yahwe and of religion, but having no longer any outlet upon earth, it turned towards heaven. Essentially human, experimental, psychological, it now applied its whole store of observation and meditation, already penetrated by the divine word, to the theological problems in which man found himself concerned. It came just at the right time to attack the problem which the exile and ruin of Jerusalem created for the religious conscience of Israel in the soul of a man like Jeremias: the problem of evil and of innocent suffering, a problem to which the Book of Job applied all the resources of this Wisdom which, in Job, now soared above the confines of the earth for the first time. And for the first time Wisdom itself came to sense that this problem ended in a mystery, in a secret of which God alone had the key.

Concurrently there came about an inevitable transformation of the very idea of Wisdom. Solomon, the wise king *par excellence*, had already been shown to us as seeking wisdom not so much in experience and consideration but in prayer. Wisdom now became a gift of God, which he alone gives to whom he wills—which does not in any way mean that wisdom neglects experience or underestimates the need for personal effort. Finally it was to rise to such a height that it would be no longer a view of man which man had gradually built up from the elements of his experience, but the eternal plan of God, which he allows man to glimpse in the measure in which he wills it and as it pleases him. Already, for Job, it seemed that God was the only Sage. The Wisdom known as Solomon's would show us its providential design working itself out in history, to the refutation of the pretensions and calculations of the wise of this world.

At this point there is only one more step to take to reach the 'wisdom in mystery' of St Paul. This wisdom remains unknown and unknowable for men. The Greeks, who in their own fashion have pursued the development of purely human wisdom, cannot lay claim to it, any more than the Jews, who strive to reduce the Torah, the divine law, to merely human explanations. But it is so transcendent, so proper to God alone, so hidden in God, that the Archontes themselves, the spiritual powers who rule the cosmos, have no access to it.

The divine Wisdom comes forth as the great reconciler, dominating, surpassing all the conflicting human wisdoms, which separate man from man, which separate men from God, in the breaking up of their rationalism which is the result of sin. It gives the lie to all the fallacious pretensions of man, who relies on his worldly reason and experience. But it brings the salvation which all the 'lovers of wisdom', all the 'philo-sophers', sought in vain. It reconciles man with himself by surmounting the division caused by sin, it reconciles men among themselves, it reconciles them with God. Thus it finally brings about that co-ordination of human existence which the royal wisdom had sought after from the beginning. But it is God who brings this about, and he brings it about from within.

It is in Jesus Christ that this Wisdom has been revealed. But to say that he is the revealer of it is to say too little. He himself is divine Wisdom for us. And he is so precisely in the mystery of his death of reconciliation, which is so to speak the centre of the divine plan. In this mystery we find life through his death, so that it is no longer we who live, but he who lives in us. The mystery, indeed, is precisely that the scattered children of God be gathered up into a single body, that of Christ crucified and risen again. Thus Wisdom, if it identifies itself with Christ, is identified even more with the Church, in the sense that the latter is the fullness of Him who is completed fully in all. The great mystery that is at the heart of Wisdom is really this union and conjunction of Christ and the Church which make of the two one flesh, in the rending of his cross.

Texts, supremely mysterious, of the old sapiential literature of Israel prepared the way for these final identifications. They showed us in Wisdom, as it were a second, feminine personality, present at the side of God and in God, his help and his model in the creation of the universe, at the beginning and at the close of history. Thus, of the Wisdom revealed in Jesus Christ, the Christian tradition was to see a first appearance, a kind of first-fruits, in the Virgin Mary, the created Mother of Christ and in him of all the new creation, and a final manifestation, in the Church of eschatological times, the final fullness of Christ all in all.

Yet, when the 'Wisdom in mystery' was thus offered to man, what had become of the original, human Wisdom? What development had it been able to pursue outside the radiating influence of the divine Word? Passing into Greece through Asia Minor, where it encountered the positive and curious mind of the Ionians, it had experienced in an initial phase an unexpected development, on the planes of the study of nature and of rational abstraction. From the accumulation of the practical knowledge necessary for commerce and agriculture, the Ionians advanced to a first attempt at the science of cosmology, of a systematic understanding of φύσις, that is of the vast natural world in which human society is immersed and from which it draws all its resources. From the processes of mensuration and land-surveying which up till then had been purely empirical, they drew up at the same time an outline of rational mathematics.

Later, in Attica, the Sophists reacted against these off-shoots of Wisdom which tended to make it lose sight of its original objective. They brought it back once more to the art of guiding men and at the same time making a way for itself in society. But the change of direction was so sharp that they very nearly wrecked it by turning it into mere practical knowledge, a temptation which had always more or less fascinated it. With the resources of subtle and captious speech—resources inexhaustible so far as the Greek mind was concerned—they created an art of persuasion which was in danger of no longer having much in common with the art of discovering truth.

Socrates effected the decisive rectification. Turning dialectics against itself, he compelled young, ambitious men like Cebes or Simmias to ask themselves, before wishing for success in life, what such a success was worth. Magnified by the brilliant metaphysical imagination of Plato, his method ended by making of the search for the truth as such, eternal truth, the Idea of the Good, the objective of the wisdom which was seeking itself, of the 'philosophy' which Socrates had substituted for the successful but fallacious wisdom of the Sophists.

Aristotle reacted in his turn, bringing back Platonic thought, which had become lost in the mists of the world of the mind, closer to reality. Without neglecting—far from it—the ethical element, he restored to the cosmological, scientific element its fundamental position.

After Aristotle, however, Greek philosophy soon tended to break free from the positive rationalism in which it had sought to enclose itself. With the decadence of a thought in which reason come to be undermined by its own action, the breaking up of the city of antiquity and all its trappings created a religious disquietude which transformed philosophy into a search for salvation. Plotinus, most loyal heir to both Plato and Aristotle, did not escape from this any more than did the others. But he sought salvation within rationalism, in the most extraordinary attempt at rational mysticism which has probably ever been seen. Around him, however, there was no care at all, or very little, for the true Greek heritage. It was by a resumption of contact with those elements retained by the East which were farthest removed from rationality that men rather sought to escape destiny. Nevertheless, in such research, Greek intellectualism, if not Greek rationalism, remained unshaken. It was still from knowledge that salvation was expected: from *gnosis*.

What, in fact, is this gnosis which appeared almost at the same time as Christianity and with which Plotinus more or less confused it? An effort to wrest its secret from the universe, to decipher in the symbolism of the religions of the East, in the 'Mysteries' which then moved towards the West, the key to all things, to the world and to man. Men formed an almost magical idea of this knowledge by which the mind of man, like that of the gods, would master the universe. By this, it was thought, man would be equal to the gods. If only he could acquire the knowledge they had of supreme reality, he would become divine and thereby be immortal.

To this gnosis, which resorted to any shift, and, in its universal syncretism, even tried to assimilate the truths of the Gospel, St Paul opposed what he called ἐπίγνωσις, 'super-gnosis'. Such ἐπίγνωσις was in no sense a work of magic of men, but the free gift of God. It is granted to the humble and not to the pride of arrogant minds. Faith is the only means of acquiring it. Obviously, then, it is not a conquest by the mind independently, but a grace granted to prayer and purity of heart. It is in no sense a knowledge which can be acquired by means of intelligence alone. It presupposes, on the contrary, a gift of self, for it is inseparable from love. Is it not the discovery of the love of God, of the love of God who first loved us, but who seeks and creates our love? It is, in fact, the recognition, at the heart of the Wisdom of God, of that 'mystery' which is its centre and its all. The 'mystery of Christ', the 'mystery of his cross', is not only the unheard-of love which God has for us and to which it points, but it is that God *is* love.

A certain love also prompted the search for gnosis: it formed the soul of Plotinian mysticism, after having been the great cosmological law of Aristoteleanism, and the magnet of Platonic reminiscence drawing souls to rediscover the Good, contemplated in a previous existence and lost by the fall in this. But the love which the wisdom of the Greeks knew was *eros*, the unappeased desire which excites the creature to no purpose. The love that the Wisdom of God discloses in the Gospel, in the mystery of the Cross, is *Agape*, the gift God makes of himself to his creature, the Gift which is also his eternal 'nature', to use the original term on which Hellenic wisdom was focused.

St Paul's ἐπίγνωσις effects the divination that gnosis had dreamed of. But this metamorphosis of the creature into its divine model is not the product of a magic sympathy: it is the fruit of the gift freely given by Him to whom the creature abandons itself in return. It is as it were an exchange of looks in which hearts recognize and give themselves to each other, for eternity.

*   *   *

There is no need to say much more in order to understand how monasticism is both the heir and the fulfilment of the whole sapiential and gnostic tradition. Wisdom sought an art of living, but an art of living that was essentially 'political' in the old sense of the word: not that which saves the individual from the multitude but that which saves the multitude by reason of the success of the privileged individual. Gradually it learnt, in Israel, to receive this art, now recognized as eminently supernatural, from God, at the same time welcoming divine grace with the open embrace and understanding of which mankind, now come to full consciousness of itself, alone was capable. In monastic Christianity, that is simply Christianity at its maximum purity and intensity, the 'Wisdom of the Cross' finally takes possession of a now willing mankind, therein to fulfil those thoughts of God which are not our thoughts, in accordance with his ways which are not our ways.

Gnosis, an off-shoot from Wisdom, sought not directly to live, but to know. Yet its knowledge, of man, of the universe and of their common mystery, irresistibly tends towards life under its highest form, by the fact that it tends to what we call to-day mysticism: to a knowledge which shall be identification, identification with the supreme intelligence who is also the supreme Being. In the mystery of the bleeding yet radiant heart of divine Wisdom, the epignosis of the monk discovers, in an experimental knowledge of the Cross to which it brings him, the secret of salvation, the secret of immortality.

Thus the monk is the sole genuine inheritor of the whole movement which has borne our Western humanity along since the awakening of its consciousness. He alone is in the direct line of its highest and deepest, its most constant aspirations. He alone touches and realizes its most intimate desires, those which move a whole existence, but of which, perhaps, we shall never have a clear perception. The monk, by his vigilance, fortified with asceticism and nourished by prayer, has arrived for mankind at that awareness of self which is only fulfilled in the discovery of the Other. He has recognized, and finally assumes the true face of man by becoming clothed with the Image of the ultimate man, of the final Adam, of God made man.

The monk is thus the only true humanist. For he alone gathers from the thought of antiquity not only fossilized debris but the soul which ran through it. He alone leads it at last to see the light towards which, striking against the roof and walls of Plato's cave, it vainly struggled. As we said at the beginning: what man seeks when he thinks he is only seeking an earthly fatherland is the heavenly home, as Plato dimly

sensed, for that is the only one which can be his: it is more than a
fatherland, it is *the* Father. And the secret which the insatiable curiosity
of his mind seeks to decipher, is not the secret of a dead universe: it is
the secret of a word, of *the* Word which the Father utters to us in all
things. But we only discover the mystery of the Word, we only meet
the Father, if we are moved by his own Spirit. It must not be to a cold
and bookish knowledge that we consecrate ourselves, but to the knowledge which leads us to love—which is already love, for it is realized
to be kinship with the loved one—which awakens recognition of him
as having first loved us. The *via crucis* alone enables us to advance in
this knowledge, or rather this recognition, as it alone permitted the
other to come, through that knowledge, even so far as to meet us on
our own plane. That is why the only humanism which can wholly and
finally succeed must be a radically eschatological humanism: not one
which capitalizes dead treasures around a heart fossilized by sclerosis,
but one which sacrifices the dearest affections to find them again, one
hundredfold, after death.